MAXIMILIAN AND CARLOTA

By Gene Smith

Maximilian and Carlota: A Tale
of Romance and Tragedy

The Shattered Dream: Herbert Hoover
and the Great Depression

Still Quiet on the Western Front: Fifty
Years Later

When the Cheering Stopped: The Last Years
of Woodrow Wilson

The Life and Death of Serge Rubinstein

CO-EDITOR (WITH JAYNE BARRY SMITH)
The Police Gazette

For Young Readers
The Visitor
The Winner

MAXIMILIAN
AND
CARLOTA
A Tale of Romance and Tragedy
BY GENE SMITH

WILLIAM MORROW & COMPANY, INC.
NEW YORK 1973

Printed in the United States of America.
Library of Congress Catalog Card Number 70-182969

ISBN 0-688-00173-4

1   2   3   4   5   77   76   75   74   73

To my dear collaborator, J.B.S.

CONTENTS

I think he was well-nigh the noblest of his race, and fulfilled the promise of his words, "The fame of my ancestors will not degenerate in me."

—LORD ACTON

Europe

1

As much the Corsican clansman as he was the French military genius, Napoleon the Great had by 1808 placed all but one of his brothers and sisters upon a European throne. From Spain in the south to Holland in the north and eastward into Germany and Italy they reigned as satellite Highnesses of a France intended to stretch from Hamburg to Rome.

But something was missing. The Emperor had no direct heir. Josephine was less than eighteen when she married her first husband, Alexandre de Beauharnais, and she seemed to have exhausted her childbearing potentialities by the births of her son Eugène and her daughter Hortense. Made a widow by the Terror's guillotine and an Empress by the Revolution's General Bonaparte, she took the waters at fashionable spas, consulted eminent doctors, prayed at shrines. But there was no issue from her second marriage.

Josephine was soft, unintelligent—but sweet. Napoleon loved her. When he had to leave her to be with his troops, he cried in her arms. She deceived him, had others, lied—as he did himself—but he always came back to her. He used to say that he loved his wife because of her lovely bottom. But there must be someone to rule when he was gone. She knew him, and perhaps to bind him more strongly to herself, she arranged the marriage of her daughter Hortense to Napoleon's brother Louis. The marriage was a disaster. Napoleon had raised his younger brother, sharing the thin fare of a junior officer's pay with him, and then, as higher position came his way, taking Louis along on his campaigns. Before he reached his majority, Louis appeared talented militarily, and also physically attractive. But by the time he passed twenty-five, he was a hopeless hypochondriac, everlastingly seeing doctors and taking cures. He hobbled along, talking in an old man's piping voice. Napoleon, exasperated, said it must be syphilis.

The marriage of Hortense and Louis produced two children. After that they separated. Their first child died and, for a little while, they drew together in their shared grief. Shortly Hortense was delivered of another child who may or may not have resulted from the reunion—for she had numerous lovers. But the child was accepted as the son of Louis. He and Hortense had named their surviving child Napoleon Louis; this last issue they called Louis Napoleon.

Napoleon regarded the two little nephews, Napoleon Louis and Louis Napoleon, as his heirs. But he grew thoughtful when one of his mistresses had a child. It came to him that it was not his fault that Josephine was barren. He shattered the armies of the Austrian Empire, and took up residence in the summer palace of Schoenbrunn outside Vienna. There he received into his bed in the magnificent Lacquer Chamber the lovely Countess Maria Walewska of Poland, who hoped she could win from him Poland's freedom. That he could gain solace, find even bliss, with another woman, meant that he did not need Josephine. In the arms of Countess Walewska he decided that Josephine must go. Soon the Countess was pregnant with his child, but she could never hope to be his Empress. For one thing, she was married to an aged nobleman whose grandchildren by a previous marriage were older than his eighteen-year-old wife. For another, her rank was not nearly what Napoleon sought. His new Empress could only be of the highest aristocracy, someone to whose irreproachable heredity he could weld his great achievements.

He decided it must be a daughter of the Austrian Emperor. No prospective father-in-law could have hated the man seeking his daughter's hand as Francis of Austria hated Napoleon of the French. But Francis was the father second, the dynast first. His daughter, the Archduchess Marie Louise, had been raised to think that this Bonaparte thrown up by the hateful Revolution was the Antichrist. Her youth had been spent fleeing palaces menaced by his armies. But she had been raised to obey her father. "Do all that he wishes," her father said; and she bowed and went to France. Austria looked upon her as a sacrificial victim.

Napoleon, her bridegroom, could not wait in his capital to receive this offering. She was the great-niece of Marie Antoinette, the last Hapsburg Archduchess to come to Paris; through her, Napoleon, the son of the Revolution, would come to refer to the guillotined Louis XVI as "my uncle." He jumped on a horse and, clad in a simple coat, rode through the rain toward her carriage as it approached Soissons. She did not know who it was flinging open the door until someone shouted, "The Emperor!" That night he took her to bed, and in the morning told his people that German girls were the best, adding also that Henry of Navarre, whom now he termed "my predecessor," had two hundred years before also taken the favors of the girl who was to be his wife before the wedding ceremony.

Marie Louise was nineteen years old and educated only insofar as she spoke several languages. (Austrian policy dictated that a Hapsburg Archduchess, whose husband might be of any nationality, had to be a linguist.) She was bovine in her ways. Her husband in his logical fashion said that he had married a womb; and soon that womb bore fruit. On March 20, 1811, after a torturous delivery, she gave birth to a son. Cannon fire heard throughout Paris and the Empire welcomed the birth of Napoleon Francis Charles Joseph, called King of Rome in imitation of the heirs to the Holy Roman Empire. Atop the arched canopy of the silver-gilt cradle was a winged Glory extending a crown amidst palm leaves, ivy, and laurel, cornucopias, genies holding Hercules' club, and, at the foot, an eaglet. On the evening of his birth, when his deliriously happy father presented him for baptism, a very deep silence fell upon the princes and generals, the kings and lords. There were bonfires, Te Deums, illuminations, processions, fireworks in the one hundred and thirty Departments of his father's Empire. "I envy that boy!" Napoleon said. "Glory is waiting there for him; I had to run after her. I will have been Philip; he will be Alexander. He has only to extend an arm, and the world is his!"

Though the mother in her dull way disdained her son, saying, "I don't see how anybody can kiss a baby," The Eaglet was adored by his father The Eagle, who roughly but lovingly tossed him up in the air, rolled him around the carpet, gave him bear hugs. For the public baptism, which followed the private one by a few months, there were dozens of coaches carrying knights, chasseurs and mamelukes, with the King of Rome in a coat of gold lined with ermine coming last in a coach drawn by eight horses. At Napoleon's order, Hortense, the daughter of the divorced Josephine and the estranged wife of brother Louis, acted as godmother.

Napoleon's son, the King of Rome, grew up addressed as "Sire" and "Your Majesty." In the Palace of the Tuileries overlooking the great square where Marie Antoinette and Louis XVI had died, he was known as the Little King. When his father went on campaign, the picture of the King of Rome always went along; on the eve of the Battle of the Moskva, Napoleon received from Marie Louise the latest painting of his son. It was with him in his room at the Kremlin and he carried it away through burning Moscow, across the Russian snows and past the terrible wreckage of the Grand Army. On the twenty-fourth of January, 1814, no longer the unconquerable but more the animal at bay, Napoleon took the King of Rome into his study in Paris, where all afternoon he burned secret papers and worked his war games in preparation for the great campaign which would settle his fate; and the child played with the little pieces of mahogany whose lengths and colors identified the different units of his father's army.

At three o'clock the next morning the Emperor came into the child's bedroom in the Tuileries and for a while looked at him before going off to join the troops. It was the last time he was ever to see his son.

Napoleon went to meet the combined forces of Russia, Prussia, and the Austria of his father-in-law the Emperor Francis. For a few brief weeks he appeared capable of dispersing his enemies; but the odds were too great against him and the Allies began closing a circle. By March 30 the campaign was over, and Paris fell. Napoleon was not there but maneuvering elsewhere.

The Emperor Napoleon was finished, but it was by no means certain that the Allies would forbid his Throne to his son. Urged to abdicate in favor of the King of Rome, Napoleon hesitated, wandering through the dead Josephine's estate at

Malmaison and saying to Hortense how happy he would be just to stay there in peace forever. Finally he signed an abdication document making his son Napoleon II, Emperor of the French.

He was too late. The child was gone from Paris. Some of Marie Louise's advisers had told her to stay in the capital, saying that to leave meant that her son would never rule France. Others had urged her to flee before the Allied armies came in force. She decided to return to Austria. But even as their carriages were hurriedly loaded, her three-year-old son screamed over and over that he did not want to go. He was put in by force alone, crying out, "I want to go and see my Papa. I want to go and see my Papa. I want to go."

His country as the child last saw it was littered with dead soldiers and burned buildings. They took him to Parma and the Swiss frontier. He kept asking, "Why won't they let me kiss Papa anymore?"

Austrian cavalry escorted home the boy's mother, Marie Louise, with the populace hailing her as a martyr who had sacrificed herself to a monster. At the Imperial Palace of Innsbruck everyone who looked up at the portrait of Maria Theresa with the child who would become the Emperor Joseph II noted his resemblance to Marie Louise's son, and when they came to Schoenbrunn she wordlessly pushed him forward at his grandfather. "I don't want to be a German!" the child cried. "I want to be French!"

But Napoleon's son had to be a German. His French attendants were fired and replaced with Austrian tutors, most of whom were former officers whose careers had been dominated by Austria's wars with France. When he persisted in speaking French he was lashed, by order of his grandfather the Emperor Francis. His French toys and his books with the French Imperial Arms were taken away. A little six-year-old French playmate was ordered to leave. "St. Cloud is nicer than Schoenbrunn and I like French soldiers better than Austrian soldiers," the child said, everlastingly asking when he could see Papa again. But by order of his grandfather he was called Francis or Franz, never François and most certainly never Napoleon. "I'm not a King anymore! I'm not a King anymore!" he would say to himself, sometimes sadly and sometimes gaily.

Spring of 1814 came, and his father went to Elba. In the fall the Congress of Vienna met. For a while Marie Louise spoke of joining her husband; but Austrian policy dictated that it must not be. An Austrian officer, Count von Neipperg, handsome, dashing, a lady-killer, was assigned to make her forget Napoleon. Soon she ceased to speak of going to Elba.

In Paris the brother of the guillotined Louis XVI reigned as King, but the restoration of the Bourbons was so unpopular that Prince Metternich, the Austrian Chancellor, was reliably informed that if the son of Napoleon came into France riding an ass, the first French regiment he met would lead him straight to Paris. Metternich's abiding mission in life was to restore the stable Europe that existed before the French Revolution and the Napoleon Bonaparte it produced. He ordered descriptions of "the Archduchess's child" sent to every police station and customhouse in the Austrian Empire to make difficult the spiriting-away of a child who might be set upon a Paris throne and whose name might inspire a new generation of Frenchmen to make war on Austria. There began that never-ending flow of reports from servants, aides and tutors, all of them in Metternich's employ, detailing everything Napoleon's son said, his progress in his studies, his interests and abilities, tempers, caprices, amusements.

His father escaped from Elba in February of 1815. An Eagle flying from church steeple to church steeple, he alighted in Paris, the Bourbon King's soldiers coming over to him by battalions and divisions. It was his son's fourth birthday. Louis XVIII fled and Napoleon's people ripped the fleur-de-lis from the carpets and wall hangings where they had been sewn to conceal Imperial bees, the symbol of the Emperor. They then placed Napoleon on their shoulders and carried him into the Tuileries. His eyes were closed in rapture; he held his arms out in front of him. Hortense came with her two sons, and he fondled them affectionately. He went from her and them, and from Paris itself, to Waterloo to meet the Duke of Wellington and the Prussian Field Marshal Blücher.

In Vienna, Marie Louise wondered what to do, and ended by doing nothing. The Hundred Days which followed the flight from Elba ended, and with it the Napoleonic Era. "Tell him that I still love him very much," his son whispered to a man who said he would be seeing the boy's father.

They took Napoleon to St. Helena. Two passions consumed him there: one, that history remember him as he hoped it would, and two, that his son rule France. But perhaps it was more than just the wish for a dynasty to follow him, for many of his feelings for the boy were less grand, less the productions of the Emperor and more the thoughts of the father. Everywhere he went on his island prison he carried a snuffbox with his son's face etched on it and once, when he dropped it, he sighed with relief when he saw it was not damaged.

Napoleon thought constantly of his son, the prisoner of Metternich. "Poor little devil," he muttered. In Vienna the boy's instructors were ordered to banish all memory of his life in France. They were forbidden to speak of what his grandfather the Emperor Francis termed "his former situation." He must not, wrote his chief tutor, "hanker after the life he might have led." He must have no thoughts of the French, a "people to whom he can no longer belong . . . must be considered of Austrian descent and brought up in the German fashion."

Four and a half years old, he called Paris "home" and was beaten for it. He learned, Metternich's people taught him, that when he was asked his name he must answer that it was Franz. But always there was a silence before he said it.

He rarely saw his mother, for she had been sent off to be Grand Duchess of Parma in Austrian Italy, which once had been one of her husband's one hundred and thirty Departments but now did service as her realm. Soon she had illegitimate children by her Count von Neipperg.

Napoleon the Great died at St. Helena with his eyes on a picture and bust of his son. His will left the boy the sword carried at Austerlitz, his dagger, his hunting knife, his pistols, the gold dressing case used on the mornings of Ulm, Jena and the Moskva, his camp beds, field glasses, his saddles and bridles and spurs, the blue cloak worn at Marengo, his sporting guns. Metternich forbade the boy to receive the bequests. They gathered dust in a storeroom in the Austrian Embassy at Paris.

He had to have some sort of title. He was, after all, the grandson of the Emperor Francis, the son of the Emperor's daughter. Several titles bearing income from far-off Imperial lands were suggested, but from Parma, Marie Louise rejected them as being unpronounceable. Finally they gave him the

Duchy of Reichstadt in Bohemia. To her German ear it was appropriate. He was seven years old.

The Duke of Reichstadt grew up as the most intelligent royalty at the Court of Vienna. Preternaturally silent, he made judgments with a maturity far beyond his years. Infinitely more handsome than his father or his mother, he exerted upon all who knew him a great fascination, and a hush fell upon Court balls when he entered. Considered witty and quick-minded, he was also the most self-contained of children. Yet it brought a chill to Austrian hearts when, playing at soldiers with the other Court children, the son of Napoleon ordered "March!" No one knew what he was thinking, and though he said that he hoped to have a career as an Austrian officer in his grand-father's service, the closest reins were kept on him. Everywhere he went Metternich's detectives shadowed him, and he was dis-couraged from making friends, for those friends might end as partisans of a boy whose picture was sold in France with "Na-poleon II" written under it.

He contrived, against his tutors' wishes, to learn all that he could of his father's career, and finally they had to permit him books on that great subject. He devoured them. From then on he read little else but works on military matters, and stayed up nights studying plans for fortifications and troop deployments.

Even as a child he understood his situation, understood his poor weak mother and forgave her. He was never permitted to visit her in Parma, for Austrian Italy might well burst into rebellion if a Napoleon should ever appear there. When he learned that his mother had illegitimate children, conceived when her husband was still alive, he silently absorbed the fact and never let her know that he was aware of their existence.

His grandfather, the Emperor, loved the Duke of Reichstadt beyond all other members of his family, including his own two sons, the brothers of Marie Louise, Crown Prince the Arch-duke Ferdinand and the Archduke Francis Charles. The Em-peror himself was far from an imposing personality, his main interests being woodworking and talking with his cooks, but the sons were worse. Crown Prince Ferdinand, an epileptic, was mentally retarded. ("Next thing to an idiot," said Eng-land's Lord Palmerston.) He was unable to remember names and had to be pushed up and steadied in the saddle when he wanted to mount a horse. The Crown Prince found his greatest pleasure in playing with his young nephew, a part of their sport being that the Heir to the Throne of Austria stuffed himself into a wastepaper basket and rolled through the endless halls of the Hofburg and Schoenbrunn. That happened when the Crown Prince was well past the age of maturity. The other son of the Emperor was accustomed to taking his pleasure in gossiping and exchanging dirty jokes with whomever came his way. He taught the little Duke of Reichstadt indecent expressions.

Austrian policy in time demanded the marriage of Crown Prince the Archduke Ferdinand to a rather simple Italian Princess. They had a mutual interest in religion, and prayed together. Policy determined at the Congress of Vienna married the younger brother, the Archduke Francis Charles, to the daughter of the future King of Bavaria. Her name was Sophia.

Sophia—or Sophie—was highly intelligent and a strong personality. She exploded when she heard whom her parents had selected for her future husband. "That imbecile!" she raged. "Never!" But she was a Bavarian Princess and Austria was Bavaria's most powerful neighbor; all had been decided in advance. It would be unthinkable for her family to risk offending the Hapsburgs. She consulted with herself and told her parents she would marry the Archduke. "I have decided to be happy, and I will," she said.

But of course Francis Charles, stupid, weak, a total nonentity, could not make her happy. She was far too clever for him. After a couple of months he utterly bored her. A pretty girl with a happy smile and light chestnut-brown hair arranged in loops, she refurnished her apartments in the Hofburg in a gay and airy fashion, read widely and practiced on the several musical instruments she played. Yet she found a soulmate in only one person in Vienna—her nephew through marriage, the Duke of Reichstadt.

He was fifteen to her twenty-one, but already six feet tall, different from his father but with something of Napoleon in the longer, thinner face and in the manner of walking with hands clasped behind. He almost always dressed in the uniform of an Austrian Whitecoat, with the sword worn at the Battle of the Pyramids at his waist. It was the only souvenir of his father Metternich permitted him to have.

He learned to talk of his father only with the Archduchess Sophia. She encouraged him to do so, saying also that school-days would not last forever and that one day he would sit upon the Throne of France. She was the wife of the second in line to the monarchy of Austria. As it was extremely unlikely that the hopeless Crown Prince Ferdinand could ever produce offspring, any child Sophia bore would one day rule. In addition, her half-sister was the Austrian Emperor's wife. Before such qualifications even Chancellor Metternich quailed. And of course she was the only member of the royal family even remotely the Chancellor's intellectual equal. In front of him she dared to speak of her hopes for Reichstadt.

Sophia brought out the humor of her nephew (which was his own, for his parents had none) and they used to laugh and joke for hours together. When she was away—he of course was never permitted to travel more than a few miles from Vienna— they exchanged merry letters. She loved to end her notes by making fun of the officer who, as much spy as tutor, supervised Reichstadt: "Adieu, my dear Francis. I kiss you with all my heart. Adieu. She who loves you deeply. My regards to your wife."

The Duke of Reichstadt saw Sophia every day, sitting by her while she played the piano. When the Court was in residence at the Hofburg he came each evening to her little salon and they took tea together, reading aloud or talking. He would be wearing his uniform of Lieutenant of Tyrolean Chasseurs and she would be dressed in a low-cut gown, with her hair in a veil of white lace and a pendant containing a miniature of her father at her throat. At Schoenbrunn they walked in the gardens, past the trellises, pergolas and fountains, she in simple muslins and India prints with flounces floating about her, and he tall and soldierlike in Austrian army white.

Napoleon's son continued his self-dictated military education, and Sophia, mindful of the future, submitted to her husband and bore him a boy, the Archduke Francis Joseph, the future Emperor of Austria. Reichstadt was by then coming into his full maturity, but he did not pursue the many women who wished to tempt him. He preferred to drive with Sophia in the Prater and walk with her through Schoenbrunn's Tyrolean gardens and out into the countryside.

In October of 1831, Sophia found herself pregnant. The child would be a boy. He, like his brother Francis Joseph, would also be an Emperor. All of Vienna would say his father was the Duke of Reichstadt.

Reichstadt was an active young man. But he was not well. There was something unhealthy about his fair, transparent skin. Sometimes he perspired and coughed in alarming fashion. He thought that the trouble could be cured by hard work, and galloped his white Arabian horse for hours. Promoted Lieutenant-Colonel of the Wasa regiment, he threw himself into drilling his men, shouting out commands in a voice which, as his twenty-first birthday approached, became increasingly muffled. He was terribly thin.

It was obvious to all who saw him that he was sick. Rumors circulated that Metternich had procured women for the Duke of Reichstadt to distract him from any political thoughts and that he had become enfeebled through dissipation, or that Metternich had arranged for arsenic to be put in his food. Sophia had her doctor examine him, and the verdict was that he suffered from a liver complaint but that it would pass. It did not. He began to cough constantly. Ever more feverish and pallid, he forced himself into longer and wilder rides through the mists along the Danube and through the chill of the surrounding hills and woods, returning bathed in sweat.

In January, 1832, a full colonel, he asked his grandfather for permission to command his regiment at the funeral of an Austrian general. In the bitter cold his voice failed him as he tried to shout out the orders. He raised his father's sword to signal a salute and his voice completely broke. Coughing, he relinquished the command to another officer and went away with tears in his eyes. Blood trickled from his mouth.

He was terribly sick. Alone of all the people at Court, the Archduchess Sophia understood that new doctors had to be brought in. They could not help. On his twenty-first birthday, March 20, 1832, he ran a high fever and was unable to get out of bed. Sophia, six months pregnant, brought her first son, little Francis Joseph, aged two, to see him; the child shouted

"Ava!" his name for Reichstadt, and handed over two camellias as a present.

Reichstadt should have gone south, but Metternich would not permit it. Once another Napoleon had gone to Italy, and to expel him had in the end cost Austria millions of florins and tens of thousands of casualties. On May 22, 1832, in a closed carriage, Reichstadt was taken from the Hofburg to the summer palace of Schoenbrunn to stay in Sophia's rooms, which she had turned over to him. He was placed in the high white bedroom with a gold ceiling that adjoined the Lacquer Chamber where once the conqueror, his father, had slept in the arms of the Polish Countess Walewska and decided to divorce Josephine. In that room his father had slept after Austerlitz and Wagram. In the distance was the arched pavilion called The Gloriette and on days when he was able, Reichstadt made his way there with Sophia, moving slowly through the sunshine. At night he perspired so freely as he lay under a tapestry showing the march of Austrian cavalry in an Italian setting—his father had slept under it also—that the sheets had to be changed every few hours. They gave him mare's milk, cow's milk. Nothing helped.

All who saw her with him thought Sophia an angel of loving-kindness. She had a special chair made for him; with him she prayed in her oratory; she guarded his sickroom door; gave him medicine and was always calm in his presence and always smiling. Away from his sight she wept when she spoke of him.

Even on warm days his teeth chattered, and coughing fits woke him at night. Weak, almost skeletal in appearance, he was carried each morning to Sophia's private garden, where there were bowling greens, fountains, terraces with flowers and a pavilion open to the air on three sides. He lay there each afternoon in an army chair, wearing a dressing gown of red and white stripes. She read aloud, pausing when he broke into coughs which ended with his pressing a handkerchief to his lips so that she would not see the blood. She pretended that she did not see. At their feet played the little Archduke Francis Joseph and often Sophia lifted the child onto his lap and he softly stroked the fair hair. Then his lips would compress with the pain from his chest. It was tuberculosis.

Now when it was too late, Metternich gave him permission

to go south, and excitedly Reichstadt talked to Sophia of how, when he was a little stronger, he would travel to Naples. He would have a special carriage made to take him there. Far gone into her pregnancy, which was very difficult, she listened and encouraged him. Too weak to read—his eyes gave out after a few moments—he could not walk more than a few steps before collapsing from the ominous pains in his chest. At Court it was freely said that the time had come for him to be given the Last Sacraments. Sophia forbade it.

But Napoleon's son was dying. At last Sophia faced it and consented to a final Communion on condition that it be done in conjunction with herself. So she suggested to him that they go to church together and unite their prayers, he for the return of his health, she for a safe delivery. On June 20, 1832, in the chapel of Schoenbrunn, they knelt together at the altar, Sophia physically supporting him. Court protocol demanded that when a Prince of Austria received the Last Sacraments all the Archdukes, their chamberlains and advisers be present. Sophia would not permit him to know they were there. So the Court went up the staircase to the chapel in perfect silence. Behind an almost closed door, unseen by Reichstadt, they noiselessly prayed as he knelt with Sophia before the priest. "She felt in the transfiguration of her sorrow," it has been written, "as though she were becoming Reichstadt's bride in a sort of mystic marriage, performed under the eyes of all, yet without their knowledge."

On July fifth, Sophia did not come to his sickroom. Alarmed, he asked where she was. They told him that her confinement had begun. He asked for the little Francis Joseph, and when the child was brought, held him dreaming in a protracted tight embrace, stroking his hair.

Sophia was a long day in giving birth, while Reichstadt, with staring, hollow eyes, spent it on his balcony, asking hour by hour for news of her as he gasped out, "Air, more air!"

His death agony came on. Sleep was beyond him. His gathered attendants caught his last coherent words: "Harness the horses! I must go to meet my father! I must embrace him once more!" He died as the sun rose above Schoenbrunn Palace.

When they told Sophia she fainted and was unconscious for

hours. Her life was despaired of. Reichstadt, booted and spurred and wearing the white tunic of the Wasa regiment, was buried with his father's curved saber at his side. Sophia, far too ill to attend his funeral, was in her bed as the procession moved to the Capuchin Crypt of the Augustiner Church, where Hapsburgs went to their final rest. "Those who knew her thereafter," it was said, "no longer found the gay and simple Archduchess. All her gentleness seemed to have left her. There was a sting in everything she said. The truth was that her youth had died with Reichstadt. She was to have intrigues, love affairs, ambitions, cares of state. But she had changed in spirit. . . . Within her heart's depth, a regret and a bitterness which would endure until her death."

As soon as she heard of his passing, her milk dried up. A wet nurse had to be found for her infant. It was a boy. They christened him Ferdinand Maximilian Joseph, but in the family he was always called by his middle name.

2

DEFEAT AT WATERLOO in 1815 and the end of the Napoleonic Era brought the Great Emperor to his island prison in the South Atlantic four thousand miles from Paris, to hot tropical afternoons spent brooding on the past which was his and the future which would be his son's. "If Jesus Christ had not died on the cross, he would never have been worshiped as God. . . . If I die on the cross and my son lives, all will be well with him," Napoleon said. The Great Emperor died at St. Helena in May of 1821, but there was never to be a future for his son the King of Rome who had become Duke of Reichstadt and had gone to his grave on a hot July day in 1832. The Bonapartist succession then passed to the offspring of Hortense—the daughter of Josephine and the wife of Napoleon's strange brother Louis.

Hortense had fled France, as all the family had done. (King Joseph, Napoleon's oldest brother, ran the farthest distance, finally coming to rest as a gentleman farmer in Bordentown, New Jersey.) Hortense ended in a rather nondescript villa along Lake Constance in Switzerland. Estranged from her husband, she raised her two boys in an atmosphere where the Great Emperor was a household god, where it was their task in life to contribute as best they could to the continuation of his dynasty. The older son, who stood second in the succession behind his cousin the Duke of Reichstadt, died during an ill-planned uprising against Papal and Austrian rule in Italy. Hardly more than a year later, the Duke of Reichstadt, who stood first in line, followed. That left Louis Napoleon, Hortense's younger son, the Pretender. He had not seen the dead

Duke of Reichstadt since the moment, eighteen years earlier, when they both fled Paris. He had never seen the little boy in Schoenbrunn's nursery. But he and the child would be one another's destinies.

Louis Napoleon was twenty-four, not handsome or graceful —he had stumpy legs—but a spectacular horseback rider, a good shot and a good swimmer. He had last seen France at the age of seven, and had been educated by tutors at home in Switzerland and by teachers in a boys' school in Bavaria. As a result he conversed in French with a noticeable German accent. He was a very poor speaker, extremely slow and hesitant, dreamy and reserved. Long pauses punctuated his conversation, and people who did not know him thought him somewhat dull in intellect. Some believed him to be a secret drunkard or opium fiend.

But Louis Napoleon's silences were those of a thoughtful scholar. All his life the atmosphere of the library clung to him. Placid, imperturbable, no matter what the provocation, he was like some provincial German professor musing over a specialty. Dreams, wanderings, fanciful vagueness characterized him. But he was a Pretender to a Throne; his own mother now deferred to him and at their home it was he who led the guests in to dinner. He wrote heavy little pamphlets on political theory and in imitation of the uncle whose political heir he was, chose artillery as a military specialty, becoming a part-time captain of the Swiss army.

Like the uncle, the nephew was promiscuous. He was eclectic in his tastes—from chambermaids on up. When, after not seeing her for a long time, Louis Napoleon met his first cousin, the Princess Mathilde, daughter of Napoleon's foolish brother Jerome, he fell in love. She did not care to have him, so he went back to a series of meaningless seductions.

With his heavy-lidded eyes and dull manner, Louis Napoleon seemed to be perpetually half-asleep. He was not. He was plotting. After Waterloo the Bourbons had been restored to their French Throne. But they fell from power in 1830 to be replaced by their cousin, the Duke of Orleans, Louis Philippe. The Bonapartists aimed to replace him. Sublimely dull, Louis Philippe, The Citizen King, exuded middle-class complacency. He carried his own umbrella in the street, he rode public omnibuses. The motto of his regime, addressed to a

nation raised on the Great Emperor's glory, was: Enrich Yourself. France was bored with him from the first. Opposed to his
dreariness, Louis Napoleon, the Bonaparte Pretender, had the
great name which had led France's armies to the ends of half
the earth. Early on an October morning in 1836 Louis Napoleon crossed over into France from Switzerland and presented
himself to the Fouth Artillery Regiment in Strasbourg, his
uncle's unit when he was in the Royal army as a junior officer
before the Revolution of 1789.

The colonel of the Fourth was in on the plot, convinced of
its rectitude by a beautiful contralto singer who made her
favors available to him only on his promise of cooperation
with her friend Prince Louis Napoleon. "Soldiers," cried the
colonel, "can the nephew of the Emperor put his trust in you?"
There were scattered shouts of *"Vive l'Empereur,"* and the
regiment marched through the streets of Strasbourg with the
Prince at its head. On his finger he wore a ring given him by
his mother Hortense; on it were inscribed the names of Josephine Tascher and Napoleon Bonaparte. It was their wedding
ring.

The column marched to the barracks of the Forty-sixth
of the Line. There someone yelled out that the man was an
impostor, the bastard son of the colonel of the Fourth Artillery. A subaltern refused to parade the battalion and several
privates yelled insults. There was a scuffle and the Prince and
his adherents were taken prisoner. One man was wounded in
the hand. By eight in the morning it was all over. Louis Napoleon was tossed into prison.

King Louis Philippe chose to treat the whole thing as a
silly farce. He ordered the Prince put on a boat and shipped
to America, where adventurers belonged. The boat crossed to
Rio and lingered there for a month, the prisoner forbidden to
go ashore. Then it made for New York, where Louis Napoleon
landed. Society took him up, and he made conquests of several
feminine hearts. But people thought insane a man who sat
around cafés with a faraway look in his eyes as he murmured,
"When I am at the head of the government in Paris . . .
When I am Emperor of the French."

For all his apparent confidence in his ultimate destiny he
thought of permanently locating in America. He wrote to his

Uncle Joseph in New Jersey inquiring about the purchase of land; Joseph ignored the letter. When word came that his mother Hortense was seriously ill in Switzerland he took his leave, grandly writing President Martin Van Buren that he regretted he must go before having the pleasure of an audience.

Back at the villa by Lake Constance, Louis Napoleon found Hortense dying. He revered her memory for the rest of his life. After her death King Louis Philippe suggested to the Swiss that the Prince should be banished from that country. The Swiss refused. A French army corps was ordered to the frontier. Trouble was averted when Louis Napoleon, with an air of royal grace, withdrew himself to London. There he made conquests, was feted by society, and permitted himself a carriage with the Imperial eagle on its doors. He stayed in England for two years and acquired as his mistress an extremely rich blond courtesan who went by the name of Miss Howard. With her money he organized another assault on Louis Philippe's government.

This one was even more opéra bouffe than the first. With nine horses, fifty-five men—including his chef, butler, tailor and fencing master—and one bird, he made for Boulogne on a hired English excursion steamer. The men wore French military uniforms rented or purchased from a British costume house. The bird—either an eagle or a vulture who would be taken for an eagle—was given the assignment of hovering in the air over the Prince's head. To insure the bird's assistance, Louis Napoleon put a strip of bacon in his hat.

On August 6, 1840, at five in the morning, Louis Napoleon and his followers landed at Boulogne and marched through the streets to the local garrison. The troops of the Forty-second of the Line refused to join them, so they left the barracks, striking a minor official of the city government in the chest with the brass eagle of a regimental standard. The police and National Guard appeared, and in a panic Louis Napoleon and his supporters fled toward where they had left their excursion steamer. But the customs officials had impounded it. With a few shots sounding from behind them, the invaders floundered out into the surf. They seized a lifeboat and put to sea, but it cap-

sized and dumped them overboard. Louis Napoleon was rescued rather than captured.

This time Louis Philippe, The Citizen King, was seriously
annoyed. A trial was ordered before the Chamber of Peers.
The Prince was sentenced to perpetual imprisonment. "How
long is perpetual?" he asked. They sent him to the fortress of
Ham in Picardy. It was always cold and damp there, and afterward he never really felt warm again.

He used to say, later, that he went to the University of Ham
for six years. And indeed he studied during his confinement,
devouring books, conducting lengthy correspondences, hatch-
ing schemes in his slow, vague fashion. The terms of his imprisonment were not onerous; he was allowed horseback
exercise on the ramparts of the fortress, and the daughter of
the local shoemaker became so frequent a visitor and so intimate a friend that she bore him two children.

Louis Napoleon was the dreamer supreme. In those years
there flitted through his mind the images of the fields of glory
his uncle had known, and those he might know, a new Austerlitz . . . Friedland . . . Wagram . . . the rolling drums, the
Cuirassiers trailing sabretaches, the Lancers and the Guard in
schapskas. The old Imperial dream was not his alone, for on
the very day he entered prison King Louis Philippe's son
arrived at St. Helena to take home the body of the Great
Emperor so that it might lie by the Seine in the Invalides, in
Paris. Louis Philippe was practical. The gesture could not hurt
him, with Napoleon's son dead, his relatives scattered and his
heir sentenced to "perpetual" imprisonment. When the coffin
was brought home, crowds massed in a November frost un-
thawed by bright sunshine and flung into the air a roaring
"Vive l'Empereur!"

Louis Napoleon in prison dreamed of that cry, but mixed
with it were business schemes, plots for books and his correspondence with a group of Nicaraguans interested in creating
an interoceanic ditch across their country. It would be called
The Napoleon Canal. They wanted him to lend his name
to the enterprise in order to help raise the monies which
would be needed. He saw the proposed canal as the means
by which Nicaragua would be elevated to the heights among

the nations of the world, with the ports at both ends of the waterway becoming the equals of London and Constantinople. He doodled sketches of the proposed passage, began to write a pamphlet on it and, his vivid imagination aroused, saw the country as a bar to the further expansion of the United States of America. He dipped more and more into the histories and situations of all of Latin America, including the former Jewel of the Crown of Spain, Mexico.

In the spring of 1846, word reached Louis Napoleon that his father, the Great Emperor's brother, was dying. There had been little intimacy between the two men, one of whom was quite free in saying the other was less likely his offspring than the product of some lover's liaison. But Louis Napoleon petitioned the royal government for permission to leave his prison for his father's bedside. It was refused. He decided his honor was impugned by the ruling, and determined upon an escape attempt.

On May 25, 1846, Louis Napoleon's physician, Dr. Conneau, reported to the warden of the fortress that the Prince was ill. The warden looked in and saw a huddled figure lying in bed. He went away to return an hour later. The figure was still there, attended by the anxious doctor.

At that moment a roughly clothed workman carrying a wooden plank on his shoulder passed through the gates of the fortress to the road outside. Dr. Conneau was bending over a dummy, and the workman was Prince Louis Napoleon, moustaches shaved and his face rouged so that his habitual paleness would be effaced. As he walked through the gates, the pipe in his mouth fell and shattered on the pavement. He coolly stooped, picked up the pieces with the plank still on his shoulder and went on his way. A carriage waited nearby, and in a few hours he was over the border into Belgium and heading for England.

Free, he took up again with the rich blond Miss Howard. He drifted along, seemingly a lifelong Pretender and failed conspirator, no longer even terribly valuable as a social ornament. But across the Channel in France was a race once the heroes of the world, they whose fathers marched as conquerors across Europe. King Louis Philippe, dull in his finest days and now slipping into senility, permitted his Ministers to forbid a Paris banquet at which the parliamentary opposition was to hold forth against corruption, unemployment, the potato blight and a bad harvest. The heroes and sons of heroes rose up and paraded in favor of the banquet and against a monarch who forbade them to hear him denounced with French eloquence and fire. The King ordered up troops to make a counterdemonstration, but as the soldiers mustered into line they shouted slogans which could not have pleased the King's Ministers. It was February 22, 1848. The crowds in the streets grew rambunctious.

It was said of Louis Philippe that he began each day by praying, "Give us, O Lord, our daily platitude." He had no answer for what suddenly looked like a mindless and leaderless Revolution. His troops gave way for the demonstrators in every case save one; in that one, they fired a murderous volley. Very likely it was because they were frightened. Victor Hugo said the whole thing took place because people at the back pushed forward at the people in front who, shoved against their will, nudged the troops. But within a few hours Paris was a mass of barricades, and paving stones were flying through the air. Less than forty-eight hours after the moment when the prohibited banquet was scheduled to begin, King Louis Philippe was fleeing France.

The mob took possession of Paris. At least once before a mob had owned the streets of the city. That had been in the wake of the Revolution of 1789, which had thrown up Napoleon the Great. This Revolution was also to bring a Napoleon to power; and like the earlier one, it was to reach its influence all across the Continent: to Italy, which erupted into insurrections, to Hungary, to Prussia, whose Crown Prince William so conducted himself that he became known as The Cartridge Prince, to Bavaria, Denmark, Holland and, perhaps most dramatically of all, to Vienna, in Austria.

3

IN THE YEARS which followed the death of the Duke of Reichstadt in 1832 the Archduchess Sophia, the wife of the Archduke
second in line to the Austrian Throne, reconciled herself
to her fate. That was to make do as best she could with her
dull husband, and to bring up her children. Perhaps *reconciled* is not the word; for she had always recognized her husband, the Archduke Francis Charles, as a fool. Royal Princesses
could not expect to marry for love, or find soulmates in their
husbands. The new Empress of Austria—the Emperor Francis
died in 1835—was a case in point. When she met for the first
time her feeble-minded fiancé, then the Crown Prince Ferdinand, she was unable to look at him without tears coming to
her eyes. Age and his accession to his father's throne did not
improve Ferdinand; servants had to help him shuffle through
the halls through which he had often rolled in a wastepaper
basket as he played with the Duke of Reichstadt, and of course
he was ruler in name only.

The real power in Austria was still the all-powerful Prince
Metternich. Superbly elegant, coldly brilliant, he had survived
Napoleon the Great's victories over Austria and he intended
to survive and even thrive on the accession of the pitiful new
Emperor Ferdinand. Austria stood in first place on the Continent, with Metternich ruling it through press censorship,
theatrical censorship, police spies, a suffocating bureaucracy,
passes, checkpoints, the threat of the Whitecoats—Austria's
army. There was no constitution in his almost feudal state, no
free expression of any kind. Metternich interpreted defeat of
the radical ideas of the French Revolution as Divine support for

his ambitious return to the medieval past, and the years after Waterloo appeared to bear him out. He was the Coachman of Europe. Archdukes stood aside when he walked by.

The explosion which came in 1848, ignited in Louis Philippe's Paris, arrived at speeds unimaginable before the age of railways and the telegraph. Suddenly, because of a far-off canceled banquet, all of Vienna seemed to be taking to the streets. There was no method to it. As in Paris, the street orators were vague in their demands. They asked for some sort of parliament, some loosening of the chains. There was no concerted movement against the sad, vacant-faced Emperor Ferdinand— on the contrary, the Viennese, understanding his weakness, treated the mention of his name with affection. The target was Metternich.

The restive crowds had an ally at Court. The Archduchess Sophia hated Metternich. He had killed Reichstadt. She gathered the forces of the Austrian Empire and, "the only man in the Hofburg"—so she was called then—she ruled there would be no fight made to save the Chancellor. While men screamed for Metternich's head, Sophia strolled along the Hofburg bastions and was greeted with cheers. She bowed and smiled.

The royalties and the Ministers, almost completely under her will, sent for Metternich. He came by foot from his palace, unarmed and unguarded, carrying his walking stick and strolling at a slow pace. None of the assembled great of Austria greeted him. He leaned against a windowsill and casually gave in his resignation. Someone remarked that the crowds contained people who were rather well dressed; he replied: "Rabble." He was never more truly himself in his behavior and in what he said, but he was wrong. For this was what would be called the Imperial and Royal Revolution, and its leader was hardly of the rabble. Sophia believed the government should grant the calling of an assembly and promise a constitution, and doubtless that would be enough. The soldier Prince Windischgraetz wanted a state of siege proclaimed and troops unleashed; Sophia forbade it. But the people in the streets grew more violent. It was announced that the Emperor Ferdinand would give more concessions, freedom of the press—"everything, everything," he cried out—but now that was not enough. The workers and students rose and rioted, sacking and burning

Prince Metternich's palace—the Prince had fled—and sending to the skies, along with the flames and smoke, the rumor that the Imperial palace at Hofburg would be next. Musket fire sounded through the twisting old alleys of Vienna and it was said that the mob was pillaging and destroying everywhere. The radicals had taken over from the moderates.

All over the vast Austrian Empire the subject peoples rose up. In Prague they shot to death Prince Windischgraetz's wife; in Hungary they announced secession. Francis Joseph, Sophia's oldest son and Heir to the throne of his uncle the Emperor Ferdinand, went to Italy as the Austrian soldiers mustered together to fight off the crowds supported by regular troops of the neighboring Italian principalities.

Vienna no longer was safe. The Imperial family fled. The Archduchess Sophia was cured once and for all of any of her liberal opinions. They went to the Tyrol, the Archduchess burning with rage. "I could have borne the loss of one of my children more easily than I can the ignominy of submitting to a mess of students," she said.

It had taken place with incredible speed. On February 21, 1848, Paris and all Europe were peaceful and seemed stable; a month later Louis Philippe was gone, the Danish and Dutch monarchs were promising their subjects the world; Berlin was raked with shot and shell; a mob was marching on London, where among the Special Constables appointed to deal with the situation was found the figure of Prince Louis Napoleon, Pretender to the throne of France, who arrested a drunk on London Bridge; and in Italy, Marshal Radetsky, with his future monarch Francis Joseph at his side, was pushing back the rebels while Prince Windischgraetz bombarded Prague in support of the same objective.

The two tough old soldiers appeared to have damped the fires and the Imperial family returned to Vienna in three carriages. It was a degrading homecoming. The Emperor Ferdinand's wife sat by her husband and wept as the horses pulled the carriages through the streets. Sophia's husband, the weak Francis Charles, looked dejected. Her oldest son, Francis Joseph, appeared completely impassive. His mother, tears of rage and humiliation in her eyes, held up a lorgnette so that no one could see.

They had come back too soon. When the Minister of War ordered up local regiments to go to Hungary to fight the rebels there, a mob slashed him to pieces and hung his body by the feet, while thousands of people danced around waving torches. The next morning the Imperial family fled again, not even taking changes of clothing. There was only time to get out a single carriage, so the young Archdukes Francis Joseph and Maximilian were put on post-horses and told to keep them running alongside. They put those horses and their own bodies between their mother and the crowds yelling "Death! Death!" at her from the sidewalks. They wandered in the direction of Olmütz in Moravia, where Prince Windischgraetz promised to meet them with troop detachments he considered loyal. Behind them the mob took possession of Vienna.

In Olmütz the Imperial family took up residence in the gloomy old Archbishop's Palace. Windischgraetz passed through and went on to take Vienna at the point of his bayonets. In Hungary the troops of the Czar came in—the Russians were always happy to help crush a revolution anywhere —and broke the back of the resistance in Budapest. (When the Russians handed over prisoners to the restored Austrian authorities it was suggested that mercy be shown, to which Prince Schwarzenberg, Windischgraetz's brother-in-law and adviser, replied, "Yes, yes, a very good idea, but we must have a bit of hanging first." The rebels swung from Budapest's lampposts, save for those who escaped to England and, in the case of the leader, Kossuth, to America.) All over the Empire the police whipping posts were put back into place.

The Hapsburgs had put an end to Revolution and disorder. Within a year or two the Metternich system would be completely reestablished, and the Prince himself would come back to live out his years peacefully. But now it was time to make a change in the dynasty. For one thing, Ferdinand had compromised himself by promising his rebellious subjects all sorts of liberties: the right of public assembly, freedom of the press, a constitution; and for another thing, he was still Ferdinand, epileptic and half-idiotic.

The order of succession called for the accession of Ferdinand's brother the Archduke Francis Charles, Sophia's husband and Francis Joseph's father. But Francis Charles, still the jokester he had been when he taught the young Duke of Reich-stadt indecent expressions, was almost as useless as his older brother. His wife, the Archduchess Sophia, was capable of using epithets when she spoke of Ferdinand, but when asked if Francis Charles could better replace him, she bit her lips.

So it would have to be her son, Francis Joseph. On December 1, 1848, Francis Joseph and his three brothers, Maximilian, Karl Ludwig and Ludwig Viktor, met with their tutor to study the regulations of ecclesiastical law. Very early the next morning, they were told to don uniform and come to the Emperor's apartments in the Archbishop's Palace. Alone with his oldest son there for a few moments, Francis Charles told him that he himself had renounced his right of succession and that in the next moments Francis Joseph would become Emperor.

Francis Joseph, his brothers and relatives and the closest attendants of the family filed in to where Ferdinand awaited them. They formed a half-circle around him. Outside in the corridors the summoned courtiers wondered what was happening.

Prodded, trembling and stammering, Ferdinand laboriously read out the words written for him: ". . . lay down our Imperial Crown in favor of our beloved nephew, the Most Serene Archduke Francis Joseph . . . our beloved brother, the Most Serene Archduke Francis Charles, father of our above-mentioned most serene nephew, having irrevocably renounced his right of succession in favor of the above-mentioned son."

Francis Joseph came up to the silly old uncle and knelt before him. Ferdinand stroked his cheek. "Bear yourself bravely," Ferdinand got out. "It's all right. God will protect you." Francis Joseph, Emperor now, kissed the hand making the sign of the Cross.

"Then my dear wife embraced and kissed our new master," Ferdinand wrote later, "and then we went to our room. Afterward I and my dear wife heard Holy Mass. . . . After that I and my dear wife packed our things."

Most of the people went out to tell the courtiers they had a new ruler. The Archduchess Sophia remained behind in a Court gown of white moiré, with a rose made of jewels in her hair. Around her neck hung a necklace of turquoises and diamonds. Her son went to her and sank sobbing into her arms.

"Good-bye to the days of my youth," he had said to his father when, not half an hour earlier, he had been told he was to be Emperor. He was eighteen.

His Apostolic Majesty the Emperor Francis Joseph the First, Imperial of Austria and Royal of Hungary, has come down to posterity as a never-changing old man with muttonchop whiskers. He was not always so. Once he was a child rushing to the dying Duke of Reichstadt, yelling, "Ava!" and once he was a child awaiting the visit of his grandfather, the Austrian Emperor, who was coming to see Francis Joseph's week-old brother, the Archduke Ferdinand Maximilian Joseph. Even before the birth of his brother it was freely said in Court circles that the baby, Maximilian, was the product of an illicit liaison between the Archduchess Sophia and her lover, the Duke of Reichstadt. The chief governess of the Imperial children referred in her letters to Francis Joseph as "the big one"; the younger child, Maximilian, she invariably called "the stepson."

On July 25, 1832, the Emperor Francis came. The chief governess had already unhappily taken notice that Maximilian was larger than his brother Francis Joseph had been at the same age, and that he was better looking. She was worried about what the Emperor would think. "If only the big one will still please him," she wrote in a letter. "I'm not concerned about the stepson. For the latter I have no ambitions and I am angry to see that he will be more beautiful than the older one. This is the common reaction among all the people at the Court. Nobody wants to know anything about him and he will have difficulties to work his way into their hearts."

When the Emperor came into the nursery the two-and-a-half-year-old Francis Joseph took him by the hand and led him to the cradle where Maximilian was. "See small boy," he said to his grandfather. The governess remarked to the Emperor that the infant Maximilian would be better looking than the first child, Francis Joseph. "You think so?" asked the Emperor. "I liked the big one from the start."

The governess, old-maidish in her ways, thought her job a difficult one. The Empress liked to carry Maximilian around in her arms; the governess found it hard work to tell her that this would make the child nervous. At official functions the two little boys were forced to stand outside in wind and cold; and the governess, feeling she simply had to speak the truth, would tell their mother the Archduchess Sophia that they ought to be taken inside. Matters like cold and wind did not exist in Sophia's lexicon, and she would disagree. As a result the boys always had stuffed-up noses and coughs. The long, drafty corridors of the Hofburg did not help; nor did the suffocating Austrian bureaucracy which made the obtaining of simple luxuries an ordeal even for those charged with the well-being of the likely Heir to the Throne and his younger brother.

But the children had other compensations, such as magnificently garbed guards of honor who, clanging, came to attention when they ran down a staircase; and they had at the summer palace of Schoenbrunn the private zoo of their uncle, Crown Prince Ferdinand, and they had gardens, ponies, sleighs, dogs, toy guns and noblemen's sons to be put through the rifle drills of the Whitecoats. The older brother, Francis Joseph, was given a wooden riding-horse and he named it "Max," explaining it was as tall as Max. The governess reflected that the gesture spoke of something very kindly in one who, although yet a child, was likely to rule millions.* How nice he is to Max, she thought. How pretty to see them walking hand in hand.

Two more sons and a daughter were born to the Archduchess Sophia, all indubitably the offspring of her husband. The girl died. The third son, after the Archdukes Francis Joseph and Maximilian, was the Archduke Karl Ludwig; the fourth was the Archduke Ludwig Viktor. These two were always considered appendages to their older brothers. Karl Ludwig was a nonentity whose sincere interest in religion was his only redeeming feature. Ludwig Viktor, called Bubi in the family, was to grow up a homosexual banished to a remote castle where the only servants were women.

Francis Joseph and Maximilian—Max, Maxi or Maxl to the family—were extremely close. When Max fell ill with a contagious disease and was put into quarantine, his brother wrote to him every day, adding drawings to the letters, to tell of his activities and those of the other boys. Francis Joseph wrote his

* Modern psychiatrists might disagree.

younger brother that their tutor had been telling them stories about robbers and Princesses. He and Karl Ludwig were building a castle and a theater. "I will try to cheer you up as much as I can by my writings and drawings. Farewell, dear Brother." He wrote of how he and the other brothers had eaten pastries, almonds, bonbons and other sweets, how they had laughed when a servant misunderstood a word. Wearing donkey hats they "ran around terrible and rushed around with the little cannon and laughed until we were half dead. Good-bye, Franz." Sometimes it was, "Your most loving brother, Franz."

Their mother, Sophia, looked to their education personally, reading *Gulliver's Travels* and *Swiss Family Robinson* to them and directing the rehearsals of the ballets, playlets and recitations they offered at family feasts, birthdays and name days. Maximilian generally took the leading part in these performances; he could sing and had grace. As a very young child he had been somewhat sickly and reserved, but his mother saw and encouraged in him the makings of a lively personality.

The two older boys—Francis Joseph and Maximilian—studied the same subjects selected for them under the supervision of their mother. They learned Latin and French, Hungarian, Czech, Polish and Italian—all the main languages of their great Empire—and, of course, German. In the school of the Josefstadt Barracks they practiced equitation; Max was by far the better horseman. Together they were put through the regulation drills of the three branches of the Austrian army, gunner, lancer and liner. They studied art, religion, dancing, geography, swimming, fencing, music, gymnastics, mathematics, natural sciences, philosophy, literature, law, physics, chemistry, government, logic, technology, the building of military fortifications, bookkeeping, newspaper analysis.

Francis Joseph early emerged from this routine with the personality that stayed unchanged for the rest of his life. He was obedient, tidy, punctual. His only gaiety was drawing, and when he became Emperor he would put that away forever. Francis Joseph was duty personified. He arose early and immediately began whatever work he was directly engaged in. Imperial pomp meant nothing to him other than a force to indicate the strength and glory of the House of Hapsburg. His valet wore better underclothing than he, and when his mother gave him some magnificent furniture used by the Duke of Reichstadt, he said it was too luxurious for him. The mature Francis Joseph put away the paints and brushes of his childhood and had no recreations other than hunting and dancing and no real feeling for nature or music. He lived through the greatest period of Austrian music and German opera and never said anything more at the end of a performance than, "It was very nice. It pleased me very much." He was not a gourmet, preferring only the simplest meals, a little cold sausage (often taken at his desk while he worked) and a glass of beer. He had no small talk, no delicacy of expression. Self-contained and cold in his treatment of everyone, he had only one friend in his maturity, his cousin Prince Albert of Saxony. They went hunting together. If he was anything in this world, he was consistent, never omitting to thank the servant who awoke him each morning, always correctly attired in the uniform he inevitably wore. Sentimentality, poetry, romanticism and mysticism were equally absent from his soul. He was a true Hapsburg, the purest representative of the most bourgeois of royal families.

His brother Maximilian was more the Wittelsbach of their mother, the Archduchess Sophia. (And of course it was said of him that if indeed he had any Hapsburg blood in him he got it through Marie Louise, the mother of the Duke of Reichstadt.) The Wittelsbachs of Bavaria had always been free souls, prey to fantasy, emotional, extravagant. They tended to be outgoing, ambitious, fanciful, romantic.

Maximilian was all of these. He loved nature, the sea, animals, food, poetry, music. Francis Joseph was very careful with money; Maximilian threw it away. They appeared, the two boys, to love each other very much, but really they had nothing in common. Maximilian would quickly open his heart to people; Francis Joseph never. Maximilian was emotional, and tears often came into his eyes. Francis Joseph almost never cried. Maximilian had great charm and an easy smile. He was witty and could be very funny. He loved to mimic people and always saw the laughable side of things. He loved gossip and chitchat. In him the easiness of Viennese coffee-and-whipped-cream in the afternoon and champagne and the waltz at night came to perfect fruition.

His mother adored him. He was her "absurd and darling Max." He sent her roomfuls of flowers on her birthday; he could write poetry and speak of Destiny and Honor. Francis Joseph always did the proper and correct thing, but that was all. And where Francis Joseph was calculating in his estimates of people, Maximilian trustingly formed short-notice friendships calling for the revelation of deepest soul thoughts and for exchanged confidences. From childhood on Maximilian was a collector—seashells, paintings, rare plants, experiences. He loved to travel and exulted in the romance of foreign places. He dipped into botany, sculpture, the world of the sea, art and the writing of long and full-blown descriptions of his travels.

Maximilian was far more lively, infinitely more charming than his stiff brother. He was physically more competent. When they had their schoolboy fights, Maximilian won even though he was two years younger. But there came a moment in the Archbishop's Palace at Olmütz on December 2, 1848, when suddenly one of the brothers was a sixteen-year-old student and the other, at eighteen, was His Imperial Majesty the Emperor of Austria. Their love for each other did not long outlive that moment. Francis Joseph, the older brother and now the Emperor, continued to live with his mother and father and three brothers, and his mother regulated his eating hours and directed the refurbishing of his rooms; but everything was different. Maximilian might build a snowslide in the Hofburg garden and the Emperor might go down it with their youngest brother Bubi in his arms; and together they might try spiritualist seances complete with table tappings—but one was addressed as "Maxi" by the other and was in turn addressed as "Your Majesty" or "Sire."

Perhaps the Emperor regretted that it must be so. He appeared aware of his growing isolation, and gave intimate family dinners. At the dancing which followed the brothers had fun throwing firecrackers on the floor to make people jump about. The Archduchess Sophia knew that she was faced with two healthy young men—one being the Emperor and the other his Heir; and she arranged certain other distractions for them: parties with "hygienic Baronesses." Both her sons were very active with these young noblewomen.

The Archduke Maximilian, young and ardent and a dreamer, wanted to serve, help, lead, be at the heart of events. His brother, the Emperor Francis Joseph, was even at nineteen and twenty amazingly self-reliant. Within a short while he politely disdained even his mother's advice and went about his work as if he had been ruler for decades. He had advisers, but he used them, drained them and remorselessly dropped them to one side. In such a situation one brother had no place in the official and public life of the other brother.

But in Paris a new ruler came to the throne of France. If the rumors about the Duke of Reichstadt and the Archduchess Sophia were correct, that new French ruler was a blood relative of Maximilian. Their possible kinship could not be discussed by the two men; but the new Imperial Majesty was to be the maker of Maximilian's destiny.

4

FOUR YEARS TO THE DAY after Francis Joseph knelt before his silly old uncle to arise as Emperor of Austria, the Prince Louis Napoleon, twice-failed conspirator, was proclaimed Emperor of the French.

Louis Napoleon, the fiascos of Strasbourg and Boulogne behind him, had no role in the seemingly mindless uprisings which toppled King Louis Philippe and then spread across all of Europe in 1848. When the Revolution came the Prince left the arms of Miss Howard and rushed from London to Paris. The provisional authorities indicated his presence was unwelcome. He retreated to England. From there, in the elections held in the autumn, he got himself elected to the French Chamber of Deputies. He had not done any campaigning, of course, but he let it be known that his name was his program. The thought was disquieting and also exciting, and his appearance in the Chamber of Deputies was awaited with the greatest interest by a nation still thinking of his uncle the Great Emperor.

Louis Napoleon came and made his maiden speech. It was a disaster. Slow and mumbling as always, he droned his way through lackluster phrases ruinously delivered in his German-accented fashion. No one took him seriously after that.

An election was held to pick the President of the new Second Republic. (The first one had been ended in 1799 when General Bonaparte proclaimed himself the Emperor Napoleon the First.)

This new Napoleon who could not talk and had made a fool of himself upon at least two well-publicized occasions appeared to be a vehicle ambitious men might yet control. "A cretin whom we will manage," said Adolfe Thiers, a future President of France. "An enigmatic, somber, insignificant numbskull," said Alexis de Tocqueville. Prince Louis Napoleon became a candidate for the presidency.

He was elected by an astounding majority and was thenceforth called the Prince-President. He had just reached his fortieth birthday. Thirty-three years had passed since the first Napoleon went to St. Helena; now, escorted by dragoons and lancers, the new Napoleon went to the Élysée Palace, where he installed Miss Howard as his unofficial hostess, invisible to the public but recognized as his mistress in well-informed circles. He had no experience or past which could be looked to as a guide for predicting his future course, and certainly there had been no experience in government in his life. But he appeared interested in public-works projects and spent his time making endless tours of the provinces to open up new railroad sections and depots. He sent a contingent of French troops to Rome to protect Pope Pius IX from the Italians who had turned rabidly anticlerical following the abortive uprisings of 1848. He put through legislation to limit to twelve the hours workers could be kept at their jobs each day, and improved aid to the poor. At the same time he spoke in so conservative a manner that France's business interests looked upon him as their own.

Throughout the truly miraculous transformation from failed adventurer and ex-convict to ruler of the strongest nation in Europe, he remained the same as he had always been, with the same heavy-lidded and dull-eyed stare and vague murmurs, the same impenetrable silences. "How I wish I could break his head, to find out what goes on inside!" said his cousin whom he had loved, the Princess Mathilde. The Princess and her father, Napoleon the Great's dandified brother Jerome, and all the other relatives had come hurtling back to Paris from exile with the accession to power of the Prince-President. They were all given positions, money, honors. With the legitimate children came the illegitimate. One was Count Walewski, the bastard offspring of the Polish Countess who had enlivened the Great Emperor's stay in the room at Schoenbrunn Palace which years later would witness the death scene of his son. Count Walewski came to the side of the Prince-President and was well received. The illegitimate son of the Prince-President's mother, who called himself de Morny, appeared. At first Louis Napoleon was shocked to learn of his half-brother's existence, but soon he learned to work closely with him.

On the second of December, 1851, the Prince-President staged a coup d'état which threw away the Second Republic's constitution and made him virtual dictator of France. His half-brother de Morny managed the affair. It was conducted very brilliantly. Louis Napoleon had no taste at all for violence, and the petty bloodshed of his coup d'état bothered him all the days of his life. But in fact there had been far fewer lives taken in 1851's coup than in the 1848 Revolution.

One year to the day after the coup, four years after Francis Joseph became Emperor of Austria, on the anniversary of the day the Great Emperor won his sublime victory at Austerlitz, Louis Napoleon was elected Emperor by the people of France. The vote was 7,800,000 in favor and 250,000 against. He called himself Napoleon III, saying the dead Duke of Reichstadt had been Napoleon II.

Europe trembled at the spectacle. The first Emperor Napoleon had unleashed war, revolution, turmoil. This one, however, masked as his intentions appeared to be, indicated he wanted peace and quiet. The various Courts gathered themselves to send greetings and congratulations beginning in the traditional fashion by which reigning royalties addressed one another: "Sir my Brother." The Czar of Russia, remembering the invasion of his country and the burning of Moscow, balked. His letter began "Monsieur and Good Friend." The new Emperor of the French might have set Europe afire for that. Instead he said to the Russian ambassador presenting this most equivocal letter that he was highly flattered; that after all we are born with our Brothers but we choose our Good Friends. He would pay the Czar back before very long.

The very essence of an Empire is that there be an Heir. Miss Howard, a courtesan and the mother of an illegitimate son by a former lover, was of course unacceptable as a wife. And Napoleon III was after much higher game. He applied to Vienna for the hand of Princess Caroline Wasa. The Archduchess Sophia begged her son the Emperor to refuse the request. For Reichstadt was never far from her thoughts, and, so it has been said, "she could not bring herself to seeing the son of Hortense occupying a place that should have belonged to the King of Rome, whom she had loved."

Turned down, Napoleon III sounded a niece of Queen Victoria, who declined, partly because the Queen would not have him. He tried in Prussia, but the Hohenzollern he desired did not want him either. He was forty-two, paunchy, unreadable, a Sphinx who with his waxed moustaches was commonly described as looking the part of a Mississippi riverboat gambler—not a great catch. In addition his reign could hardly be called a stable one; in a half-century France had seen numerous forms of government—monarchy, republic, Empire, monarchy, a different monarchy, a republic and now a Second Empire. Thinking and saying that he might as well admit himself to be a parvenu, he announced he would follow, not the dictates of state, but rather those of his heart.

And his heart was indeed engaged. There had appeared in Paris, in the days of his Prince-Presidency, a Spanish lady of doubtful antecedents and even more doubtful reputation. Of partially Scottish descent, she had married a Colonel de Montijo, the son of a noble Spanish family who in time inherited title and fortune. By then his wife was notorious in Madrid for unpaid debts and lovers. It was wondered aloud who had fathered the two daughters, Paca and Eugenie.

Paca had made a brilliant marriage with a man whom her sister had desperately loved, the Duke of Alba. That marriage did not embitter relations between the two girls. But Eugenie was a very long time recovering from it. Perhaps because of it and her ardently religious Spanish nature and perhaps in reaction to her mother's long series of adventurous love affairs, she had remained determinedly virginal. Eugenie de Montijo was twenty-six when she arrived in the life of the Prince-President who was momentarily to become Emperor of the French. He met her at the salon of his cousin, the Princess Mathilde, and shortly had her to dinner with her mother. After the coffee was served he made as if to escort her away; she reminded him that her mother, the older woman, deserved the honor of strolling on his arm. He dolefully complied with the proprieties of the situation, and Mlle de Montijo walked behind with an aide.

Louis Napoleon had Eugenie to a hunting party at Compiègne and she was magnificent. The fiercest horse in the stable could not frighten a girl who had ridden bareback across Spanish plains. In her perfect jaunty attire she was in at the kill of the stag and showed no squeamishness at the sight of blood. She had always loved the bullfight.

Eugenie was very beautiful, both sitting sidesaddle and in formal dress at the evening ball. She had sapphire eyes set in a flawlessly white oval face surmounted by shining auburn hair. Her dancing was fiery. Impatient, quick to irritation, proud, a religious bigot, she stirred Louis Napoleon's blood as had no other woman of the very great number in his life. He sallied forth to make another conquest, but she was more than equal to the challenge. The members of the household, noted the British Ambassador to France, were laying odds on the day "on which the fortress would surrender," but they did not know her. "Yes," she was heard to reply to his passionate pleas, "when I am Empress, yes."

Eugenie raised questions among the people surrounding the French Emperor-to-be. Her mother, after all, had moved Paca and Eugenie from one school to another, from this hotel to that resort. The word *adventuress* was heard a great deal in Paris in late 1852. Louis Napoleon continued to importune and Eugenie to decline. Everyone knew that she had told him that there was only one way to her bedroom—through a church.

At a formal affair Eugenie felt herself insulted by the wife of one of Louis Napoleon's Ministers and with her blazing temper burst out in front of all present that she would take her leave from Paris upon the morrow. He replied in his quiet fashion that on the morrow there would not be one person in France who would insult her. The next day her mother received a note asking for her hand. Some people said that it was because he had been told that a rare plant in the Botanical Gardens which had blossomed only in the year Napoleon Bonaparte married Josephine Tascher had suddenly flowered again; but, "She has played her game with him so well," wrote the British ambassador, "that he can get her in no other way but marriage."

Louis Napoleon became Emperor in December, 1852; he married her in January, 1853. In his speech to the Legislative Body announcing the impending nuptials, he boldly said new times demanded new ways and that the time for politically inspired marriages of convenience was past. In addition, he pointed out, Eugenie had no royal relatives who need be provided for. (And it was made clear to her mother that Spain, not France, would be the better place for the older woman's abode.) Upon the announcement of their engagement the shares on the Stock Exchange dropped.

For such an Emperor marrying such an Empress-to-be, the trip to Notre Dame for the ceremony could only be in the coach used for the coronation of Napoleon and Josephine, and, later, for the marriage of Napoleon and Marie Louise. Eugenie took her vows speaking French in the Spanish Castilian accent; Louis Napoleon with his German one. "I was faithful to her for six months," he would say later.

In Vienna, the Archduchess Sophia went matchmaking. Her son the Emperor Francis Joseph had permitted himself to fall in love with a nineteen-year-old Hungarian, and appeared at a state ball wearing the uniform of a Hungarian Hussar, but the Archduchess was not having any half-Hungarian grandchildren. Her son turned to Princess Anne of Prussia, a niece of the King; but a Berlin tentatively thinking in terms of eventual leadership over the German-speaking world did not wish to ally itself to the main German rival.

There remained the Bavarian royalties, the Wittelsbachs, of whom the Archduchess was herself a member. Her sister Ludovica had five daughters. That each of the girls was a first cousin to her son did not concern the Archduchess. Ludovica greeted with enthusiasm the expressed hope of her sister Sophia that one of the girls might marry Sophia's oldest son, the reigning Emperor of Austria.

The most likely candidate was Helena, whom the family called Nené. All the girls were high-strung, given to fits of rage and passionate tears followed by uncontrollable fits of laughter, but Nené was at least minimally amenable to discipline. In the summer of 1853 the Archduchess Sophia wrote her sister Ludovica inviting her to bring Nené to the Austrian resort town of Ischl for a visit. She herself would be there with her son the Emperor.

Francis Joseph was entirely aware of the reason for his

mother's invitation. He hardly remembered Nené, for he had not seen her since the days of 1848 when he and his family had been driven out of Vienna by the mobs screaming for blood. She had been only a child then. He himself was, in the summer of 1853, twenty-three years old, tall, slim and handsome. He would have been a completely distinguished-looking young man even if he had worn the uniform of a mere lieutenant rather than, as he did, that of an Austrian general officer. Nené by contrast arrived in Ischl wearing a black dress which emphasized her pale face and made her seem drab and mousy. The Archduchess Sophia took one look and immediately ordered her own maid to dress her hair, liven her up. It was too late. In came the Emperor, to see a thin-faced girl, pale and tense. The matchmaking was not going to work.

But standing with her governess in the background was Nené's fifteen-year-old sister Elizabeth, Sisi to the family. She looked wonderful in black, as indeed she looked wonderful in anything. She was a child, but a child in whom the spectacularly beautiful woman-to-be shone forth. Sisi was by far the freest spirit of Ludovica's children. Erratic, wild, unstable, neurotic to an alarming degree, willful, she was like some untamed little animal. With a glance she made Francis Joseph her servant. Between his first look and the moment when the world knew that Elizabeth of Bavaria was to be Empress of Austria, only four days elapsed.

They were married in the spring of 1854 in Vienna. Sisi came to Francis Joseph as a sixteen-year-old schoolgirl who wrote romantic childish poetry and lived for her horses and dogs, her pet ducks and rabbits. She knew nothing of Austrian politics or history other than the little which had been drummed into her in the brief time which elapsed between the meeting at Ischl and the day when she came sailing down the Danube in a yacht bedecked with roses. The crowds and cheering, the old ladies of her Aunt Sophia's suite kissing her hand, all terrified her. She had written to her aunt and future mother-in-law using the familiar *du* and had been reprimanded by her fiancé, who told her that he himself had never in his life addressed his mother by other than the formal *sie*. To the Archduchess the whole thing was wrong. "Little monkey," Sophia said. "Nasty old woman," the child learned to call her.

The wedding night was a catastrophe. For one hundred and more years since then Vienna has said that the bridegroom, too experienced with "hygienic Baronesses," killed in his child bride his and his country's hopes for a successful marriage. In the morning, by the orders of the Archduchess Sophia, the new Imperial couple had to appear at early breakfast; and it is said Sophia's blunt questions shattered Sisi.

The child bride who had become Empress of Austria was never meant to be happy. The half-mad daughter of a half-mad Bavarian father, Sisi was trapped in a world that served as her prison. Her father, unhampered by responsibilities, could wander Asia Minor and Greece at his leisure and return to produce execrable writings. He had been free to take his daughter into villages where they were not known, there to play his fiddle while she danced for coins the peasants threw at her. No such freedom existed for her when she became Empress. Her ladies-in-waiting were the confidantes of her mother-in-law the Archduchess Sophia, who called her "a silly chit of a girl who does not know enough to behave herself." They did not respect her. She could never be alone, never free of the stiff Court protocol of the Hofburg and Schoenbrunn. (When she became the first Empress in Austrian history ever to wear a pair of shoes twice, courtiers threw up their hands.)

The Empress of Austria took refuge in insane exercise regimes which called for hikes lasting fifteen hours, in endless horseback riding, in mad diets which saw her subsist for a week at a time on carrots or milk or grapes. She conceived a dangerous inner life in which she believed she left the dull and business-like existence of the nineteenth century and journeyed with heroes and poets of old. In public she habitually covered her face with a fan or handkerchief.

Francis Joseph the man she briefly loved; Francis Joseph the Emperor she cared not a whit about. He on his part worshiped this uncaught and uncatchable prize. No whim of hers was left unsatisfied. She took, in time, endless trips to far-off Mediterranean islands where she built immensely expensive castles only to abandon them; she went to follow the hunt in Ireland, taking along half-a-hundred Imperial Stables horses for her exclusive use; she went on cruises. She left him lonely. No man was ever lonelier.

In all the Court, Sisi found but one sympathetic soul. It was her husband's brother, Maximilian.

The Archduke at twenty-one was tall, slim, very blond, with light-blue eyes. He liked to be called, and called himself, a sailor Prince. That was the work that had been found for him. He had needed something to keep him occupied. Francis Joseph had originally seen him as the family's poetic dreamer and patron to the arts. The Viennese would like that. But Maximilian felt in himself the need for something greater, saying in his romantic way that he wished to soar above the clouds, that he could not walk or trot, but had to gallop. To be simply and solely an Imperial Prince living on his appanage was, he said, the most ignoble thing in the world. The Archduchess Sophia, feeling her oldest son slipping away from her even in the first months of his reign, encouraged the hopes of her favorite child. Within two years from the moment at Olmütz when Francis Joseph became Emperor, Maximilian had become a serious problem for him. Francis Joseph's first love and first dependency was his army, the Whitecoats. Officers surrounded him. He had come to his position, after all, by way of the bayonets of Windischgraetz and Radetsky. Maximilian, an idealist, was repelled by soldiers. Hurt by his brother's disinclination to allow him any real role in the monarchy, he became increasingly liberal, permitting himself to say that the Emperor was too narrow, too strict, too much the successor of Metternich.

Maximilian was the Heir to the Throne. It was intolerable to the Emperor that his brother permit himself the too-free expression of such thoughts. They argued. But the argument could have no resolution. Francis Joseph had the power to retain or dismiss the members of the Archduke's household and to regulate his movements. But Maximilian, a Prince of Austria, could not be disciplined beyond a certain point. The solution was to send him away. Let him become the sailor Prince of a navy which had not fought an important engagement since the Battle of Lepanto in the sixteenth century.

The Archduchess Sophia approved of the plan. Two years before Francis Joseph met Sisi, Maximilian had fallen in love with Countess Paula von Linden. Paula was seventeen and dressing for a Shrove Tuesday noon-to-six dance at the palace of the Prince Auersperg when Maximilian made his intentions known. They were in the form of flowers delivered to the Vienna residence of her father, the Minister from Wurttemberg. There was no note attached but Paula knew who the sender was. Her father said she could not wear flowers sent anonymously, but she innocently said she supposed they were from an old noblewoman of her acquaintance. Her father made no more objections. She went to the dance, where she found Maximilian deputizing for his brother as guest of honor. He came to her before the first cotillion and asked her to dance, disregarding the protocol which dictated that the Princess Auersperg be his first partner.

At six Paula went home to change for the evening ball at the Hofburg. The same messenger who had delivered the first bouquet arrived with an even more stunning offering. She put it on and when she entered the Imperial Palace she saw Maximilian's younger brother Archduke Karl Ludwig leaning against a door. He winked at her. So he's in on the secret, she thought. Maximilian came to her and together they danced almost every dance. They were observed very carefully by the Archduchess Sophia, who did not like what she saw. Paula was no catch in the eyes of Maximilian's mother. As the clock began to bang out the twelve strokes which would mean midnight had come and Lent with it, the Archduke and Countess moved at an ever-slowing pace, and when at the final stroke Johann Strauss the Younger lowered his baton they stood motionless together. The next day Maximilian was ordered to Trieste for a cruise on an Austrian navy ship.

He found the commander's cabin of the *Novara* decorated with what he called "arsenal taste," with the colors of the furniture and curtains "in too glaring contrast with each other." But as the *Novara* headed south along the Italian coast, the Archduke became enraptured with the sea and the sunsets and storms: "The overawed soul feels the littleness and vanity of man."

He tried ocean swimming and felt upon his first try that he was like "a swan on the blue waves." All of the south captivated him; he saw himself as one with the ancient German tribes who wandered from the north and were struck by "the mighty spell of Italy." At Vesuvius he covered his face with a handkerchief to peer into the volcano from which sulphuric fumes issued, and thought the deposits surrounding the mountain spoke of the earth as it must have been before the "foot of a race of sinners" appeared, when the land was not yet animated "by the breath of the Most High."

At Pompeii, Maximilian exulted in a "gloomy ruin such as I love . . . the objects in a mystical dusk." Naples excited him: "Where will your jubilant sensual life end—where are you dancing to, you joyous Neapolitans?" He went on, "To Sorrento. To Sorrento! What melody is in that name. . . . Throne of the poet's love." On the eighteenth of August, Mass was held on the ship to celebrate the birthday of the Emperor, the first one the brothers had spent apart.

After that, all through the early 1850's, Maximilian was constantly away on his cruises, sometimes with his younger brother the Archduke Karl Ludwig along. Almost always he took a professor or scientist with him to aid in assembling souvenirs for his growing collection of plants, animals, rocks. He went to Spain and saw a bullfight. Before it began he had qualms and half-decided to leave, but when it started he was immensely stimulated and thought it a vital and moving sight remindful of braver, more gallant days and symbolic of the ways of the heroes of old: "I love the olden time! . . . The times of our ancestors when chivalrous feeling was developed." The matador dedicated a bull to Maximilian and he fancied himself back in the days when the Hapsburgs ruled the Spanish people. Something of the same thought came to him when he stood by the graves of Ferdinand and Isabella—his ancestors—and held the ring and the sword of Ferdinand the Catholic, thinking what it would be to reconquer their lost dominions in the New World: "What a lovely, glittering dream for a nephew of the Spanish Hapsburgs!"

He was in Vienna not long after the marriage of his brother and Elizabeth of Bavaria. There Maximilian would talk to her for hours about his adventures and travels. And he aroused in his brother Francis Joseph a hellish feeling of jealousy as the Emperor watched Sisi excitedly hang on Maximilian's words and respond to Maximilian's full-blown courtly ways and gay, laughing manner. The Archduke left Vienna after a short visit.

Maximilian sailed to Greece and took long horseback expeditions through the mountains, saying it was a glorious thing that bandits still lurked in the crags and caves, for without them "Where, then, would be the last remnants of romance?" At the Parthenon he took a bottle of Austrian wine brought especially for the purpose and opened it in front of King Creon's throne. Then with the members of his party he offered a toast to the mythological gods, took "a mighty draught" and dashed the bottle to pieces on the marble before the throne.

At Smyrna he conjured up the spirits of Alexander the Great and Richard the Lion-hearted; in Albania he dreamed of wandering in the long grass for hours; in Algiers he longed for the depths of the African jungle. His thoughts were never for the drab present. Factories depressed him—they leveled all men to mere automatons—railroads were "the ruin of all poetry."

Maximilian became perhaps the best traveled royalty of his day, and certainly the best traveled Hapsburg of memory. The Emperor Joseph II used to wander in commoner's attire during the days before the French Revolution, riding stagecoaches and talking with the passengers. Francis, his grandfather, had walked through Vienna chatting with whoever approached him. Their wanderings served a purpose; they sought, Joseph through intelligent perception and Francis from idle curiosity, to gain some insight into the minds of their subjects. But they were Emperors and rulers, while he was but the Heir of a young and virile brother married to a girl who would surely have children. He was a questing, unhappy young man.

5

Two years an Emperor, Napoleon III paid off his debt to a Czar of All the Russias who declined to call an Emperor of the French *Sir my Brother*. A French expeditionary force went to Gallipoli and the Dardanelles and the Heights of the Alma and to the Fortress of Sebastopol. The Crimean War's origins no one could quite identify and its entire meaning was unclear; but it was a war which saw the Tricolor again floating at the heads of columns of troops rushing forward as the heirs of the Great Emperor to expunge their country's memories of the Moskva and Berezina. It was given to the Chasseurs d'Afrique to rescue what was left of Lord Raglan's Light Brigade when its charge shattered on the Russian artillery.

The Empress Eugenie emotionally saw the troops off to their transports and then went with her husband to confer with their opposite numbers in Windsor Castle. Her Britannic Majesty had expected to detest these parvenus on sight; to her great surprise she found them charming. Eugenie deferred to her in all things. The Prince Consort, born a German, sang Teutonic duets with the Emperor of the French brought up as one. The French rulers left Great Britain as firm friends of Victoria and Albert, ignoring the cruel comparisons which were current, one being upon the fashion in which the royalties seated themselves. The British royal family simply sat down when they were tired of standing, for they knew someone would be there holding a chair. Napoleon and Eugenie looked first.

In 1856 the troops came home from the Crimea, victors in their own eyes and in the eyes of Europe. Even as Italian military victories had consolidated the Empire of the Great Napoleon, so the Crimea solidified the Empire of his nephew—

who was by his enemies called Napoleon the Little. What the enemies said did not matter. France was enormously prosperous as it embraced the Industrial Revolution; France's army was home from the wars with its laurels. The world flocked to a Paris being rapidly rebuilt and modernized. The medieval old city was, under Napoleon's direction, cut through with magnificent boulevards—ideal for straight artillery or musket discharges—and the old cobblestones were replaced with asphalt which would not be so easily pulled up and flung and the open-drainage ditches which might hinder cavalry charges were replaced with covered sewers. The total effect, beyond reassuring the mind of a ruler retaining the outlook of a revolutionary conspirator, was magnificent. The Second Empire came into flower.

It was glorious—and vulgar. Upon the plush and silken banquettes of the Tuileries the courtesan sat by the princess, and mixed in the stunningly elaborate balls at St. Cloud were stock market confidence men and the grandsons of the Great Emperor's marshals. The Faubourg St.-Germain, where the old royalist aristocracy lived, never accepted any of it. To them the Empress Eugenie was not even Mme. Bonaparte—she was referred to as "She," "The Spanish Woman" or "Mademoiselle Montijo." Eugenie tried to swamp what they said in the flurry of brilliance and activity which surrounded her Court. Bowing right and left, she traveled only in a four-horse coach complete with postillions, outriders, a troop of cavalry; with her husband she loaded honors and glory upon all remindful of the great days of the Great Emperor. De Morny, the Emperor's half-brother, became richer than ever and head of the Legislative Body on his way to a Dukedom; Count Walewski was Foreign Minister; the Great Emperor's silly old brother, Jerome, was addressed as "Your Majesty" and given the post of Governor of the Invalides along with a stipend of two hundred thousand francs a year. A magnificent statue was erected over Hortense's grave and a cult of the nobility of Josephine became fashionable.

But Eugenie was not happy. She brooded over the fate of Marie Antoinette and collected all the samples she could find of the Queen's jewelry, lace, fans, statuettes, books. She talked endlessly about the Queen, her childhood in Vienna, her life in the Tuileries, her children, her execution. The Empress had an almost morbid interest in Marie Antoinette's death, and spoke of it endlessly. If the mob should ever get her, Eugenie said, she hoped they would kill her outright. It was humiliation she feared the most, that they might lift up her skirts and expose her—might touch her.

The Empress looked wonderful in her muslin gowns equipped with flounces, puffings and paddings over multiple sets of petticoats, but there was something frantic in her determination that everything must be perfect—that her ladies-in-waiting be the most beautiful women in France and her horse equipages the finest to be seen in the world. (The Faubourg St.-Germain said, of course, it was all the unmistakable sign of the parvenu.) Her vermeil service, her footmen in powdered wigs, her gold, satin, plush, her embroideries and knickknacks everywhere—it was overdone. She had always been high-strung, and palace chamberlains throwing open doors declaiming, "Her Majesty the Empress!" as the music began did not allay her nervousness.

It was her marriage, of course. She screamed at him in front of other people. It was his unfaithfulness. Emperor of the French and middle-aged, Napoleon III could not resist the temptations. He moved through great Tuileries rooms adorned with majestic portraits of all the marshals of the France of the First Empire, and murmured to the wives of his Ministers, his wife's ladies, to courtesans and opera singers and dancers that they would come to him that night or the next. They always consented. "Half an hour sufficed to make me an Empress," one of them said. (The next day the girl saw the Emperor had a new favorite, and fiddled with the new one's merry-go-round wooden horse so that it would fall and hopefully fling her head over heels.)

" 'Ugenie, 'Ugenie, you go too far," he would mumble when his wife ranted at him or wept incessantly. He did nothing to change his ways. But after all nothing could stir up Napoleon III. "The other day a servant squirted a siphon of seltzer water into his neck and he merely set his glass on the other side of his plate, without a word and without the slightest sign of irritation," said Princess Mathilde to a friend. "He never loses his temper and the angriest word of which he is capable is 'It's absurd!' He never says anything more than that. He doesn't even whisper anything worse."

The Emperor appeared to have no nerves and no emotions; he was always kind, always dreamingly attentive to the desires of the people around him. It was impossible to dislike him. The Empress, on the other hand, lived on her nerves and could be haughty and vindictive. People feared her. She took water cures and immersed herself in Marie Antoinette and in a study of sartorial fashions which resulted in her becoming, beyond doubt, the best dressed woman in the world and the acknowledged pacesetter for women everywhere, but it did not help. Their marriage continued downhill.

Mercifully, Eugenie became pregnant. The accouchement was very difficult and her screams were plainly heard from her chamber. When finally she was delivered and the infant was seen to be a boy, her husband went into ecstasies of delight, running from one person to another, showering at least a half-dozen with kisses.

The birth of the Child of France, Louis Napoleon the Prince Imperial, meant the dynasty was cemented into position. In its splendor, with its army bedecked with shining jackboots, gleaming gold breastplates, with plumes and pennons and sword knots, the nation stood in first place on the Continent, its Emperor referred to by Pope Pius IX as "the Constantine of Christian France, the Charlemagne of modern times."

No two men could have been more different than the volcanic Napoleon I and the stolid Napoleon III. But the Second Empire was forever harking back to the First, everlastingly holding celebrations of the Great Emperor's victories. Those victories had to a great extent been gained over Austria. In Vienna it came to the Emperor Francis Joseph that he must have more knowledge of this new Napoleon, some insight into his thinking, and, if possible, some sort of arrangement with him. The Austrian Ambassador to Paris, Count Hübner, was not the man to send telling dispatches. He seemed too much under the spell of the Second Empire's glitter and splendor. Someone else must go and see and report back. Francis Joseph thought of his brother Max.

The Archduke Maximilian arrived at the railroad station in Paris on May 17, 1856, and then went on to the suburban palace at St. Cloud escorted by Napoleon's cousin, a dilettante who was universally called "Plon-Plon." The forty-eight-year-old Napoleon III was waiting at the top of the steps. His lengthy silences, his mumbled responses, his numb manner, were not calculated to impress the Archduke. Maximilian, tall and elegant, looked down and saw a man who in his view was characterized by short and unimposing stature, a shuffling gait, ugly hands and sly, lusterless glances from hooded eyes. It was not difficult to form an unfavorable impression.

Maximilian was taken in to see the Empress Eugenie, still a semi-invalid recovering from the birth of the Prince Imperial. Led by chamberlains in red and gold through the rigid lines of the Cent Gardes in breastplates of polished steel and high plumed helmets, he found her reclining upon a chaise longue in a darkened room. She wore a blue silk robe with white lace at the neck. There was a rose over her ear. He bent to kiss her hand and she appeared abashed at the gesture. She disappointed him. He thought her anxious to be outgoing—"she took extraordinary pains to be nice," Maximilian wrote Francis Joseph —but she seemed embarrassed. He thought her undeniably beautiful but there was something about her which spoke too much of hairdressers and makeup. She was, the Austrian Archduke thought, "quite thoroughbred, but essentially lacking the august quality of an Empress." He thought to himself of his Imperial sister-in-law the Empress Elizabeth, and his comparison to the Empress of the French did not favor the latter.

Owing to her convalescence, Eugenie did not appear at dinner that night. The Archduke thought the food was badly served. The conversation did not go well, for the Emperor was so taciturn that Maximilian found it difficult to bring some liveliness into the proceedings. After the meal the Archduke visited the Empress, and then, the next morning, walked in the gardens with the Emperor. Napoleon talked at some length of his uncle the Great Emperor and made kind references to Francis Joseph. "Much archness," thought Maximilian. They spoke of the recent Crimean War and it seemed to Maximilian that Napoleon was delighted that France had done so much to humiliate Czar Nicholas and Russia. But why had not Austria joined in, wondered the Emperor. "Had we drawn the sword," the Archduke replied, "the war would have been endless." His assignment to Austria of a position which was too great to fight a limited war such as had been undertaken by France and England seemed to set the Emperor back on his heels.

They discussed England, the Archduke saying that Austrian principles rested upon a firm foundation of upright conservatism, while England, "the great nation of shopkeepers," was opportunistic. "Yes," said Napoleon, "it is a misfortune." He did not seem to Maximilian to be well informed. His ignorance, in fact, "astonished" the Archduke. He did not know how long the Emperor Ferdinand's reign had been; he did not know where Ferdinand now lived.*

At luncheon the Empress came to table. Following the meal the Archduke called upon Napoleon Bonaparte's foolish old brother, the former King Jerome, who struck Maximilian as looking like "an old Italian dentist"; Jerome's daughter, Princess Mathilde, who seemed of a "common appearance" and Jerome's son, Plon-Plon. He had been Maximilian's original surly welcomer to Paris; now on their second meeting the Archduke found Plon-Plon's amiability no more striking than it had been at the railroad station. He was in Maximilian's eyes the perfect image of a "worn-out *basso* from some obscure Italian opera house."

That evening the Emperor and Empress offered their guest a state dinner at St. Cloud. It seemed to the twenty-four-year-old Maximilian that the forty-eight-year-old Napoleon had incredible "lack of ease." He put it down to Napoleon being "in the presence of a prince of more ancient lineage." But Maximilian tried to make things easier for the French monarch and concealed as best he could his feeling that the affair had none of the quality of Imperial entertainment, that nothing went smoothly, that the "parvenu etiquette keeps coming through everything." It was unnecessary, he wrote his brother, "to assure Your Majesty that I take pains to be very nice and to let no sign appear of the unpleasant impressions which strike me here and there."

Maximilian spent twelve days with Their Imperial Majesties, making an agreeable impression on the curates of the Louvre, who found him possessed of an excellent knowledge of the fine arts, and on the people of Paris, who cheered him

---

* Eating and praying to his heart's content, the former Emperor lived quite happily in Prague.

when he went about the city. But he did not change his mind about the Second Empire: it reeked of the nouveau, it was all transitory and overdone. The Imperial couple did not know how to behave in the presence of servants; they spoke too freely in front of subordinates and permitted the members of their suites to act too freely, allowing them to shake their hands. Versailles was too grandiose and not as dignified as Schoenbrunn, the theatrical piece presented in the Imperial theater was improper and not fit for showing before ladies, the behavior of the Empress was shockingly parvenu. When Maximilian bent to adjust a hassock at her feet her apologies for his trouble and thanks for his solicitude were so overwhelming that even her husband said, "It's too much."

"There can be no question of a good or bad tone here," Maximilian wrote Francis Joseph, "for this Court is absolutely lacking in tone." The state ball at St. Cloud "produced an irresistibly comic effect upon me. . . . The society was inconceivably mixed, and distinguished for its disgusting dress and tactless behavior. Adventurers swarmed, which is a leading characteristic of this Court."

But to a certain extent he found the French monarchs palatable. He decided that Eugenie had freshness and openness, that Napoleon was easygoing and informal. He thawed to them, thinking to himself that the Emperor could be manipulated. What was needed were fine phrases for his social climber's ears. Maximilian "fired off at close range" a few earlier thought-out compliments and had the satisfaction of deciding he had conquered Napoleon. "We are like old friends," the Emperor said when the Archduke was leaving. The Imperial couple lent him their yacht, *The Queen Hortense,* to continue on his way. For his trip was not finished. On its first leg he had met the man and woman who would one day make his destiny. Now on their yacht he went to meet the girl who would share it with him. *The Queen Hortense* took him to Belgium. He was glad to be back among people of his own kind, who lived a well-bred existence. He felt at home with the Belgian royal family.

The head of that family was the King of the Belgians, Leopold I. The son of the German Duke of Saxe-Coburg-Saalfeld, Leopold had married the daughter of the future King George

IV of England, who ruled as Prince Regent on behalf of his mad father, George III. The daughter's name was Charlotte. Upon the accession of her father to the Throne of England, she would be his Heir. Leopold's future seemed assured: his wife would be Queen one day and a child of his would rule England when she was gone.

But his wife died giving birth to their stillborn child. Overnight Leopold was a foreigner with no future, living off an English allowance. His sister had married the Duke of Kent and given birth to a daughter; and he stayed in England assisting in the upbringing of his niece and wondering what to do with himself. In 1830, in the wake of the French uprisings which chased away the brother of the guillotined Louis XVI and brought in Louis Philippe, the people of the southern section of the Netherlands revolted and broke away to form the new country of Belgium. After carefully considering the question he consented to come and be King of the Belgians.

Solemn, conscientious, exceedingly thoughtful of his every act, he made a magnificent ruler for the stolid and hard-working Belgians. Under his reign the new country prospered mightily. He sought to ally himself with the France of Louis Philippe and proposed a marriage with the daughter of the Citizen King. He was forty-two; the French King's daughter, Princess Louise Marie, was twenty. She came to him as a Princess of France under orders, feeling, as she said later, "absolute indifference." In time they learned to love each other. Louise Marie was small, blonde, blue-eyed, discreet. She did not wish to shine in the limelight but knew how to win people's hearts. She was a reader and thinker and good adviser. She made her husband very happy, and he called her "my angelic Louise." The people of her new country loved her. Every railroad station, hotel salon, restaurant carried her picture on the wall.

Their first child was the Duke of Brabant, born in 1835, the Heir, named Leopold for his father. Philippe, Count of Flanders, followed two years later. In 1840 Queen Louise Marie gave birth to a girl. Her husband had wanted another boy and his disappointment was obvious. Queen Louise Marie spoke of that to her mother, the wife of the Citizen King, and her mother wrote back from Paris that there need be no worry;

that this Princess would be the pet of her father. That was the way older men were.

At the insistence of Queen Louise Marie, the infant was named after her husband's first wife, the English princess who died bringing forth his stillborn child: Charlotte.

She grew up in the eyes of the people of Belgium as the little girl seen in hundreds of thousands of pictures hanging in innumerable homes. Her brothers, one slim in his Grenadier's uniform and the other chubby in his Guards attire, stood by her; she smiled from under her big ribboned hat: "Our good little Princess."

By Charlotte's fourth birthday her grandmother's prediction had been fulfilled. Her father loved her the best. The girl was "a little better received this morning than four years ago," Queen Louise Marie wrote her mother. She was "lively . . . petulant . . . talkative . . . astonishingly intelligent . . . wanting absolutely from the age of two-and-a-half to learn to read." Well-spoken but "willful without a doubt," Charlotte was also capricious and temperamental. She was active and persevering. She read all the time and went to Te Deums where she conducted herself well, carrying her part in the service very nicely. Princesses are always said to be beloved of the poor and humble, but in Charlotte's case it was so; her mother the Queen was very active in charitable work and invariably took little Charlotte with her wherever she went.

Sometimes her mother took her to Paris to visit her grandfather and grandmother, writing ahead to say that no arrangements need be made for the child to be in the same room as herself, for although she was with Charlotte all day at the Palace of Laeken, Charlotte was used to sleeping alone. Indeed she was very little worry to her mother, unlike the sardonic Heir, who was already giving signs of the chilling although brilliant personality which, full blown, he would inflict upon the world once he gained the Throne.

In 1848 the Revolution which banished Louis Philippe to England and retrieved the future French Emperor, Prince Louis Napoleon, from English banishment, swept through France and from France to all of Europe and to an Austria which turned against Prince Metternich. Abandoned by the

Hapsburgs operating under the leadership of the Archduchess Sophia, Metternich fled Vienna and ended in the only stable country left in Europe, Belgium. There all was serene. Very briefly King Leopold had wondered if his people would turn against him as the people of so many other European monarchs were doing. With arrogant astuteness, he offered to abdicate if that was what Belgium wanted. But because of the intelligence of his rule his subjects begged him to stay. His dynasty was safe when every other Throne was in jeopardy, a fact that made Leopold a figure of awe. Across the Channel in England his sister's child, born into a position quite remote from the British Throne, became, through the deaths and childless marriages of the closer Heirs, Her Britannic Majesty Queen Victoria. She was eighteen when she took up her duties, and very much dependent for advice of all kinds upon her uncle in Belgium, to whom she wrote with the greatest regularity. A matchmaker, Leopold tactfully introduced her to his nephew, Prince Albert of Saxe-Coburg-Gotha, with whom she fell in love and blissfully married. She was now his niece twice over. Leopold reached heights of influence throughout Europe from which he was never to fall. He began to call himself, and to be called, the Nestor of Kings.

His wife, Queen Louise Marie, more human, warmer, more approachable, was truly loved by the millions of strangers who were their subjects. All of Belgium sorrowed for the Queen when in 1848 her sad old mother and father were chased from the Tuileries into a horsecab which took them to safety, followed by exile in England. Extremely upset at their plight, Queen Louise Marie sought consolation in her children, particularly in her daughter Charlotte. Every day they worked together on the Princess's studies. The little girl was particularly good at German, English, music and religious studies. Of course there were other influences in Charlotte's life, including the teachings of her father, and the kindness of her first cousin the Queen of England, who in that Revolution year of 1848 sent her a dollhouse—but her mother of course came first. The Queen's importance to her daughter was beyond that of the usual mother. For a Princess of Belgium was protected from outside influences—school, neighbors, numerous playmates. Queen Louise Marie was at once Charlotte's best friend, teacher and loving mother. Charlotte was taught good manners; she wrote Queen Victoria to thank her for the dollhouse and doll, saying, "Every day I dress my doll and give her a good breakfast; and the day after her arrival she gave a great rout at which all my dolls were invited. Be so good, my dearest Cousin, as to give my love to all my dear little Cousins, and believe me always, your most affectionate Cousin." She was eight.

Two years later, in 1850, Queen Louise Marie's father, the former King Louis Philippe, was dead. His daughter, the Queen of the Belgians, did not long survive him. She sank into her last illness saying that her only sorrow was that others suffered for her; and when at last the doctors told King Leopold it was over he sobbed, "Her death is as holy as her life." Victoria in her letter of condolence did not mention the dead woman's two sons but told Leopold how often and how touchingly Queen Louise Marie had spoken to her of Charlotte.

Ten years old, the little girl deprived of her mother turned in upon herself. Her gaiety was gone. Her tutors, noblewomen selected by her late mother, saw this and tried to counteract the shock of the Queen's death, but nothing could be done. In the summer Charlotte went to the British royal family's seaside residence of Osborne as Victoria's guest, and Victoria tried to reach her, but in vain. The child was appealing and charming, but she could not be treated like a child. She was more like a small adult. With an intelligent adult's reasoning brain, Charlotte saw she was disconcerting the Queen, and so she went running and jumping through the grass in order to please her cousin. Victoria wrote King Leopold to indicate that all was well. But it was not. Charlotte entered adolescence as a very thoughtful, extremely pensive child. She was very much like her father, "a miniature Leopold." Her brothers were entirely different. Philippe was gay, a good dancer, a great hunter. Everybody loved him, including his sister. "My big Philippe," she called him. They were the best of friends. The older brother, the Heir, called Leopold after his father, was murderously cruel and violent, and in his pride forced recognition of his position even from his sister, who disliked him. It was not hard to do so. The tiniest real or imagined slight would make him sulk for weeks.

Their father gave each of the children the same general education. He told his daughter that each night one must make a moral judgment upon oneself and recapitulate the day's doings. One's motives should be examined and the motives of others considered. He warned Charlotte against vanity and pride and the acceptance of flattery, for it came too easily to those in high position. As he had with his niece, the Queen of England, he told his young daughter that the security royalty held before the French Revolution could never be regained and that frequent falls from high estate could now be expected. Character therefore must be built so as not to be crushed by bad fortune or unduly exalted by good.

Charlotte's precise and reasoning mind translated her father's teachings into an ineradicably held feeling that God had imposed upon her an injunction to be worthy of the bounty which attended a Princess of Belgium. To fill her role would require the greatest exertions of mind and spirit, and in pursuit of her objectives she was by the age of thirteen reading the deepest religious tomes and the lives of the great men of the past. She was extremely strict with herself and with others. Aware of her demanding views, she worried that perhaps she was too exacting in her judgment of others, and asked her tutor to give her sermons whose point was that she should not judge people too quickly or harshly. Charlotte's way of looking at herself, however, was not to be modified by any kind of forgiveness. She looked to God to help her live up to her high ideals for herself, but she thought herself lazy and irresolute. She did not understand herself enough, she said, and, Puritan-like, she worked harder. She studied calculus, Kings of England, music, math, in an almost feverish fashion.

She worked far more than she played. In fact even her play became work. Saying that it was important to have a strong constitution, she never paddled about when she swam, but practiced her strokes religiously. The same was true of her horseback riding. It was not for fun but for study that she mounted the animals in her father's stables. One became "all cotton" without hard sports, she said. She took her needlework very seriously, working like a slave on a pair of tapestried bedroom slippers for her father or a purse for her brother Philippe.

Charlotte's strong will was extraordinary for so young a girl. Sometimes there came into her somewhat melancholy eyes a sudden flash of emotion, but it seemed to the people of the Belgian Court that she subjugated it instantly in her desire to remain calm and in possession of herself. It was banality or vulgarity or laziness of body or spirit which brought out those flashes. Such wastes shocked and horrified her. She tried to live up to her mother's performance as patron of charitable works, and was the exact opposite of the kind of royalty who plays her life away. Such a Princess, it seemed to her, was the Archduchess Henriette of Hungary who married her brother Leopold. Henriette was interested, Charlotte thought, only in music. Her new sister-in-law, she wrote, was "about to break my heart with concerts. . . . It's insipid." She thought her brother's wife frivolous and empty.

The Princess was not the type of girl conventionally described as beautiful, although her father thought her to be so. But intelligence shone forth from her somber features. People meeting Charlotte for the first time were invariably struck by her command of many subjects, her seriousness and analytical manner.

The Princess took official visits seriously, as she took seriously all things, and so when the Court of Vienna formally asked if His Imperial Highness the Archduke Ferdinand Maximilian Joseph might not come to Brussels after his visit to the Emperor and Empress of the French, the Princess Charlotte wrote a former tutor that it was her hope that "subjects of conversation will not be lacking," and that "I certainly hope the inhabitants of this House will conduct themselves correctly." Perhaps she was thinking of a particular inhabitant of her House, her odious brother Leopold, Duke of Brabant. As the Heir, he was sent to receive the Austrian Archduke alighting from the yacht of the Emperor of the French. Maximilian thought him "rather Machiavellian" and suspected the depth of his "guise of overwhelming friendliness" as they traveled toward the capital.

To Charlotte's astonishment her brother Leopold was charmed by the Archduke. She was almost suspicious of the practically unique display of generosity her brother manifested when he wrote her that "the Archduke is a very superior being from all points of view. If I had one thing to say in his disfavor I would have said it. But there is nothing. You can be sure of it."

Charlotte's father advanced upon Maximilian in his Nestor-of-monarchs fashion and at the conclusion of the welcoming state dinner offered a lecture as the two men sat in a window embrasure. "Interminable," Maximilian wrote Francis Joseph. They parted with the King promising to come see the Arch-duke the next day for a further lecture on political science, "an offer I received yawning in spirit."

In the morning the King, true to his word, came to the Arch-duke's apartments. He was sixty-six to Maximilian's twenty-four, and Maximilian looked upon him as a pompous old party seeking to be the Pope as well as the Nestor of monarchs, "before whose pronouncements all of Europe must bow." The lecture went on for an hour while everyone waited lunch. He was a well-bred old man, Maximilian thought, and the Palace of Laeken was lovely, although the palace in central Brussels didn't even have stone staircases. But when Maximilian traveled through the little kingdom, he forgot this omission, for Belgium was a model country, neat, prosperous, with every-thing well laid out. Despite himself he was impressed.

The daughter of the King of the Belgians was instantane-ously and totally impressed by the Austrian Archduke. He was after all tall, handsome and very gallant. And he was so different from the men around her, her solemn aging father, her light-weight brother Philippe and the sinister Heir to the Throne. Maximilian was both outgoing and yet a thinker interested in many subjects. He talked of his plans for the Austrian navy, of the great port he hoped to construct in Trieste, the fortifica-tions he would install; but he could also talk of art and his botanical collections. His piety appeared to match hers, and she loved that in him. Princess Charlotte was an analytical and reasoning being, and a very intelligent one—but she was also sixteen years old. She fell head over heels in love.

Maximilian, on his part, found it "quite incredible that the young Princess should be so much in advance of her years in intelligence." And he liked her appearance, thinking she might make a beauty when she got older. But he suspected her mo-tives, thinking that her crafty father might have stage-managed an attempt to ally his family with that of the Emperor of Austria. Maximilian was taken with Charlotte when he left Brussels, but he was wary too.

In fact the King of the Belgians was pressing the matter, urging people he knew in Vienna to encourage Maximilian to ask for Charlotte's hand. The Archduke knew and resented it. Word of his attitude soon reached Brussels. King Leopold averred that the Archduke was mistaken. "My dear and most gracious prince is a little inclined, I think," he wrote Maximilian, "to take me for a great diplomatist, who has some special political reason in view in every step that he takes. This, however, is not the case, and in May you had already won my confidence and goodwill, quite apart from all political considerations."

Maximilian was not the only royalty who questioned the match. Queen Victoria wrote her uncle that Charlotte could do better. She should marry Pedro of Portugal, "*the* most distinguished young Prince there is." Charlotte would be a blessing for Portugal and it would be far wiser for her to be given to Pedro "than to one of those innumerable Archdukes." Leopold wrote back, perhaps not entirely truthfully: "My object is and was that Charlotte should decide as *she* likes it, and uninfluenced by what I might prefer. *I* should *prefer* Pedro, that I confess, but the Archduke had made a favorable impression on Charlotte; I saw that long before the question of an engagement had taken place."

Victoria discussed the matter with her husband the Prince Consort and wrote Leopold: "I *still hope* by your letter that Charlotte has not finally made up her mind—for we both feel so strongly convinced of the immense superiority of Pedro over any other young Prince. . . . If Charlotte asked *me* I should not hesitate a moment."

Charlotte was not asking her. By the fall of 1856, six months after his visit, the Princess had decided. She did not dwell upon her choice's physical charms, but translated his great appeal into proof of his moral and spiritual qualities. Maximilian on his part permitted himself to be taken into camp. He formally wrote her father to ask for her hand. His petition was granted in November, and he wrote his fiancée:

"The gracious response of His Majesty your august father

which made me profoundly happy authorizes me to address myself directly to Your Royal Highness to address to Her the most grateful and most cordial and the most deeply felt sentiments. . . . Assures the happiness of my life. . . . Express my gratitude to Your Royal Highness. . . . I sign myself, Madame Your Royal Highness, the most affectionate Maximilian."

A month later he came again to Brussels. Dressed in the uniform of an Austrian admiral, Maximilian arrived at the Gare du Nord, where both Charlotte's brothers waited. Galas, operas, receptions, a Court ball for fourteen hundred persons followed. The Princess found the Archduke even sweeter than she had remembered, "charming on every point of view." He showed her the designs of the palace he was planning near Trieste. He was going to call it Miramar. It would be located on a little spur reaching into the Gulf of Trieste. Maximilian had been blown ashore there once while sailing in a small boat, and some humble fisherfolk had given him shelter. This was where, he had decided that day, he would build his home. "Ravishing," Charlotte said, looking at the plans for a terrace with a fountain and a Moorish kiosk in the park, at the projected greenhouse with all kinds of birds, at the winter garden. "He promised me a Mass every day," Charlotte wrote a former tutor. He was so considerate. Even the servants would have their special place in the chapel of his Miramar. "Exquisite," she said.

Christmas came during Maximilian's stay; he gave his fiancée a bracelet with a lock of his hair in it, and a pair of diamond earrings and a diamond brooch. On the first day of the new year of 1857 he stood with the royal family at the Court reception, amused by the declarations of loyalty of various groups which were encouraged in a constitutional monarchy. The address of a little rabbi bent over backward the better to deliver his speech was hilarious, he wrote Francis Joseph, as was the stammered-out bellow from the leader of the civic guard. The whole thing was a comedy, including the responses of the King, who "kept gliding to and fro with his characteristically slinking shuffle, nodding his head amiably."

Unamusing, however, were the negotiations concerning the dowry of the Archduke's bride-to-be. Maximilian had brought with him an old friend to discuss the matter with King Leopold's financial adviser. The talks did not go well. Leopold's representative offered nothing but Charlotte's inheritance from her mother plus an allowance from the Belgian Parliament. Maximilian through his agent requested a contribution from the King himself. Leopold declined, stiffened in his attitude by his son and Heir, the Duke of Brabant, who, despite his liking for Maximilian, was against anything that might reduce his patrimony. The King's position was that he was contributing a trousseau and jewels to his daughter, and that ought to be sufficient. The agents reached an impasse until, just before his departure for home, Maximilian personally wrote the King a note. It said, Maximilian told Francis Joseph, that Austria would not receive favorably the information "that the King was not able to resolve himself to put his hand into his pocket for his darling daughter." The note had its effect, for the King's negotiator came to see the Archduke and said on behalf of his master that something would be done, but that the King could not at the moment indicate the exact sum he would offer. But at least it would be something. The Archduke had bested the redoubtable King of the Belgians. "I am rather pleased with myself for having at last wrung from the old miser something of that which he has most at heart."

Maximilian left behind him an entirely captivated Princess. "My Archduke. He is so good!" The Archduchess Sophia wrote Charlotte, addressing her as "My dear child," and ending with "Your tender mother." The Princess's grandmother, her mother's mother, wrote saying she gave thanks to God to know that her Charlotte would be happy.

The marriage was set for July of 1857. The bridegroom-to-be spent the last days of his bachelorhood in traveling, primarily in Austrian Italy. By then the wedding arrangements had been settled. King Leopold, assisted by the Belgian Parliament, would, along with a trousseau, jewels, one table service in gold and one in silver, contribute a dowry of one hundred thousand gulden and an annual allowance of twenty thousand gulden.*

A month before the nuptials Queen Victoria, in compliance with the request of her uncle in Brussels, invited Maximilian

* The gulden at the time had a value of approximately forty cents in American money.

to call upon her in London. After he had been with her for a few days she wrote Leopold: "I cannot say how much we like the Archduke; he is charming, so clever, natural, kind and amiable, so *English* in his feelings and likings. . . . I wish you really joy, dearest Uncle, at having got *such* a husband for dear Charlotte, as I am sure he will make her happy, and is quite worthy of her."

Presents for Charlotte began to arrive from Vienna: from the Emperor Francis Joseph a diadem, necklace and bracelet set with diamonds, from the Archduchess Sophia an antique brooch with a miniature of Maximilian enclosed. On July 23 the Archduke arrived in Brussels; and four days later his bride-to-be came to him in the Blue Room of the royal palace, wearing a robe of white satin embroidered with gold and an immense veil that was the masterpiece of the Brussels lace-makers and fell in undulating folds over her shoulders, with a diadem of orange blossoms and diamonds intertwined and attached to her coiffure. Charlotte's father escorted her in the uniform of a lieutenant general of his army. The bridegroom wore the dress uniform of an admiral of Austria. The mayor of Brussels officiated at the civil ceremony and then the party adjourned to the chapel, where Cardinal-Bishop Dechamps gave the benedictions. Victoria had sent her husband the Prince Consort as her representative. The English Queen wrote Leopold that she felt through the Prince Consort as if she were there herself, and that she had ordered wine for her servants and grog for her sailors to drink the health of the new couple.

Maximilian and Charlotte signed the marriage contract bound in red velvet with a magnificent wax seal five inches across and attached with tasseled cords in the colors of Belgium—black, red and gold—with ribbons streaming from the silk-lined cover enclosing the hand-lettered pages stipulating the conditions of their mating. Then they went with all the company to a dinner and ball. In the morning, in accordance with the marriage contract, Maximilian handed his bride thirty thousand florins—the *cadeau de noce,* the gift for the night which saw the consummation of their marriage.

That day there was a gala concert in the royal theater followed by a luncheon, and in the night, singing and feasting.

Venetian illuminations lit up the nearby portions of the canal of Willebroek and made it seem on fire. Throngs of boats blazing with magic lights came through the water with bands blaring; at the end a boat carried their portraits surrounded by roses and orchids and, above, written in giant letters: *Happiness*.

A day later, alone, Maximilian and Charlotte went to the Church of Laeken, there to stand before the opened grill of her mother's grave. She had always been such a solemn and reasoning girl; but now all her restraint fell away, and kneeling where her mother lay she burst into impassioned sobs. Charlotte had not cried like that since her mother died; but now, married to a man she adored, she released herself of that Puritan and grave manner she had worn for so long. He raised her to her feet and led her from the chapel; but at the moment when they were about to cross the threshold she turned for one last look and then went to her knees again. Unemotional since the day after her mother's death she now at this moment permitted herself to return to emotion again. Maximilian had done that for her, or rather the picture of him that she had: a handsome, deeply feeling, wonderful man who would love her and take care of her forever.

He raised her once more to her feet and they went away.

6

In January of 1856, four months before the visit of the Archduke Maximilian to the Court of Their Imperial Majesties the Emperor and Empress of the French, a woman known as the most beautiful in the world had arrived at Paris.

Born Virginia Oldoini in Florence, Italy, she had become the Countess de Castiglione. Her husband, an Italian nobleman seeking a wife, had been told that if he wished to be the husband of the most glorious woman in Europe he should go to Florence and there he would find her. The man who gave Count de Castiglione this advice was the Count Walewski, the bastard son of the Polish Countess who seduced the Great Emperor in the vain hope that he would grant freedom to her country. Count de Castiglione did as Count Walewski suggested. Virginia—"Nicchia," as she was called—told the Italian Count he was making a mistake. She would never love him. He said it did not matter. To have her as his wife would be enough. They married. In a year or two she had dissipated his fortune. He played no role in her life after that.

The Countess de Castiglione was so beautiful that when she attended her first ball at the Tuileries the dancing actually halted and the musicians stopped playing. People jumped up on chairs to see her better. The Emperor was dancing with the Empress but after one look at the Countess de Castiglione he handed Eugenie over to Duke Ernest of Saxe-Coburg-Gotha.

The Countess had long dark curls, a magnificent complexion, arms, eyes, hands, legs, feet. Everything about her was magnificent. "Her bust," wrote Count Horace de Viel-Castel, "seems to bid defiance to the rest of her sex." "Her beauty really took my breath away," wrote the Princess Metternich, wife of the future Austrian ambassador and daughter-in-law of the late Chancellor of Austria. "In a word, Venus herself come down from Olympus. Never have I seen anyone so beautiful; never again shall I see anyone so beautiful."

Withal, this flawless creature had no friends. Hardly seeming human because of her wondrous appearance, she was at the same time the coldest of human beings. Aloof, freezing, sulky, possessed of not the slightest desire to please, she spent her time looking at herself in mirrors. She rarely danced, saying she would let "those other women" rush about and get red in the face. Showered with compliments, she showed no emotion at receiving them. "Do you wish to see my ankle, my foot?" she might ask a particularly importunate admirer. "Come to my house tomorrow and I will show you them."

The Countess almost never smiled and had no small talk. Second Empire Paris was a city where almost anyone with the gift for the bon mot or telling jest could always be assured a welcome in the palaces of the high, but in that brilliant, nervously gay and frivolous place one could rise by other attainments. Nicchia de Castiglione had no desire or ability to talk, but her appearance was enough to gain her entry anywhere. It would never have happened in Vienna. There, wrote the American Minister, John Lothrop Motley, "If an Austrian should be a Shakespeare, a Galileo, a Nelson and Raphael all in one, he couldn't be admitted into good society unless he had the sixteen quarterings of nobility which birth alone can give him. . . . It is as impossible for a professional or commercial person to enter as a mulatto into the aristocracy of Mobile."

That was Vienna. But the Countess was now in Paris, where in the very first five minutes of her introduction into society she could find herself dancing in the arms of the Emperor of the French and captivating him. But after all, that was why she had been sent there.

At the time of the Countess de Castiglione's entrance into the life of the Emperor Napoleon III, Italy was nothing but a geographical expression. That was what Prince Metternich had called it. He had, after the fall of the Great Emperor,

taken the leading part in making the peninsula a conglomera-
tion of petty principalities, tiny dukedoms and weak little
kingdoms. Even though Metternich himself fell from power
in 1848, Austrian policy adhered to his conception. Austrian
ownership of the rich Italian north, of Lombardy and Venetia,
must not be menaced by any Italian ideas of unification and a
resultant expulsion of the overlords. To this end Austria placed
petty little despots on the varied Thrones of the peninsula and
all the petty little despots danced when Austria pulled the
strings. To reinforce Vienna's desires, the bulk of her army
was stationed in Austrian Italy. From time to time patriots
dreaming of a United Italy rose up; they were crushed by the
Whitecoats. There was no Viennese charm or lightness involved where Italians were concerned. And in fact most of the
Austrian troops were tough Slovaks or Hungarians. They stood
guard in the theaters and opera so that no one might choose
to call out slogans unfriendly to Austria; they manned the
whipping posts where Italian women were publicly lashed for
having insulted Austrian officers. (The city where the incidents
occurred was charged for the price of the whips.)

In the extreme northwest of the Italian peninsula, adjoin-
ing France, was the Kingdom of Sardinia—also called Pied-
mont. It was the center of all anti-Austrian sentiment. It had
taken the lead in the Italian uprising of the Revolution of
1848, but had been crushed by the Whitecoats in 1849. After
that the dream of a United Italy appeared to be over.

But it was not dead in the mind of Count Camillo de Cavour, Sardinia's Prime Minister. He thought of little else. When
in 1854 the French and British troopships sailed off to the
Crimea to battle Czar Nicholas, Cavour told his Parliament
that Sardinia must join in the war on the side of the Allies.
The idea seemed insane. What had a small and weak northern
Italian kingdom to do with a war against Russia? Cavour said
that if Russia won in the Crimea and consequently gained an
entrance to the Mediterranean through the Dardanelles, it
would mean Russian squadrons in addition to French and
British would be patrolling what the Italians had once called
"Our Sea." His reasoning was farfetched and recognized as
such. For it was not Russia he wished to fight, but Austria.
But if he could help the Allies, and particularly his French

neighbor, France might one day help him at home. Twenty-five thousand Sardinian soldiers went off to fight the Czar and when the war was over Sardinia held an honored position among the powers of Europe and possessed an experienced army that served as the focal point for the rebellious United Italy forces and other petty princedoms.

For a couple of years Sardinia's sacrifice seemed in vain. Then an Italian threw a bomb at Napoleon and Eugenie as they arrived at the Opera in Paris. Horses and guards died in the explosion, and blood splashed onto the Empress's dress. Caught, the bomb thrower said he had done it because Napoleon was not doing anything for Italy. The act and the accusation gave the Emperor pause. The bomb thrower went to the guillotine, but another might follow his example. And Napoleon III had always been interested in Italy. His brother had died, after all, during one of the many attempts to force out the Austrians. His uncle had gained his first victories fighting the Austrians in Italy, exporting, as he put it, the French Revolution ideals of *liberté, égalité, fraternité.*

The French Emperor thought about Italy in his cloudy, wandering way, and "I will do something for Italy," he said. But he did not do anything. Cavour decided to nudge him. The Countess de Castiglione was a vague relation of the Sardinian Prime Minister; he called her to him and explained that with France at Sardinia's side, all Italy might be made to burst into flames which would expel the Austrians, but that without France nothing could be done. Napoleon III ruled France. She must work on him. "Succeed, my dear cousin," Cavour said, "by whatever methods you think best. But succeed." She spent her last night in Italy in the bed of the King of Sardinia, Victor Emmanuel, and left for Paris. Cavour, sighing to himself that if we did for ourselves the things we do for our country, what scoundrels we would be, wrote a colleague also working for a United Italy, "I have enrolled in the ranks of diplomacy the very beautiful Countess de Castiglione, inviting her to coquette with the Emperor and, if necessary, to seduce him."

The moment of the Countess's arrival in Paris was opportune, for the Empress was entering into the final stages prior to her confinement which would result in the birth of the

Prince Imperial. But of course that was not a determining factor, for Napoleon was only too accessible. "He runs after every alley cat he sees," said his cousin, Princess Mathilde.

A bird of prey in a dress of transparent muslin, with her dark hair falling over her shoulders from under an enormous hat with marabou feathers, the Countess's triumph was brutal. It took place at Compiègne during a performance of the Comédie Française. She arose from her seat, declared she had a headache, and said she was going to her room. The Emperor in his box pulled at his moustache. In the first intermission he got up, deserted his wife before the entire Court, and went to the Countess. She was waiting in a gray nightdress of cambric and lace. In the morning the entire world knew.

Within a few weeks Napoleon was going to the Countess's Paris residence at eleven o'clock at night, to emerge an hour or two later for the drive back to the Tuileries. When, four months after her arrival at Paris, the Archduke Maximilian came for a visit, he was shocked when the Princess Mathilde openly talked with him about the Emperor's romance. Maximilian wrote his brother, the Austrian Emperor, that the Countess was lovely, but seemed because of her "impudent bearing" like a dancer brought back to life from the free-and-easy English Regency days. "This person," he told Francis Joseph, "may prove dangerous to the domestic happiness of the Emperor and Empress."

There was nothing Eugenie could do. The sensual side of life had never appealed to her despite its having been a large factor in capturing her husband, and after the birth of the Prince Imperial she all but ended marital relations with Napoleon. Yet she bitterly hated the woman now monopolizing him. She took a measure of revenge at a costume ball at the home of Count Walewski. The Countess de Castiglione came as the Queen of Hearts. Forty years later, one of the ladies of the Court still remembered the dress as the "most suggestive and fanciful costume" ever put together. The Countess wore no corsets, no "artificial supports" of any kind. The dress was of light gauze. Upon this transparent material were pasted three small hearts. The Countess faced Eugenie, whose eyes slowly traveled down and came to rest. "Your heart seems a little low," she breathed.

But night after night the Countess made love to the Emperor of the French, he the aging roué and she the most stunning woman of her time. She everlastingly talked of Italian hopes. This beautiful woman would one day say that she had created modern Italy. Perhaps she did. It is certain she estranged Napoleon from Eugenie, and that Eugenie sought happiness in political adventuring, and from that adventuring came death, tragedy, tumbled Thrones.

The King of the Belgians, reluctantly, had given his daughter Charlotte a handsome dowry upon the occasion of her marriage to the brother of the Emperor of Austria. However, to be the wife of the commander of the third-rate Austrian navy was not what Leopold had in mind for his Charlotte. He wanted something in return, more specifically for the Austrian Emperor Francis Joseph to elevate Charlotte's husband to a higher position so that his daughter might thereby extend the royal Belgian influence.

Francis Joseph did not really want to raise his brother. Maximilian was an excellent observer and Francis Joseph had greatly enjoyed his letters reporting on his adventures. But Maximilian was a liberal and a freethinker in whose hands real authority might be dangerous. King Leopold delicately played his cards. He had two. First, he had the goodwill of Belgium to offer or withhold, and second, he had his immense influence with his niece, the Queen of England. Reluctantly Francis Joseph came to realize that he must do something for Maximilian. He appointed him Viceroy of Austrian Italy.

It was an extremely important position. The Austrian Empire possessed five major cities, Vienna, Budapest, Prague, Milan and Venice, and as Viceroy and Vicereine Maximilian and Charlotte would be rulers in two of those cities. The appointment meant for the Archduke a chance to do something and be somebody more than simply Francis Joseph's younger brother. It would give to Charlotte an opportunity to put to use those studious habits which had hitherto been reserved for the classroom. Maximilian reveled in the idea of glory and the opportunities for helping people; Charlotte immersed herself in an analysis of Italian history, the political situation, the language. "Great satisfactions" were in store, she wrote her former tutor. Young, physically attractive, with a brilliant future in Italy opening before them, the couple left Brussels after their wedding and went to Bonn and from there took a steamer to Mainz and then to Nuremberg and Ratisbon and down the Danube to Vienna. They left behind the old King Leopold, who never before in the experience of the British Prince Consort had shown as much emotion as he displayed at the loss of his daughter, and they went to the Archduchess Sophia, who could not get over the young girl's intelligence and charm.

Then they went to Trieste and to Venice and Verona, *their* domain now, and on September 6, 1857, six weeks after their marriage, entered Milan—Imperial Viceroy and his lady. Artillery salutes greeted them, and the sound of the Austrian "Kaiserlied" and the Belgian "Brabanconne." They had traversed northern Italy in a simple manner, but now they changed into a magnificent state carriage for their official entry into the seat of the Austrian Government in Italy. Maximilian was in uniform and Charlotte in a cerise silk dress with white lace, and on her head a crown of roses and diamonds.

The Austrian troops paraded before them and in the evening the entire city was illuminated in celebration. They took up residence in the royal palace at Monza just outside Milan. It was enchanting, with wonderful rose gardens. Maximilian had always loved Italy, and Charlotte found the country a revelation after cold and wet Belgium, the blue sky and golden light, the churches, galleries, the marble and mosaics. She had never been as happy in her life. "Max is perfection in every way," she wrote an intimate, "so excellent, so pious, so tender. I taste perfect happiness. . . . Everybody is so wonderful to me, I'm so happy, surrounded by affection. . . . Happy in my home . . . happy in this beautiful country. . . . The good God has given me *everything*."

For years the Archduke Maximilian had urged his strict brother the Emperor to relax the hold Austria held upon its two major subject peoples, the Hungarians and the Italians. But the Austrian Emperor would not change. Now the Emperor's brother, the Archduke–Viceroy, was in a position to do something for a people with whom and in whose climate he had always felt at home. He said the severity associated with the name of Austria was dead, and he moved through the crowds with no guards or soldiers. It appeared to Charlotte that this display of simple trust was having an effect; the people seemed, she wrote, happy that her Max was not "too German."

In their palaces both at Milan and Monza Maximilian and Charlotte had chamberlains, majordomos, lackeys in livery for him and ladies-of-honor for her. One thing was missing. That was the allegiance of their subjects. Austria to the Italians still meant whipping posts, gallows, firing squads, the military crushing of the Revolution of 1848–49 and the imposition of ruinous taxes and penalties afterward. After all, said the Archduchess Sophia, Italy was an "armed camp" as far as the Austrians were concerned. She was right. Periodically the Austrian troops were confined to barracks to avoid incidents that might inflame the entire peninsula; at other moments they swept the streets in a search for United Italy agitators or propagandists.

The previous year the Emperor Francis Joseph and Empress Elizabeth had come to tour their possessions of Lombardy and Venetia, and the reception had been frightful. Prior to their arrival, the Whitecoats had imprisoned thousands of politically suspect persons and all of northern Italy was honeycombed with police spies and informers. But nothing could conceal from the Austrian rulers how they were hated by their Italian subjects. At Padua the sullen crowds dragooned into position were ordered to cheer the third carriage of the procession wherein the Imperial couple rode; they yelled, "Long live the third carriage!" In Venice, daunted by the two-hundred-yard walk from the gondola landing to the steps of the palace reception, every step dangerous because of the packed mass of cursing people, only thirty of the more than one hundred thirty aristocrats invited dared to appear. Seventy of those who failed to come did not comply with the terms of the invitation, which stated that a nonacceptance must be given in writing. At Milan every lady invited to the Imperial reception received an anonymous letter saying that if she attended, all possible details about her personal life, including her love affairs, would be widely publicized.

"For all these machinations, Cavour alone is responsible," Francis Joseph said grimly. But he knew it was only partially so. With the utmost reluctance the Emperor relaxed Austria's hold, rescinding some of the penalties laid on for 1848–49, ordering the release of political prisoners and donating money for the erection of monuments to Marco Polo and Leonardo da Vinci. The appointment as Viceroy of a known liberal who disliked soldiers seemed the final nicety. "The terrain could not be more difficult," Francis Joseph wrote the Archduchess Sophia. "Let us hope that Max's tact will do some good."

Tact the new Viceroy had in abundance. He lavishly gave alms to the poor, and when the flood times of northern Italy came he went among the people, helping to alleviate their miseries and then organizing a lottery for their benefit. He instituted movements to dry up the swamps and bring better water to the cities; he beautified the towns; he looked into educational problems. There was never a festival at which he and his consort did not appear. Charlotte posed for an artist in Lombard peasant attire. The Viceroy and his lady smiled, were charmed by Venice, in love with Monza.

The Viceroy and Vicereine were popular—on a personal level. They saw the smiles which met them (for it was impossible to dislike two well-meaning young people so earnestly anxious to be loved) and thought to themselves that from this popularity might grow a Kingdom of Lombardy–Venetia more or less independent of Vienna; and that such a kingdom might steal from Sardinia its leadership of the peninsula; and that it might come to pass that they would yet rule as King and Queen of United Italy, the descendants of the Caesars.

Two factors were going to shatter their hopes. The first was that their six million subjects did not want the Austrian Archduke and Archduchess to be liberal or kind; they wanted them to leave. Any aristocrat who accepted Viceregal attentions became a social outcast. If ostracism did not deter the man in question from dancing attendance upon Maximilian, he would find himself euchred into fighting duels against dangerous opponents. So no aristocrats came to the offered soirées. The Viceroy and Vicereine put aside the stiff Hapsburg protocol and asked the bourgeoisie to their Court. They did not come. They had their business interests to consider. The intellectuals stayed aloof from the beginning. When it was announced that the Viceroy and his lady would be attending the theater, all the boxes and half the seats were empty when they arrived. If they came into a public square the people vanished, leaving them alone with their Austrian escorts. As Francis Joseph had said, the terrain could not be more difficult.

But it was the Austrian Emperor himself who made their task even more difficult. From the very first Francis Joseph had taken the role of a schoolmaster instructing protégés. He forgot his original thought that tact would win the day and wrote the Viceroy that the Italians must be brought to heel. They had "bad manners" which must be corrected. "Get them used to the necessary respect for a Court." Francis Joseph was being true to his most narrow and unimaginative self, showing to his very worst advantage. There were student demonstrations in favor of Italian unity in Padua. Three hundred students should not be permitted to gather for such a cause. Northern Italy, after all, was the personal property of the House of Hapsburg. Francis Joseph was the head of that House. His brother must not be indulgent with his authority. The students must be punished. And it was "false clemency" to permit unfriendly articles to appear in the Italian newspapers. Flags of United Italy mysteriously appeared on public buildings. Why? The letters from Vienna to Milan contained a continual litany: "The illegal demonstrations and effronteries have to finish. . . . Everything with determination."

But the tide of what was called Italianism was reaching its crest. Maximilian did not appear to be halting it, and in Vienna it was said that the Viceroy was much too gentle. Francis Joseph sent new squads of police spies south to act as agents provocateurs in order to smoke out Austria's enemies. And the Emperor extended the draft so that no man liable for conscription could marry until he reached the age of twenty-three. The Viceroy wrote Vienna asking that Lombardy–Venetia be given a separate army and political body, its own educational system and tax structure. Otherwise it would be lost to Austria. Francis Joseph answered by depreciating the currency of Austrian Italy, and ordered Maximilian to cooperate more completely with the Austrian police and military units in the two provinces. Their commander was General Count Gyulai. He had been stationed in Italy for nearly ten years. He was a soldier. Francis Joseph raised him to the Viceroy's level, telling Maximilian to clear all his moves with Gyulai. When Maximilian remonstrated, Francis Joseph sent his complaining letters to Gyulai. The Viceroy was put in the position of competing with Gyulai and his Whitecoats for the Emperor's favor. And he was not winning that battle.

Maximilian resented his brother's attitude bitterly. Italy became for him "this land of misery, where one is doubly depressed by having to act as the representative of an inactive government with no ideas, which one's judgment tries in vain to defend. . . . I am accordingly beginning to ask myself whether my conscience will allow me blindly to follow instructions from Vienna." Francis Joseph knew what his brother was thinking, for the Viceroy permitted himself to make public his opinions on individual issues even before he complained to Vienna. "I must be assured," Francis Joseph wrote, "that once I have decided something it will be executed with zeal so that the opposition to whatever I have decided will not be encouraged by the belief that you are not in agreement with the plan which I have drawn up." He ordered the Viceroy to rely more upon Gyulai the Whitecoat: "I tell you that one hundred times."

Maximilian countered by asking for direct command of the army so that both the civil and military arms would be his. Francis Joseph refused, saying the move would be meaningless, for in the event of a war Maximilian would have to hand over the post to a real soldier.

Maximilian and Charlotte went to Vienna to argue their case for liberalism and a freer hand. The Emperor refused them everything. They returned to Italy in late 1858 to find that in their absence the situation had deteriorated. Maximilian was afraid that his young wife—she was only eighteen—would be insulted in the streets, or even that they would be assassinated. Openly hissed in the theaters, they ceased to appear in public. They were still personally popular, but in Italian eyes they remained the instruments of the hated oppressor. Their situation was hopeless. Dazed, Charlotte wandered the gardens of the royal palace. Her husband sent her to visit her family and friends in Brussels. He stayed behind, feeling "as lonely as a hermit. . . . Before me dances and whirls the carnival, but in my apartments it is as silent as Lent."

In Paris in that holiday season of 1859 the Emperor of the French at his January the First reception paused in front of the Austrian ambassador. Slightly raising his voice so that what he said could be plainly heard, the French Emperor declared that it was his wish that the thought be transmitted to Francis Joseph that whatever happened he, Napoleon III, entertained only the most friendly personal feelings for the Austrian ruler. At once Austrian troop reinforcements were ordered south to Italy. In Sardinia, Cavour must have smiled. A few months previously he had secretly gone to Napoleon for a meeting at Plombières. They had agreed to make war on Francis Joseph. If they won, Italy would be united under Sardinia—and France for her aid would be given the provinces of Savoy and Nice.

On April 21 General Count Gyulai, who had been in Vienna to see the Emperor, arrived in Milan to hand the Emperor's brother an Imperial letter. The Viceroy was relieved of his duties, which he was to turn over immediately to the Austrian general.

Two days later mobilization posters went up all over Sardinia. Francis Joseph, facing Austria's greatest crisis since the revolutionary days of 1848, had a saddled horse brought to him at Schoenbrunn Palace. Alone, with no escort of any kind, he rode to the home of the retired Prince Metternich to talk of the situation with Sardinia. "For God's sake, Majesty," the aged Prince cried, "no ultimatum! No ultimatum!"

"It went out last night," Francis Joseph replied.

The ultimatum demanded disarmament by Sardinia. In answer Cavour ordered his army into Lombardy. Behind the Sardinians, through the passes of the Alps and along the coast through Nice, marched Frenchmen. The Great Emperor had come this way. By their sides, they were told, walked the ghosts of the Grand Army. The new Napoleon was with them. He had made Eugenie regent and gone to join the soldiers making for the south.

From Vienna, happier in that moment than he had ever been since the first glorious days of courting Elizabeth, Francis Joseph went off to be among Whitecoats. He went to his infantry with their blue trousers, the Jaegers with green cross-belted greatcoats, the Hussars with yellow-trimmed shakos and the Uhlans with flagged lances. His artillerists were in brown; his Cuirassiers in high boots and crested helmets. General Gyulai and his staff wore cocked hats with light green plumes. Above the silvered bayonet points waved the banner of Austria: a black double-headed eagle rampant upon a yellow ground.

Marching south, the French moved to the beat of the rolling drums and to the quickstep of the blaring trumpets, the Dragoons with their horsehair plumed helmets, the infantry in tall shakos, the Zouaves in baggy pants with spats, the Spahis in the flowing robes of the African campaigns wherein they had their genesis, the whole befrogged, epauleted, gold-laced. "The purpose of this war is to give Italy to herself," Napoleon said. Italy was to be free from "the Adriatic to the Alps." The French army joined and merged with the soldiers of Sardinia. Almost forgotten, the former Viceroy was left to superintend what he called "four or five wretched vessels" at Venice. Even there, a useless spectator to what would be entirely a land war, he was by his brother's orders to report to the Venice fortress commander.

On an extremely hot fourth day of June, 1859, the armies met. Picking their way through the poplar windbreaks, they stumbled through the marshes of the Lombardy ricelands where it was difficult even to walk because of the swampy nature of the land, and blundered into each other at the town of Magenta. As the Great Emperor had begun as an artillerist, and as his nephew had followed him in that specialty when a part-time officer of the Swiss army, the gunners of the Second Empire had always been favored in the distributions of the military budget. When their batteries opened upon the Austrians at Magenta the power of the barrage was something the world had never seen before. The slaughter was frightful. Then the French and Sardinian infantry went in. The Austrian rifle was the best on the field that day, but its value was reduced by the very open skirmish lines the terrain forced upon the attackers. There was no massed concentration of troops at which to fire. When at last, fixing bayonets at the very front of the Austrian lines, the French and Sardinians lunged forward, the accuracy of the Austrian rifle was nullified. And as it fired in a trajectory, the defense volleys could not sweep the field.

The two armies closed with blades: bayonets and swords. They fought all day in the killing heat. Wounded men fell face down into the rice paddies and drowned. The slashed-open wounds were terrible and shook the Emperor of the French as the sight of a hundred thousand corpses would not have disturbed his uncle. Napoleon III sat on his horse and smoked one cigarette after another as he saw his men brought back in braided dolmans soaked with blood. "It's going badly, badly," he muttered.

Night fell upon one of the ghastliest battlefields of a century that had known many. In the morning the Austrians were seen to fall back. "Sire, what a glorious victory!" exclaimed an officer to Napoleon. "A victory, is it?" he asked. "And I was going to order a retreat."

Three weeks of maneuvering followed. From Vienna during that period came news of the death of Prince Metternich. On June 25 the armies clashed again at Solferino. The slaughter from the artillery and then the close-up fighting was as grisly as at Magenta. Smoking fifty cigarettes one after another, Napoleon gasped out, "The poor people! The poor people! What a horrible thing war is!" The Austrian right wing hung on a village cemetery. From behind the cemetery walls the defenders poured out fire, but French reserves came up and went over their own dead and wounded to burst into the cemetery with their bayonets. The right wing broke, and the center followed. The Austrians fell back once again, this time upon prepared positions which would require even more slaughter to take.

Napoleon III, his nerves completely shattered, welcomed the news which his wife the regent now sent him. The Prussians, she wrote, were massing on the Rhine. If they moved, they would find the way toward Paris open. The troops must come home. At once Napoleon contacted Francis Joseph, suggesting they reach an agreement. Francis Joseph had come to this war joyously, exultant in the hope that in one swoop he would chastise the nephew of the man who had twice occupied Vienna and at the same time end the Italian unrest and captiousness which plagued his tidy soul. It had not worked out that way. The two sovereigns met at the tiny hamlet of Villafranca. For a few minutes they discussed their little boys, Rudolph Crown Prince of Austria and Louis Napoleon Prince Imperial of France. Then Napoleon laid down his terms. Austria must leave Italy. Francis Joseph remonstrated and they settled it that Lombardy must be evacuated at once and Venetia later. "I hope, Sire, you will never learn what it is to lose your two most beautiful provinces," Francis Joseph said.

The armies went home. That the Emperor of the French had not kept his promise to liberate completely all of Italy enraged Cavour, but nothing could be done. At the victory parade in Paris people gasped when they saw the holes in the formations which showed where dead and wounded comrades had formerly marched; but it was still a victory parade. In Vienna they were sullen as they watched the beaten Austrian regiments straggling home. People wondered aloud if, like the idiot Emperor Ferdinand renouncing his position in favor of Francis Joseph, the time had not come for Francis Joseph to do the same in favor of Maximilian.

A bitter joke asked, "Why does the Emperor wear a triumphant laurel wreath on his brow on all the coins?"

"I don't know."

"Neither do I."

There were terrible scenes between the two brothers as they hashed over the events which had led to the disaster for Austria. It was said that, in front of the entire Court, Maximilian had struck the Emperor in the face.

Twenty-seven years old, without a job and without a future, more depressed than he had ever been in his life, Maximilian took his nineteen-year-old wife and went to their Castle of Miramar.

In that summer of 1859 the Archduke Maximilian and the Archduchess Charlotte, sometime Viceroy and Vicereine of Austrian Italy, looked at each other for the first time. What had they in common? She was precise in her thinking, rigid, logical, analytical, observant. He was light, inconstant, fanciful, romantic, with a mind that leaped from one thing to another. The supports for their marriage were gone—the excitement of the courtship and wedding, the honeymoon and triumphal entrance into Italy, the Court they had maintained there and the fight they had made together against Viennese blindness and reaction. They knew Francis Joseph would never again give Maximilian anything, "Even," Charlotte wrote her grandmother, "if he lived to be ninety years old." In Vienna, Maximilian was the irresponsible liberal who, given a chance in Italy, had signally failed. (It would never occur to Francis Joseph that it was he himself who had failed to understand the situation.) When England's Lord Palmerston remarked to the Austrian Ambassador to London that it might be wise for Francis Joseph to crown his brother King of Hungary and so give the restive Hungarians a measure of independence, he marked himself as entirely ignorant of Austrian affairs.

Alone, uneasily knowing the supports for their life and their marriage were deeply changed, the Archduke and Archduchess drew apart. While Charlotte stayed at Miramar, Maximilian escorted his sister-in-law, the Empress Elizabeth, on a trip to Madeira. Then Charlotte went to stay at the Empress's villa while her husband took a long cruise to Brazil, where he collected plant and reptile specimens. But they could not be forever going away. So they came to rest at Miramar, she choosing to regard the situation as this "present vacation" which Providence in its wisdom had given them so that, with some gifts taken away, they might learn to be happy in a more sure fashion. Having less, they now had less to lose. They were "relegating grandeur into their memories."

Charlotte painted and read. Maximilian threw himself into perfecting their home. It reflected him. Viewing it, a lady-in-waiting to the Empress Elizabeth saw something to meet "the wildest dreams of an Oriental imagination. . . . The purest, most spotless marble, the snow-white building. . . . Minarets fretted and carved like lace, pointed turrets, terraced roofs adorned by groups of exquisitely winged statues, medieval battlements, and drawbridges which savor of the fifteenth century."

Inside, the Archduke had an oaken stairway hung with panoplies of exotic weapons from the Middle Ages; from the ceiling dangled maces and battle-axes, and on the carved balustrades were wooden valets wearing the Imperial livery of five hundred years before. Eighteenth-century sedan chairs with the monogram of the Empress Maria Theresa stood by. Past the staircase was the great hall where through a blue-tinted window the Istrian coast could be seen stretching for miles. Everywhere were vaulted arches, mullioned windows, suits of armor, coats of arms, massive clocks, pianos, French doors, elaborate wainscoting. Maximilian's study was an exact replica of the commander's cabin of the *Novara*, the ship of his cruises. The library was enormous, with marble busts of Dante, Homer, Goethe, Shakespeare. The chapel was in imitation of the Church of the Holy Sepulchre in Jerusalem, paneled with cedar of Lebanon.

On the floor above were galleries, a fish pond with running fountain, several reception rooms opening one into the other, a bedroom designated to be occupied only by visiting royalties—the sovereigns' room, he called it—a drawing room, the Chinese and Japanese room used for smoking, a throne room, the seagulls' room, with birds painted on the ceiling, to be used for official dinners. The paintings that hung from the magnificently sculpted wood of the ceilings were of Kings and Emperors, or enormous landscapes.

The castle, dramatically set on a promontory over the sea, looked from its wide terraces sixty feet straight down into twenty fathoms of water in which floated ribbonlike algae, anemones of pale green-yellow, lilac and blue, starfish and angel wings. Behind the building was the park, peacocks strutting where fir trees from the Himalayas stood next to cedars from North Africa and cypresses from California. There were conifers from every part of Europe, poplars, silvery olive trees, great clusters of palmettos and cacti, date palms and magnolias and masses of shrubbery of myrtle, laurel, euonymus, viburnum and arbutus. The avenue leading up the great circling driveway to the ornately sculptured stone entrance in the castle square was lined with superb sycamores which all but shut out the light. The fountains were smaller but of the order of Versailles; in the greenhouses orchids bloomed all year long. Heroic groups of statuary were everywhere. Paths led to the terraced gardens, a pavilion, the swan pond, a little villa where they lived while the work went on, to a gun deck with cannon given as a gift by Charlotte's brother Leopold, the Duke of Brabant.

It was the residence of a profligate maharaja. Maximilian's brother, the Emperor of Austria, had never in his life built anything a tenth as grand. Francis Joseph slept on a simple army cot. Charlotte's brother, the Heir to the Throne of Belgium, argued over centimes with shopkeepers, counted his change twice and went about in clothing bought secondhand from Parisian street merchants.

The castle was not sufficient. The Archduke and his wife had a second home. It was a restored twelfth-century monastery located in the wilderness of the little island of Lacroma, just across from Ragusa on the east side of the Adriatic. In that romantic setting they rode, sailed, ate in the open. They did nothing serious, nothing real. Maximilian's younger brothers Karl Ludwig and Ludwig Viktor might fritter their lives away; Charlotte's brother the Count of Flanders might do the same— but they were different. She felt they were created to govern— she said it was *his* destiny and she but his aide—and that Providence intended that they work to make people happy. The day would come, she said, when those gifts so briefly displayed in Italy would be permitted to flower again.

Meanwhile the Archduke and his wife listened to the sea and watched the fishing boats go by. On Sundays they opened the gardens to the public of Trieste and, with a band playing in the castle square, ate on the balcony where they could see what was going on and note the admiration aroused by the wondrous grounds. Sweet aroma from the flowers filled the air and birds sang. Often they asked strangers in to see the paintings and hear the Archduke play the great organ. "But are we in this world to pass our days in silk and gold?" she asked her grandmother, the former Queen of France. Was her husband always to be nothing but "an individual who occupies himself with building programs, gardening and voyaging from time to time?" As for herself: "I have known too little of life not to desire something to love and something to do outside of my household."

Her father understood. It was terrible for a girl who had loved hard study to be simply a meaningless royalty. Her grandmother understood—"they cannot spend their lives on that rock by the sea." But Maximilian's brother Francis Joseph did not care to understand. And it was only the Emperor of Austria who could save them and give to their gilded existence some meaning. And of course he would not.

Maximilian and Charlotte drew further apart. There was no bond of children to hold them together, for after three years of marriage it appeared she was barren. He sought diversions elsewhere but the women meant nothing to him. He felt aged and useless. He drank too much. Her face tightened and she went about with lips compressed. And so, they drifted.

7

THERE WAS A CHARMING BUTTERFLY who often came to the Madrid home of the future Empress of the French when Eugenie was simply the young daughter of a mother who liked company. Some of the guests at Señora de Montijo's salon were eminently respectable; for example, the writer Stendahl, who talked to little Eugenie and her sister Paca about the history of his country, France. Another guest was the writer Prosper Mérimée, who one day heard from the mother a Spanish tale which he amplified into what became the opera *Carmen*.

Some of the guests, however, were more raffish. One such was the butterfly. His name was José Hidalgo. It was said of him that he was one of a group of gentlemen who helped amuse Señora de Montijo and her friends by getting down on all fours to be mounted by the ladies, who then tilted at each other like the knights of old or played polo like the playboys of more contemporary note. It was also said of José Hidalgo that he was the lover of Señora de Montijo.*

Whatever he was to Eugenie's mother, he was gay and obliging in the best drawing rooms of several European capitals. He represented, people said, the graciousness and sunniness of old Mexico transplanted, apparently permanently now, to the Old World. For he did not go to Mexico where his estates had been taken over in the wake of Mexican troubles. There had been trouble in Mexico ever since the Spanish colonies revolted against the mother country after Napoleon

---

* He was not the only man of whom this was said. Rumor has always had it that Eugenie's father was not Señora de Montijo's husband, but Lord Clarendon, Great Britain's Ambassador to Spain at the time of her conception.

Bonaparte's removal of the Spanish royal family in favor of the kingship of his brother Joseph. Too weak to combat the Great Emperor, the Spanish had no strength to fight revolutionaries in their colonies. The Spanish Empire faded away. Mexico, the former jewel of that Empire, vanished from European consciousness. One heard the Mexicans had revolutions. President followed President. There had been, what, fifty, fifty-five, sixty of those Presidents since the breakaway from Spain in 1810? That made an average of about one President a year. And there had been an Emperor and a personage who called himself Serene Highness at the head of what was called the Mexican Government. Either these men got themselves and their supporters shot or they were banished.

Mexican exiles were scattered all over the Caribbean area, in the United States and Europe. José Hidalgo was such an expatriate. So was a friend of his named José Maria Gutierrez de Estrada. Gutierrez was a forbidding character. He traveled all over Europe saying that Mexico was going to ruin and anarchy under the weight of revolutions directed against one President after another, that no one was safe, that brigands ruled the roads and that the Catholic Church was being despoiled. What was needed, Gutierrez said endlessly in letters sent to anyone who might read them, was a European Prince, a monarch, to take charge.

Gutierrez had been saying that ever since 1842, when he had been exiled from Mexico. In his time he had gone to Prince Metternich in Vienna and King Louis Philippe in Paris. Both of these men had expressed some vague tentative interest in finding a royalty of their respective countries to go to Mexico, but the Revolution of 1848 had removed them both from power. Gutierrez went on to their successors, particularly Napoleon III. But where Hidalgo, "Pepe" to his friends, was charming and appealing, Gutierrez was so fierce and intense that he made people uncomfortable. After one interview he was not asked back, for he was a bore.

After becoming Empress, Eugenie had lost track of Pepe Hidalgo. But one day in the summer of 1857, driving from her villa at Biarritz to Bayonne to view a bullfight, she saw a man step into the street and raise his hat to her. It was Hidalgo.

She ordered the carriage to halt and chatted with him. Would he come to see her on her yacht the next day?

On deck the following day Eugenie found him as agreeable as he had always been. Hidalgo became a courtier of the Imperial family of France, traveling to the great hunting parties at Compiègne and staying with them weeks at a time at their palaces at St. Cloud, Chantilly, Fontainebleau. Sometimes he talked to the Emperor and Empress of his unfortunate country torn by unending wars and revolutions, and he introduced into their presence his friend Gutierrez, who in his customary long-winded and driving manner put them off. Gutierrez lectured the French rulers on how it behooved them to do something for Mexico, a Latin nation and a Catholic country. They were interested in what he said, but not in him because of his manner. They told Pepe Hidalgo to keep his fanatical friend away from them. Pepe complied, but went on where Gutierrez had left off. Wouldn't the consort of the mighty Emperor of the French, herself a Spaniard, want to do something to help a country of Spanish culture that would, if left alone, inevitably come under the sway of the Anglo-Saxon, Protestant United States?

Eugenie listened to Pepe Hidalgo. It was a distraction for her to do so. She needed diversions. The image of the Countess de Castiglione hovered over her marriage, for while Napoleon had fleetingly dallied with other women, the superlatively beautiful Countess had lasted. Eugenie could not force him to be faithful—nobody could have achieved that—but she could make him listen to Pepe Hidalgo. It was not hard. Memories of an earlier interest in Nicaragua came back as Hidalgo's flattering Mexican charm poured over Napoleon. Indeed the French Emperor would like to do something. "How is it to be done?" he asked Pepe. There seemed to be no answer. Alone, France could hardly do very much about a land three thousand miles away, on the other side of an ocean. The matter rested there.

In 1860, with Savoy and Nice now the property of France as payment for her part in the war against Austria, the Emperor and Empress went off on a triumphal tour to their new provinces. They then crossed the Mediterranean to France's Departments of North Africa, and were there when Napoleon received word of the death in Paris of Eugenie's dearly loved sister Paca, the Duchess of Alba. The telegram was handed to the Emperor just as they were about to go to a dinner offered by the ruler of one of their African possessions. He put it away. Only after the Empress had charmed the African officials did he break the news to her. She was horrified that he had let her laugh and waltz as Paca lay dead. It took years for that hurt to vanish.

Distraught, Eugenie returned to Paris and ordered the immediate destruction of her sister's residence there, saying she could not bear that anyone else should live in it. When Paca's body was returned to Spain for burial it was a sign of her feeling for Pepe Hidalgo that she asked him to assume the somber task of escorting her sister home.

He did so and returned to be constantly in her company and that of her husband and their Court. Then in the summer of 1861, four years after Pepe Hidalgo raised his hat to her as she went to her bullfight, he received advance notice through Mexican emigré circles that the homeland was going to default on the payment of its immense debts to the European powers. He went to the Empress and told her. Mexico was now outside the pale of civilized nations. The country had lost what honor it once possessed. Europe must surely act. Would not the Emperor of the French lead?

Eugenie took Pepe Hidalgo into the Emperor's study after dinner. Napoleon stood up and lit a cigarette. Eugenie picked up a piece of embroidery. "Tell the Emperor what you have just told me," she said to Hidalgo.

He began.

"Your Majesty, I had long lost hope . . ." He said that surely the English, infuriated by a default on prodigious loans, would order battleships to the Mexican ports, which were very few in number and easily blockaded by even a small European flotilla. Surely Spain would not permit Mexico to act in such a fashion, not let the former colony simply announce it was not going to pay its just debts. And France? Hidalgo had the answer. "Destroy the demagogues, and proclaim a monarchy, which is the only salvation of the country." And the United States and the Monroe Doctrine? There was no need to fear the Yankees. The First Battle of Bull Run a month earlier had sent the Union army flying in retreat. The Americans had their hands filled with their own troubles. "They will not move," Hidalgo said.

Napoleon remarked that it was a certainty that Spain and England would have to do something about the Mexicans, and that if the interests of France demanded it, he would move also. "I shall lend a hand."

Hidalgo spoke again of going beyond a mere intervention aimed at collecting just debts and reiterated that this was just one of endless indications of the hopeless state in which the Mexicans found themselves. The country needed complete overhaul, the righting of countless ills, a new regeneration. The Mexicans could never do it by themselves. They desperately needed a monarch who could rise above the eternally contending parties and unite the country. "Will Your Majesty permit me to ask whether you have a candidate in view? The Mexicans would accept him from Your Majesty as their own choice."

The Emperor turned aside to light another cigarette. "I have none," he said.

Hidalgo looked at the Empress. Her husband had not said that he would *not* help set up a monarchy. "We cannot think of a Spanish Prince," Hidalgo said tentatively.

"It is unfortunate," Eugenie said. They talked of two or three German Princes, but agreed that their religions were wrong—Protestant—or their states too small and insignificant. They turned to Austria. "But which Archduke?" asked Eugenie.

"I believe the Archduke Rainier was mentioned," Hidalgo ventured.

"Yes," she said, "the Archduke Maximilian would not be willing."

"Oh, no," said Hidalgo, "he wouldn't be willing."

"No," said Napoleon, "he would not accept."

There was a silence. Then Eugenie lightly tapped herself on the breast with her fan. "Well! Something tells me that he will accept."

"We can but try," Pepe Hidalgo said.

Mexico

8

Hernando Cortes landed in what was to be called Mexico on Good Friday of the year 1519. He had five hundred men, harquebusiers, gunners for his seven bronze cannon, cavalrymen for his fewer than twenty horses. He was authorized by the captain-general of Cuba to reconnoiter the coastal areas to arrange trade with the natives. That was not his aim. Conquest was. Cortés burned all his ships and sent word to King Charles V that His Most Catholic Majesty's soldiers on the shore at the place now called the city of the True Cross, Vera Cruz, would press on for the glory of God and Spain.

His men trembled when he burned the boats, but Cortés was a great captain commanding their hearts. They followed him away from the coast and into the interior and into battle against some tribesmen to whom they gave musket fire, artillery shells and Toledo steel. Through his interpreter, the Indian maiden Malinche, Cortés reasoned with the defeated tribesmen. They hated the great warriors of the interior, the Aztec-Mexicas. He asked them to join him as he marched inland. More than a thousand resolved to go with him to face a glittering Empire of two million.

Inland three hundred miles across the mountains on his island capital in the middle of the great lake, the ruler Montezuma heard from his spies that the men were coming who traveled on the water in great buildings and joined themselves on land to monstrous four-legged creatures. The news paralyzed him. The suzerainty of Montezuma's Aztec nation was two hundred years old, and its destruction had been foretold even at its birth. The Aztecs had been a wandering barbarian

93

tribe, despised by others because they ate the flesh of the victims they sacrificed to their god Huitzilopochtli. No one knew from where they had come, but they settled in a snake-infested dank island in the middle of a great lake. They chose it because their god Huitzilopochtli had spoken from the skies to their leader Tenoch: "O sublime priest! Lead my beloved followers in a pilgrimage, through mountains and valleys, and when you find an eagle devouring a snake, there shall be established our dynasty. I with the assistance of the gods will accompany you in spirit through the golden roads." On a green cactus of the island in the shimmering waters they found their eagle and, in his claws, their snake.

The Aztecs conquered almost all who lived within a thousand miles and cut out the hearts and ate the arms and legs of a hundred thousand victims. They fought wars not so much for conquest as for hearts to offer their god, for if he were not so appeased he would halt the sun's progress. But they knew all the time that one day Quetzalcoatl, the god their Huitzilopochtli had chased away, would return. Quetzalcoatl had sailed to the east in a boat made of serpent skins, saying he would come again one day. He was light-skinned with blue eyes and a fair beard. He would deliver his children from the warriors of Huitzilopochtli.

Now such a being was coming toward the island-city Tenochtitlan. Great palaces sat there, an immense majestic temple and the homes of tens of thousands of people. Long causeways led to the mainland and all luxuries crossed them. Montezuma possessed an army that had never tasted defeat; he was worshiped as semidivine and even the heels and soles of his sandals were of gold. But he was doomed. It had been foretold. In recent years the lake surrounding the city had for no apparent reason rocked, and comets had been seen in the skies while fires drenched with water continued to burn. Montezuma had asked his soothsayers to tell what the signs meant, and they said that the end of the Empire was near. He sacrificed the soothsayers to his god and ate their arms and legs, but afterward he fell to brooding and wondering. Now his fate was coming over the mountains.

At Cholula the Tlaxcaltec Indians plotted to attack the strangers they pretended to welcome as friends. The maiden

Malinche found out and told Cortés. He asked three thousand Indians to come to him to discuss his departure. When they assembled, his guns opened upon them and his war horses charged. He left their bodies heaped one on the other and marched inland.

That Cortés seemed able to read minds was the final evidence of his divinity. There was no opposition offered when he topped the mountains and came to look upon the great city on the island. The causeways were undefended and, borne by his nobles, Montezuma came to him. He alighted and walked to meet Cortés, Aztec lords going before him with brooms so that he might not touch dust. Montezuma gave Cortés his late father's palace, which was so vast that all the Spaniards and their thousand allies slept there comfortably.

For a while Cortés lived peaceably in the palace. Then with six officers he went to Montezuma and told him, politely, that he was to become a prisoner. Montezuma went with him in chains and was unable to protest when Cortés hanged certain Aztec nobles who displeased him. But the people were able to do what their ruler was unable to bring himself to do. They rose against the strangers. Montezuma stood on a balcony and appealed to them to return to their homes. They stoned him. He was not seriously hurt but the stones destroyed his will. He lay almost trancelike in his depression while outside his people attacked the palace. In two weeks Montezuma was dead. By then the situation was desperate for the Spaniards. A handful of men surrounded by three hundred thousand enemies, they had to flee. At night, in the rain, the Spaniards stole out of the palace and made for one of the causeways. But they were seen. The terrifying pounding of the great war drum of the temple sounded through the city and the Spaniards were forced to slash their way through legions of Aztec eagle warriors. They gained the causeway and stumbled across it, those who fell off being dragged into canoes and borne away for sacrifice. When at last they halted on the mainland and Cortés saw the ravages in his forces, he burst into sobs. Spain remembered it as The Sad Night.

The dead Montezuma was succeeded by another ruler who shortly died, the victim with thousands of others of the smallpox the Spaniards had brought. Cuauhtemoc, Montezuma's nephew, married to Montezuma's daughter, became the ruler. Cortés obtained reinforcements from Cuba, gathered more Indian allies, and laid siege to Tenochtitlan. For three months he pounded the city. Indian bodies choked the canals. There was no choice but surrender. Cuauhtemoc asked Cortés to kill him with the blade the conqueror wore at his waist; his request was denied. The Spaniards seeking the vanished treasure of his uncle Montezuma tortured him by putting his feet into fire. He said nothing beyond mildly inquiring of another victim who cried out for him to reveal the hiding place: "Do you think I am enjoying this foot bath?"

They never found the treasure, but Spain and her cavaliers now owned the country. They tore down the great temple and upon its foundations and with some of its stones built the Cathedral of what they called the City of Mexico. They sent troops to subdue the few Indian tribes who failed to swear allegiance and behind those troops and all over New Spain came their priests and their missionaries. The whole conquest, Cortés said—and for three hundred years Spain echoed him— was made not for gain but for the glory of God and to bring the true faith to a people who had been led astray by Satan. In their way the Spanish were loyal to that claim. Other colonizing nations wiped out the natives or drove them away like wild animals, but the Spanish did not. Perhaps it was because they realized the wealth of their new acquisition could not be exploited without native labor. Perhaps also it was because the Indians so readily adapted their fervent ecstatic religions to Catholicism. Twelve years after the conquest a simple Indian peon, Juan Diego, walking on a hill in Guadalupe, just outside Mexico City, thought he heard a voice telling him to go to the Spanish bishop to say there must be a shrine to the Virgin built on that spot; that he should take his wrap and put in it the roses which blossomed at a time when no roses were in flower. When he unrolled the wrap to show the bishop his roses it was found to bear the picture of the Virgin. Her face was dark, an Indian face. The shrine that was built became the shrine of all Mexico; the picture of the Virgin of Guadalupe hung in every home.

Despite the fact that its citizens were now universally the coreligionists of the overlords, economic Mexico existed solely for the aggrandizement of Spain. No industry was permitted which would compete in any way with the mother country, no vineyards, silk spinning or tanning of hides. No shipment of anything was permitted to any but Spanish ports. Mining was the only real occupation. Billions of dollars of silver and gold, mostly the former, sailed from Vera Cruz in the galleons of the Silver Fleet that went along the Spanish Main to Florida, Bermuda, the Azores, Cadiz. There were three classes of citizens: the Spanish-born, who ruled and held all important positions from Viceroy on down; the Creoles, who were of Spanish descent but Mexican birth; and the Indians, the People of No Reason, who labored. The People of No Reason had no education, no rights, no land, no historical memory in the wake of the intense effort to burn their records and destroy their temples and their ancient idols. The Creoles had money but no high social position. The steel-encased Spaniards had sedan chairs and four-inch standing collars, boots to the hip, silver-gilt helmets with floating plumes, capes topped with ermine, sword scabbards encrusted with gems.

In their calculations the Spaniards forgot another class: the mestizos. The mestizos were the offspring of Spanish men and Indian women, and their numbers soon grew very great. For women did not come out from Seville or Madrid. Spanish women were not colonizers. Mestizos possessed the quickness of mind and drive of the Spaniards but they also had learned from their Indian mothers the silent, joyless ways that suddenly and impulsively could be broken by a terrible mindless violence. There lived in them something of the Indian reticence to speak of emotion, feelings, thoughts—Indians communicate through gesture, through attitude of body, hints instead of statements, or through things said to third parties—but there were also in the mestizos wildness and great ambition. It showed in the fiery fiestas, the guns fired into the air, the boasting speech-making which suddenly gave way to self-effacement, the smiles to answer threats. Mestizo ambition took the form of a hatred and jealousy of the pure Spaniards—the *gachupines*, those who wear spurs. Mexican songs ended in a howl of sadness, and the falsetto singing was very much like the sound of crying.

What the mestizos had undergone for three hundred years

surfaced on the sixteenth day of September of the year 1810. Three thousand miles away, in 1808, the Great Emperor of the French had sent his troops across the Pyrenees to conquer Spain for his brother Joseph (it was the day Queen Hortense gave birth to a son of Napoleon's brother Louis), and the reverberations reached to New Spain. Father Miguel Hidalgo, fifty-seven years old, bald, Creole, stood in the pulpit of his church in the little town of Dolores lost in the immense deserts of the great plateau and cried, "Mexicans! *Viva Mexico!* Long live Our Lady of Guadalupe! Death to the *gachupines!*" Three hundred men followed him and together they marched through the long, dusty main street, past the square, window-less adobe huts filled with the odors of cooking and the sounds of the Stone Age—the sharpening of obsidian knives. They went forward into the desert carrying the image of the Virgin of Guadalupe. They would never have carried a representation of Jesus Christ, for Christ was a man, and as such remindful of the Conquistadores who had shattered and raped. Mexicans pray to the Virgin.

Father Hidalgo and his 300 followers took the road to San Miguel, a few score miles. They moved across the wild, rolling, empty land, so green when the rains came but beginning in September to turn brown. At San Miguel the Spaniards had barricaded themselves in the city hall. They came out when it was promised to them that they would not be harmed. But Hidalgo's followers sacked and butchered. And when they finished they marched on to Celaya and as others joined them they grew to 4,000. They were barefoot, ragged, carrying ma-chetes, clubs and slings. With them were women and children and chickens and baskets of beans and corn, and when they came to Celaya they ripped it open. Twenty thousand now, they poured upon Guanajuato. The *gachupines* were en-trenched in the great communal grain warehouse. They died at the hands of the great roaring mob, to the last soldier. Eighty thousand Indians and mestizos went through Toluca and up the mountain passes toward Mexico City. The Viceroy sent royalist troops to meet them at the Mountain of the Crosses and there in October's mists and amid tall evergreens the two forces met. The battle appeared undecided, but Father Hidalgo, who was no soldier, chose to withdraw his forces.

When he did his men began to fade away. The Spaniards attacked and captured Father Hidalgo, who was defrocked by his Church. His head was put on a pole atop the communal grain warehouse in Guanajuato.

His successor was Father Morelos. Morelos had military ability. He fought a guerrilla war against the weakening Spanish forces, darting in and out. He also convened a congress which declared for independence. The Spanish rule in its last throes fashioned itself into an imitation of the conquerors of the past and sent Peninsular War veterans to hunt Father Morelos down and put him before a firing squad. As with Cuauhtemoc and Hidalgo, Father Morelos was a man who had not succeeded in his task but who met death well. He gave candy to the men of the firing squad and asked they aim at his heart, not his face. Always involved with death, with dying, with the end of life as the point of life, Mexico ever after revered the three. *Tell me how you die and I will tell you who you are* is a Mexican saying.

Father Morelos was shot in 1815. In that year the Great Emperor went to Waterloo. But it was too late for Spain. Guerrilla bands were everywhere in Mexico. The leader of a force sent against one band was the Royalist officer Augustin Iturbide. He had fought very well against Morelos. He seemed loyal to the Crown. But Iturbide was ambitious. In the little dusty town of Iguala south of Mexico City, the long straight street opening upon the empty plain, his ambition seized him. Iturbide formulated what he called his Plan of the Three Guarantees: religion, union, independence. The uncountable guerrilla bands accepted him as their chieftain and marched with him upon Mexico City. The last Viceroy met with Iturbide and, in the name of his country, capitulated. It was over. The Spaniards went home. Mexico was free.

Iturbide attempted to draft some sort of democratic constitution. It was impossible. The delegates to the constitutional convention could agree on nothing and never having had responsibility they could not deal with it. They argued points of philosophy instead. The men of Iturbide's old regiment became impatient and marched through the streets of Mexico City shouting out his name but calling him, now, Augustin the First. He was crowned as Emperor in July of 1822 in the Cathedral built upon the ruins of the great temple of the Aztecs.

Iturbide had no hope of reigning successfully. His soldiers, paid in worthless paper money, turned away. Braided and epauleted generalissimos and caudillos covetous of his power pronounced against him. He could not abide the thought of more war and more slaughter and so he fled to Italy, to London, and, a year later, back to Mexico. A former officer of his Army of the Three Guarantees commanded the squad which stood him against a wall.

In the country which had been New Spain chaos reigned supreme. One regional chief backed by troops succeeded another in the National Palace next to the Cathedral, only to be sent flying by the pronunciamento of a third coming up to the highlands of Mexico City, Indians and oxen yoked together to pull his artillery train over the mountains. "He took the road to the coast and sailed from the Republic, embarking himself for New Orleans," became almost a formula to describe the end of the public career of innumerable men. Some came back again and again. One such was Antonio López de Santa Anna, dictator, President and Serene Highness. Without principle, an eruption of egotism shimmering with tinsel glory, he dominated the country off and on for a quarter of a century. In between Santa Anna's many seasons there reigned the Generals Victoria, Guerrero, Bustamente, Herrera, Arista, the Senors Gomez Farias, Peña y Peña, and others, one for a total of forty-three minutes.

In a country larger in size than France, Austria, England, Ireland, Scotland, Italy, Holland, Portugal and Belgium put together, there was not a road that was safe from bandits, hardly a business that was not in the hands of a foreigner depending on his Minister or ambassador to protect him from Mexican Government thievery. And even that did not always work, for officials left office so quickly and with so little notice that letters appealing their capricious decisions usually went unanswered. Weeds overgrew the long cobblestone roads the Spanish had built. The riches of three hundred years had traveled the road from Acapulco to Mexico City, but twenty years after the last Spaniard had gone the Acapulco–Mexico City road was impassable for any wheeled vehicle, and it took a good horse or mule to travel it; and the road to Vera Cruz was so dangerous that it was not uncommon for a diligence to arrive at its destination bearing passengers who had been robbed by one band after another, taking in order their money, their watches, their luggage and finally their clothing. Inn-keepers waited behind barricaded walls so that they could throw blankets over completely naked customers.

The descendants of the proud Spaniard and the proud Indian, mixed now into the Mexican race, sank into hatred and fear of all those not part of their little circle of family and friends. In that despoiled, hopeless mass there could be aroused no love of country, no feeling for anything but self-aggrandizement. Far to the north in their province of Texas the Anglo-Saxon settlers revolted in 1835 against Mexico City's rule, and Santa Anna threw together a ragged Indian-conscript army with women, children and goats tagging along. They journeyed a thousand miles through the desert to an old Spanish mission which Santa Anna clumsily took after killing the defenders to the last man. The Texans gathered to meet him two months later and San Jacinto succeeded the Alamo. Santa Anna gave up the province.

Two years later, King Louis Philippe, irritated by indignities against French citizens, sent his son, the Prince de Joinville, to mount a naval expedition off Vera Cruz. Part of the French complaint was that a French cakemaker resident in Mexico City had been robbed in a wretched riot in the streets —one of hundreds. A French cannonade crashed into the old Spanish fortress of San Juan d'Ulúa and a French landing party went ashore to back up the Prince as he raised his father's flag over Vera Cruz. The campaign from beginning to end took three hours. Guarantees of financial restitution assured, the French took their leave from the affair titled, in honor of the cakemaker, The Pastry War. Behind them, only partially dressed (for he had been asleep) and waving his sword, came Santa Anna. The French threw a few shells at him. One shattered his leg. A surgeon cut it off, and, a war hero in power again, Santa Anna had it buried in a vast mausoleum in the capital. Shortly later, as he flew yet once more in his cheap gilded finery from the National Palace, a mob unearthed his limb, attached rope to it and dragged it through the filth and mud of the streets.

Each petty little town or province had its slovenly group of sombreroed and sandaled men carrying rifles and bandoliers who passed for customs inspectors; and each train of mule drivers coming through had to pay tribute. The amount demanded varied with the bribe offered or the show of force displayed by the guards accompanying the wagon train. Adventurous European travelers saw in the wild landscape and untamed ways the Spain of Don Quixote reborn in the nineteenth century.

Hopelessly divided and weak, Mexico blundered into war against the Colossus of the North. Zachary Taylor came swinging in through the limitless deserts to fight at Buena Vista in February of 1847, Winfield Scott landed at Vera Cruz to follow Cortés's route to Cerro Gordo. From there Scott circled Mexico City and ranged his marines and soldiery before what had been the site of Montezuma's summer palace and, later, that of the Viceroyalty of New Spain. It was, the Americans said, Manifest Destiny. Captain Robert E. Lee personally sighted each artillery piece, and Lieutenant Ulysses S. Grant went in with the troops to attack Chapultepec Castle. The main body of Mexican defenders fled, leaving a group of cadets behind. When further resistance was hopeless, six of the boys, thirteen and fourteen years old, wrapped themselves in the flag of the Mexican Republic and flung themselves over the parapets. Their death was glorious, and something stirred even in those many Mexicans who hated best their own countrymen. The Boy Cadets became saints in Mexico's Pantheon along the Cuauhtemoc, Hidalgo, Morelos.

The peace settlement of 1848 which followed the sight and sound of the gringo * putting the Stars and Stripes atop the National Palace took from Mexico one-third her territory, California, Arizona, New Mexico.

In what was left of Mexico in the 1850's, the walls of the country haciendas crumbled under the rifle shots of marauding outlaw bands and water poured through the shattered roofs onto the discolored floor tiles. Grass grew in the courtyards of the abandoned suburban villas located outside Mexico City. Like Asian Pashas the warlords of the countryside wandered

* The word is thought to have originated from a song the Yankee marines sang, "Green Grow the Lilacs, Oh!"

just beyond the gates of every city. Smuggling and banditry were the major industries of the country. The Mexicans fought among themselves and their ancient cannons left behind by Spain set the prairies on fire during the dry season so that horses and men, wounded and dead, perished together in the flames. And after the camp followers stripped naked the dead, the vultures and wild dogs came to rip at the corpses.

The Mexicans fought with machetes, the illiterate caudillo pronouncing against the *Jefe,* the adventurers setting off against the plunderers. Their version of war was hardly distinguishable from armed robbery and murder, but in their scrambling vicious fights the majestic towers and battlements of the Spanish rule went falling into the dusty streets where no garbage collectors came. There was not a building in Mexico City that did not bear bullet marks. Bridges collapsed and fell into the stream beds and the people forgot that once New Spain had been the jewel of the greatest Empire in the world. The causeways built to sustain roads were bashed down and the best trees were felled to make barricades; the result was that mud covered the roads during the rainy season and clouds of dust during the dry months. Everywhere one saw peeling plaster, broken windows, doors hanging by a single hinge, blackened walls, unrepaired aqueducts trickling water, cemeteries with coffins broken open by men searching for loot. There were eleven changes of government in the course of the stupid bungling war of 1846–48 which lost to the Yankees what Spain had held for three hundred years. Leadership did not exist; those who were called leaders died because their own troops shot them, or they ran away with gold or the tax receipts extracted at the point of a leveled bayonet.

That a man like Santa Anna could hold office, prosper, inspire devotion, be greeted with a screaming *viva* when he went forth time and again showed what Mexico had become. The Europeans who resided in Mexico City and in the port of Vera Cruz could not understand these people who by turn were suspicious, dissimulative and exquisitely courteous. The Mexicans did not understand themselves for they all wore masks, the defense of a subjugated race whose members could not trust even their own. For one of their people might be a traitor revealing secrets to the outsiders, those of the conquest.

Their most vile term, their most unthinkable word, which pronounced aloud must result in a death, was *chingada,* which meant to be opened up, exposed.

For *chingada* meant what the Conquistadores had done. It had shown them to the others. It was nakedness, weakness, having no power, the flight of the ancient gods, subjugation. To find the return of power, manliness, domination—*machismo* —they sought leaders who were bombastic, eloquent, gallant, glorious. Such was Santa Anna. But there came a time when his magic finally failed for the last time. The fields churned up by cavalry charges were barren and the workshops leveled, and actual barbarism was the next step—and so he fled to Venezuela, flinging behind him his usual cry that he had sacrificed himself for Mexico. It was late 1855.

General Juan Alvarez succeeded Santa Anna. Very brave, a soldier humble and yet gallant in that Mexican Indian way, Alvarez knew himself. His army of peon soldiers had driven Santa Anna away, but he himself was never meant for a statesman or even a politician. President for only a few months, Alvarez stepped down in 1855 in favor of Ignacio Comonfort. Comonfort was something of a student and thinker. He had come to a conclusion. It was that the troubles of Mexico were to be laid at the door of one institution: the Church.

Catholicism in Mexico had come with the Conquistadores. It had in fact *been* the conquest—Cortés himself had said so. In the years that followed the quick establishment of Spanish rule, the priests had protected the Indians as best they could from exploitation. Some of them were nearly saints, traveling unthinkable distances through unspeakable perils to found their missions, to put their churches into the desert and tropical jungle. Soldiers of Christ, they died by the thousands to bring their parishioners the Word.

There was another side to their labors. The priests had kept the Indians in dense ignorance while they made their Church unimaginably, uncountably rich. The Cathedral of Mexico was its symbol. Every gold-encrusted chapel there, every jeweled crown, each soaring height seemed to say that *here* was the richest, the finest, the most exalted House of God in the world. In every Mexican village with its chickens pecking in the dusty roadway, with its donkeys picking at the sparse grass of the plaza, a church towered above everything. In its aisles *hacendado* sons of the grandees at their devotions sprawled face down on the floor along with barefoot Indian peons. In Mexico golden Jesus and diamond-crowned Mary received a due unknown anywhere else in the world. In the remote mountain parishes the Indians painted Jesus Christ as a cowboy with the great spurs of the *gachupines*, with a six-shooter on hip, with silver coins on the pantaloons and on the brim of the sombrero. It was their highest tribute. The Indians gave more. They gave years of labor to pay the padre for conducting a relative's funeral or for marrying them to their betrothed; they gave tithes, bequests, fees for baptisms, confessions, masses, saints' days; they gave the Church special laws which permitted the operation of businesses outside the regular laws of the land (legal suits against priests did not exist); they deposited their money with the Church because there were no other banks in the country. The Church by the time of Independence in 1821 was deeply involved in all forms of commerce, owned 50 percent of Mexico's lands and Mexico's wealth.

President Comonfort, a Catholic, believed intellectually that the Church must give up her enormous position. Steeling himself but fearful also, he authorized the laws of June 1856, which took from the Church all her lands save those on which actual houses of worship were located. A constitution followed which established secular education in a country which for three centuries had known only teachers who were churchmen. Freedom of speech and the press were granted, and a hundred other reforms passed. From Rome, Pope Pius IX sent word that anyone who signed his name to the document would be excommunicated.

But the Mexican Congress voted for the new constitution. That it had done so was a torment to Comonfort. He was relieved when General Felix Zuloaga denounced the constitution, occupied the National Palace, drove away Comonfort's supporters and ordered him to renounce the document. Comonfort did so and fled into exile.

Comonfort's followers, chased from Mexico City by General Zuloaga, assembled in Guanajuato. They accepted the fact that Comonfort had deserted them, but not that his government was dissolved. Hardly more than a handful of men, they maintained that they were the legal government of the Republic and that Zuloaga was an interloper, even though he sat in the National Palace at Mexico City. Among the Guanajuato refugees were to be found all the Liberal thinkers of Mexico, the men who had tried to take away the riches of the Church. They had all the Mexican traits: eloquence and bombast, love of finery and title, a passion for power. Yet the man who led them now was unlike them in every way. He was Mexican, too. But where virtually all the others were mestizos he was pure Indian. Perhaps that was the difference.

Benito Pablo Juarez was born in 1806 in San Pablo Guelatao, a cluster of mud huts located in the remote mountains of the southeast. In the vacant high places of the immense wilderness sierra there was nothing whose duplicate had not been there in the time of Cortés, and indeed in the time of Christ. Vague reminders of the great days of the Zapotec nation which long antedated the Aztecs could be seen, stones that might have been a temple. Nothing more. What the people called the Enchanted Lake was near the village. Its clarity was unusual; one could see almost to the bottom in even the deepest sections. There was, the people said, a water witch living in its depths.

Juarez's parents died when he was an infant; he was left with no memory of them. His Uncle Bernardino took him into his home of mud and straw and put him to watching twelve sheep who grazed near the Enchanted Lake. There was no school in the town, no government agency of any kind. The child grew up in the Indian way, almost always silent, never crying. Perhaps he seemed brighter than the others, for he tried to learn the Spanish language known by a tiny fraction of his people. The others knew only Zapotec. When he did not do well in his lessons, such as they were, he fashioned a whip from a tree branch, gave it to his uncle and asked that he be beaten.

Twelve years old, barefoot, with the limp black hair, dark eyes and tireless light step of the mountain Indian, the boy saw one day a line of muleteers come past the Enchanted Lake. They stole one of the sheep whose safekeeping was the meaning of his life. To a people knowing nothing of manufactured goods, of money, of the world beyond their own village, the loss of a sheep was a disaster. One who lost it was dishonored. That day the boy set out on foot for Oaxaca, the great city at the base of the mountain. His sister had gone there years earlier. He walked for days over the rocky hillside trails and came to the city, beautiful in the Spanish colonial fashion, with arcades and stone mansions. He found his sister working as a cook for a well-to-do family. The head of the house was a dealer in cochineal, a dye made from the body of an insect found on the cactus plant. The family sent the boy Benito to be apprenticed to a bookbinder, who taught him to read and write correctly and then sent him to school.

Juarez grew up as a determined student, not brilliant but hard working. Once, barefooted, he acted as a waiter at a dinner for Santa Anna. He was not imposing physically, remaining always the prototype of the stolid mountain Indian. Other men among the very few who rose from similar origins spoke of their pasts by saying, "When I was an Indian . . ." but Juarez never did.

His benefactor, the bookbinder, had intended him for a Church career but the seminary's teachings turned Juarez against religion. He studied law. He became a lawyer, a judge, the governor of the state of Oaxaca. His rise was truly remarkable, but it did not seem to affect his manner, for he remained slow-speaking, quiet, self-effacing. He married the daughter of the family to whose home he had come to seek his sister. "He is very homely, but very good," his wife said.

In time Juarez found himself unable to pledge his allegiance to Santa Anna, who said it was a simple matter of Juarez resenting his service as a waiter. Santa Anna, in power in 1853, exiled him. Juarez went to New Orleans, where he worked in a tiny cigar factory and ate in the lunchroom of a third-rate hotel before he moved to equally rundown lodgings, where he paid eight dollars a month for his room and eight dollars more for his meals. At home, Santa Anna, sensing another of the unending revolutions in the offing, sent word to the fanatic monarchist in exile, Gutierrez de Estrada, that he might search in the name of Santa Anna for a European Prince to come to Mexico to rule. Perhaps if one came Santa Anna could rule through him.

But the revolution led in 1855 by the simple Juan Alvarez

came suddenly, and Santa Anna fled for the last time. When word of the uprising reached New Orleans, Juarez took ship for Acapulco and joined Alvarez's forces. He did not reveal that he was the Benito Juarez who had been the incorruptible governor of Oaxaca under whose rule schools had been built, roads improved and rotation of crops encouraged and sloth in the government routed. He simply offered help. They made him a clerk. After a time Juarez was recognized and became Vice President in Comonfort's government. Then Comonfort, disavowing the new constitution, fled. And Juarez was made President. Or at least he and his supporters said he was President. But soon General Zuloaga forced him to flee to the west coast, there to take ship for Panama. He crossed the isthmus and sailed north and came safely to Vera Cruz.

There were two governments in Mexico. One belonged to General Zuloaga in Mexico City and the other was headed by Juarez in Vera Cruz. Between them there could never be peace. The Conservatives of Mexico City called themselves the Party of Decent People. What the Liberals of Vera Cruz stood for, the Conservatives said, was license and theft. They spurned Old Mexico; they wished anarchy. They would permit priests to be derided. They robbed in the name of virtue. They wanted men and women married outside of the Church. They were irresponsibly bent on tearing apart the social fabric which had endured for three hundred years. Bearing banners before them with the Cross outlined in their colors of green and white, the Conservative hosts went forward to the inevitable war. They were encouraged by priests carrying the banners LONG LIVE RELIGION. DEATH TO TOLERANCE. The Pope in Rome endorsed their fight, pointing out that Jesus Christ had said of the clergy: "He who hears you, hears Me; he who depreciates you, depreciates Me."

From Vera Cruz the Liberals came to meet them. They asked, "Had not Christ called out, 'My reign is not of this world'?" They fought, the Liberals said, not against religion but against priests grown fat and corrupt while the peons starved; they fought for the ideals that emerged with the French Revolution and culminated in the outbreaks of 1848. They fought, they said, to give their country democracy.

With "Mexico" on the lips of both, they met. It was the

most terrible kind of conflict, a war that is religious and civil. Neither side showed mercy. Each side regularly castrated dead enemies, each tied prisoners to the tails of horses and sent those horses galloping through the desert cacti until the dragged men were ripped into pulp. Both sides mashed cartridge powder into men's eyes and lit that powder with cigars. They cut off fingers and pulled out tongues so that the victims could never again fire a gun or even speak in opposition. They routinely shot prisoners surrendering under a promise of safety.

The priests in the name of Conservatism refused last rites to dying men who were Liberals and branded Liberal women married outside the Church as whores living in sin. The Liberals tore out the bells of every church they could take, maiming the building by cutting off its voice. Liberal soldiers smashed altars into firewood and used the chalices as glasses for liquor; they ripped down the lamps, censers, urns, the baptismal font, and shouted obscene songs from the pulpit.

In 1858 General Zuloaga gave way to the twenty-six-year-old General Miguel Miramon as leader of the Conservatives and President of the Mexico whose government was in the National Palace. (Zuloaga had been a gambling-hall proprietor, and his background made some of the clerics uneasy.)

Miramon was as handsome as a god, the idol of every young girl whose family was Conservative. He had military ability, and under his leadership the Liberals were forced back into a few small enclaves. But Mexico was so vast and uncharted, so trackless and wild, that Miramon's patrols, though well outfitted through the contributions of the Church, could not put down the Liberal bands who rode out of the mountains, struck and disappeared. Or were they Liberals who came burning and robbing, or only bandits who used that name? No one knew— and no one knew if ferocious killers who called themselves Conservatives were indeed of that persuasion or merely out for whatever plunder they could garner.

During those years of terror, from 1857 to 1860, mine shafts were flooded, fields laid waste and mills abandoned. Irrigation canals dried up in the countryside, and the streets of the cities were overrun with garbage and mosquitoes, and the plazas turned to weeds which grew in the manure of the cavalry horses. The ultimate depredation was reached when General Leonardo

Marquez, the second soldier of the Conservative cause after Miramon, took Tacubaya, a suburb of Mexico City. Liberals fighting there surrendered to General Marquez under a promise of no reprisals, and the doctors and students of a nearby medical school came out to tend the wounded prisoners. When everyone from the school was in the streets taking care of the Liberals, Marquez drew out his revolver. He was a worthy military strategist, soft-spoken, exquisitely polite. He went among the wounded and the dying and the doctors and medical students and opened fire. His soldiers followed him. They left not one person alive. From then on General Leonardo Marquez was called the Tiger of Tacubaya and any slight tinge of honor in the war, any hint of mercy, disappeared.

Through all the slaughter of those years of what would later be called the War of the Reform, Juarez stayed in Vera Cruz, living in a boardinghouse, where the only sign of his rank was that he sat at the head of the table. Indifferent alike to the dreary food and the killingly hot and wet climate of the city, he dressed each day in his formal Prince Albert coat and high hat. He never rode a horse. That was for the *gachupines*. He went about in the simplest of black coaches. Once the enemy was thought to be upon Juarez, and an aide urged him to order the coachman to send the horses into a gallop. "At a trot," Juarez said. "The President of the Republic cannot run." He himself, he said, did not matter, but what he represented did. That was democracy—"the life of my heart." His faith in that was "the only title that raises my humble person to the greatness of my task. The incidents of war are contemptible; the idea is above the domain of cannon."

In the end Juarez won. In December of 1860 Miramon staked everything upon one great battle just north of Mexico City. The Conservatives were routed. Miramon fled to Europe and a Liberal army took Mexico City. Ten days later Juarez, sitting in his black carriage, came into his capital with his hands on the head of a cane, leaning forward and staring straight ahead.

There was no Terror following his entrance. Instead Juarez tried to put together the shattered nation. But the Church had not given up. There would be no ecclesiastical burials for those who supported him, no absolution granted to those who purchased an acre of the vast Church estates he auctioned off.

Juarez did not back away, but enforced the constitution with the greatest vigor. The religious orders were suppressed and priests forbidden to appear on the streets in clerical garb, the books and paintings owned by the Church were deposited in museums, the novitiates were closed and girls training to be nuns forbidden to take their vows. Whatever money the Church needed would be given to it by the government. It would have no other sources of income.

The priests did not yield. It was Jesus Christ, the Son of God, they said, who gave them their powers. No man could take those powers away. The situation was a stalemate, and fifty-one members of the Mexican Congress, uneasy and fearful, signed a statement asking Juarez to resign the presidency. Fifty-two signed a request that he stay.

Even as the Church fought, so did the Tiger of Tacubaya. Marquez roamed the mountain passes between Mexico City and Toluca, fifty miles to the west. It was beyond the power of the Liberals to bring him to bay, and he showed his strength by capturing the distinguished political scientist Melchor Ocampo, who had been perhaps the most valued of Juarez's advisers. In addition to his political position, Ocampo was a leading agronomist. Marquez took him when he was on his way to his hacienda where he conducted experiments in bettering corn production. For four days, not a hard morning's ride from where Juarez sat in the National Palace, Marquez paraded his prisoner through the countryside. So terrible was Marquez's reputation and so weak Juarez's forces that not a man raised a finger to save Ocampo. In the end Marquez shot Ocampo, the gun so close to his head that powder burns covered his face. Marquez left his body hanging on a tree on the Mountain of the Crosses where fifty years before Father Hidalgo had fought the Viceroy's troops. Word reached Mexico City that Marquez had cut off Ocampo's head and strung it on the saddle of his horse; * the rumor was followed by delivery of a letter from Marquez to the Congress bewailing the death and the savage and barbarous condition in which Mexico found itself. The crocodile tears so infuriated the Congress that men screamed aloud from their places.

---

* In this case the report was untrue, although Marquez had beheaded other men on several occasions.

When word of what Marquez had done spread through the city a mob gathered to storm the prison where Conservative prisoners were held. Juarez increased the guards. He was, he said, the ruler of an enlightened society, and such do not slaughter men taken in battle. Instead, relying upon a forced loan of fifty thousand pesos—at the time the Mexican Treasury did not contain that much money—he sent the Liberal General Santos Degollado with orders to bring in Marquez alive or dead. Twelve days later Degollado was dead at Marquez's hands. His men had fled as soon as they spotted Marquez's forces. Five days later the young, idealistic officer Leandro Valle set out with eight hundred men to avenge Ocampo and Degollado. The first had died on June 3, 1861, and the second on June 15. On June 23 Marquez took Valle and cut his trunk in half. The top half of the body was found hanging by its arms from a tree on the Mountain of the Crosses and to those who saw it there was something infinitely terrible in the fashion in which the arms, twisted by the weight suspended from them, appeared to be reaching out.

Benito Juarez was the head of a government. But a great number of that government's citizens sincerely thought of it as the instrument of Satan. Unable to enforce his wishes even in the very suburbs of his capital, Juarez faced the prospect of seeing what was potentially one of the richest countries in the world degenerate into anarchy. Half a century of independence had brought Mexico to the edge of what Europe had been in the Dark Ages—a truncated wilderness of petty fiefs ruled by warlords owing allegiance only to their vassals and knowing no law but the sword. It would go on and on, raids, slaughter, massacre, provinces falling away from the central government. The government's Treasury was empty, Mexico's towns ruined and the countryside ravaged. Juarez saw money as his first and greatest problem. With money perhaps all things might be done—the peons fed, the Church placated, Marquez put to flight. Three weeks after Valle was cut down from the tree, in July of 1861, Juarez defaulted on the payments of Mexico's enormous debt to the nations of the Old World. With no money to pay his soldiers or effectively run his government he would not send a peso to Europe. He simply ignored the fact that foreigners, trusting Mexico's promise to pay, had lent money to Mexico.

Juarez might have appealed for understanding to the European diplomats accredited to Mexico, but he did not do so. It was not his pride which forbade him, for Juarez had no personal pride. It was that the President of the Republic could not appeal in Mexico's name for pity. The diplomats found out from the newspapers. All payments were immediately suspended for a period of two years. The situation would be reviewed at the conclusion of that time. Perhaps payments would be resumed then. That was all.

Immediately the act was made known—that debt service was suspended, that Mexico was outside the pale of civilization, a thief, a criminal—the Ministers of France and Great Britain broke off relations. Sir Charles Wyke wrote Britain's Foreign Secretary Lord John Russell, telling him of his boundless contempt for "this wretched government . . . constantly talking of liberty, toleration and the blessings of a constitutional system. . . . It is like a Prostitute boasting of her virtue. Their idea of political economy seems to consist of putting their hands into other people's pockets."

And the word of what Juarez had done reached Europe and the butterfly salon diplomat Pepe Hidalgo; and he went to the Empress of the French and with her to her husband the Emperor—and they talked together.

9

No GREAT POWER OF EUROPE which actively traded abroad could permit any nation in the world, no matter how far away, no matter how barbarous, to default on loans. A month after the news from Mexico had been received, England, Spain and France signed an agreement to join together in a military expedition to Vera Cruz.

The motives of the three partners signing the Convention of London were mixed. England saw the matter as a bill-collecting mission. The British Minister to Mexico, believing he dealt with "a set of fools and knaves" mismanaging a place where "anarchy and confusion" reigned, was of the opinion that gunboats and small landing parties should be dispatched. They could then seize the coastal customhouses and levy taxes on everything coming into or going out of the country. European bayonets would settle all discussions. The mass of rabble called the Mexican army could do nothing about it. After a while, the Mexican Government would see the light and be reasonable.

Spain could not look upon an expedition to Mexico in so simple a fashion. The last Viceroy had left half a century before, and chaos and anarchy had been the result of that departure. Madrid wondered whether the appearance of Spanish troops might once again bring a great triumph. Were there not very many Mexicans who would welcome their country's return home to the Spanish Crown?

The third partner, France, cared not a whit for Mexico. The amount of money owed by Mexico to French companies and investors was not so great that its loss would disrupt the French economy. Emotionally, the issue had little meaning to the population.

However, Mexico mattered to three people in France.

One was Auguste de Morny, the illegitimate son of Hortense, Napoleon III's mother, the man who had made Hortense's legitimate son the French Emperor. Napoleon's half-brother lived very expensively, lavishly indulging his whims and those of his Russian wife. They liked animals, so their home was filled with caged lions and tigers, and monkeys flitted through the drawing rooms. De Morny liked horses, and so inspired the building of Longchamps. He liked sea bathing and almost singlehandedly created Deauville. All his endeavors were on a grand scale. Immense sums filtered through his hands, money obtained from all kinds of business deals, stock market coups, purchases made advantageously by a man extremely close to the Emperor. De Morny had been one of many offered the Throne of Mexico by the grandly generous Gutierrez de Estrada, but had declined. The gamble did not look promising, and besides, he was happy in Paris. But suddenly he had a great interest in Mexico.

A certain Swiss financier, Jean Baptiste Jecker, had come to de Morny with a proposition. Jecker had a large but not very palatable claim on Mexico. Jecker had kindly consented to lend Miramon's Conservative government when Miramon was President of Mexico the equivalent of seven hundred and fifty thousand American dollars. In return Miramon had given Jecker bonds issued in the name of the Mexican Republic for fifteen million American dollars. So low was Mexico's international credit that this was the best arrangement Miramon could get from anybody. Now Miramon was gone, having used the money unsuccessfully to contest the presidency with Juarez, and Juarez sat in the National Palace. The idea of paying fifteen million dollars for less than a million he had never seen had helped Juarez to decide to default on Mexico's debts.

Meanwhile the Swiss Jecker was sitting on the bonds. He went to de Morny and told him that if the French could get Juarez or any other Mexican to pay the fifteen million, five million of it would be de Morny's. De Morny arranged for Jecker to receive French citizenship and urged his half-brother, the Emperor of France, to push ahead with the expedition to

Vera Cruz. But de Morny did not have to take the lead in praising intervention to the Emperor.

It was the Empress who did that. Somehow it seemed that all the circumstances of Eugenie's life had come together to make Mexico her passion. Born a Spaniard, she mourned for the lost Spanish Empire. A monarch now, she often thought of another woman and another monarch, Isabella, who, so it was said, had pawned her jewels that Columbus might sail. Isabella of Spain had found the New World; might not Eugenie of France reclaim a part of it from the chaos into which it had sunk?

Of all the problems Mexico faced, that of the Church touched Eugenie most. She was so devout a Catholic that she half-regretted the French victory over the Austrians in 1859. That victory had paved the way for the unification of Italy, and a united Italy would never permit the Pope the immense lands his predecessors had ruled. If France had indirectly harmed the Church in Italy, perhaps it could help godless and sinful Mexico, a land robbing the Church of its treasures. Eugenie saw herself as Defender of the Faith.

All else aside, she was at the nadir of her married life. The Countess de Castiglione was gone, but only to be followed by a score of others—statesmen's and officers' wives, actresses, *grandes horizontales,* chambermaids. She raged that she would take the Prince Imperial and go to Rome to live, which made Lord John Russell wonder if Napoleon would file a divorce suit naming the Pope as corespondent. Eugenie had scenes and weeping fits. Though the Emperor quavered, he continued in his ways. Yet he hated to see her unhappy. "He is capable of setting Europe afire to escape a domestic quarrel," remarked one of the members of the Court. Now Eugenie wanted France to go to Mexico with more in mind than a simple military demonstration. She wanted a new Crusade. She talked of nothing else. "Eugenie," her husband moaned, "you never get an idea, the idea gets you."

But Napoleon listened to her, partly as the mighty Emperor of the French and partly as a husband. He would make up to the Empress what he owed to the wife. And it was strange, very strange, reflected Lord Cowley, the British Ambassador to France, how Latin America had intrigued Napoleon ever since his prison days at Ham. But no one could deny that there was grandeur in the idea that at his behest France's army would sail for Vera Cruz, bringing redemption with it. His uncle the Great Emperor had gone to Egypt and thought of going to India. He had never done so, and now India was the British colony most responsible for England's greatness in the world. Napoleon III's uncle had by the Louisiana Purchase thrown away most of France's position in the New World. Perhaps the nephew could reestablish that position. And there was the question of getting cotton for France's mills. It was difficult now, with the Union navy blockading the ports of the Confederacy.

Always the dreamer, always a combination of gambler-opportunist and prophet-saint, there joined in him the desire to end his wife's screaming fits and an impulse to higher, nobler things. The Emperor was the culmination of the French Revolution; the survivors of the idealistic days of 1848, he thought, looked to him for fulfillment of their aims. In America republicanism and democracy had set the North and the South at each other's throats; if republicanism and democracy won in Mexico would the result there be different? Hardly. That had been proved in the fifty years since Mexican independence.

Napoleon III pondered some more. If the South won the Civil War, would it stay in its own territory, or would it advance past the Rio Grande to take a weakened Mexico? And if the North won? Representative Abraham Lincoln of Illinois had opposed the dispatch of the American army to Mexico fifteen years previously, but it had gone there and cut a third of the country loose and attached it to the United States. As President, would Lincoln, if his gigantic army overran the South, halt his soldiers at the border or send them on to Mexico City? Napoleon knew there was not a monarch in Europe who would have hesitated as to his course, put into Lincoln's position.

Napoleon III could be the savior of Mexico. France would be risking nothing. Years earlier the predecessor of Sir Charles Wyke, Britain's Minister to Mexico, had said that a group of three or four thousand European regulars could take over the whole of Mexico, raise a "native body of troops" for police duties, and rule. Other experts had agreed. France, Napoleon reflected, could simultaneously bring Latin civilization and European traditions back to Mexico, gain a great market and add fresh glory to the reign of France's monarchs. But Napoleon had not forgotten the awful slaughter of those boiling hot days at Magenta and Solferino. He wanted no blood. But all that was required was for a few troops to make a triumphal march which would assure the payment of the debt to France.* This would make the Empress happy, bring economic benefit to his countrymen and, finally, enhance his position as the spiritual heir of the Great Emperor who never hesitated to go far afield. France, he decided, would go to Mexico.

But could it be done as a simple partner in a three-cornered debt-collection expedition? No. France would have to sponsor a ruler for the beautiful but unhappy land beyond the seas. An Austrian Archduke would seem the best choice, for such a selection would go toward improving France's relations with the Austria she had humbled in the war of 1859.

The matter was not discussed by the statesmen who signed the Convention of London on October 30, 1861. The Convention specifically said the three partners, Spain, England and France, did not seek any acquisition of territory and would do nothing to influence the Mexican people in their internal affairs. But in the most technical sense the Emperor of France was *not* endorsing anybody for monarch of Mexico, for the matter was in the hands of Pepe Hidalgo and Gutierrez de Estrada. Five minutes after saying, "We can but try," Hidalgo asked if he might use the special Imperial telegraph to send word to Gutierrez that he must hasten to Vienna. There he should sound out the Austrian Government on sending an Archduke to Mexico. It was a Mexican who asked, not a Frenchman. A rebuff would not be directed at Napoleon.

Hidalgo's telegram galvanized Gutierrez. Two months previously, in his eternal hawking of a Throne for Mexico, he had suggested the name of the Archduke Maximilian to the Austrian Ambassador to Paris, Prince Metternich—the son of the dead Chancellor—who sent the suggestion on to his Foreign Minister, Count von Rechberg. Von Rechberg said he could not encourage the idea. But now Gutierrez arrived in Vienna with implied credentials from the Emperor of the French.

---

* It is unknown if the Emperor knew the exact reason why de Morny pressed the cause of intervention. He probably did, and, in his fashion, looked the other way.

Foreign Minister von Rechberg took the matter up with Francis Joseph. Ever reserved and cautious, the Austrian Emperor told him to confer with Maximilian. He did not say no to the idea that his brother should go to Mexico. Von Rechberg arrived at the castle square of Miramar bearing in effect an invitation from one Emperor and permission from another. He offered to a twenty-nine-year-old unemployed Archduke, appanaged cadet and younger son, the possible opportunity of rescuing and ruling a country more than three times larger than France and potentially richer than Austria. What else, Maximilian asked himself, did he have in prospect? What else, his wife wondered, did life offer?

They could not but leap at the chance. But the situation was delicate, for Francis Joseph, weakened by the Italian war and faced with an ever-rebellious Hungary, could do and would do nothing to help. That meant Maximilian would be dependent upon countries other than his own for aid in setting up the new monarchy. The Archduke, his wife and the Austrian Foreign Minister discussed the problem and sent word to the Mexican emigrés in Paris that Maximilian could consider the proposal only if two conditions were met: that there be substantial military support from powers other than Austria and that the Mexicans themselves indicate they wished him to be their ruler.

In Paris the emigrés knew only that a bearer of the name von Hapsburg was interesting himself in what they, lost exiles, had sought for twenty years. Gutierrez said he completely understood the Archduke's position. It was akin to the "eligible young lady" whose "role is modestly to wait until her hand is sought."

Napoleon rushed ahead, telling the people around him that it was certain that the moment European squadrons appeared in Mexican waters, the monarchial party, with its numerous members, would appear and beg for a ruler who could bring order out of chaos. He wrote King Leopold of the Belgians, Charlotte's father, to ask that he use his influence with his niece the Queen of England to assure support for the plan in London. British support would not be easy to obtain. The English had contracted to collect debts, not set up dynasties. The King of the Belgians was aware of the British view and of the difficulties his son-in-law and daughter would face. But the prospect was exciting. The Archduke wrote asking what his father-in-law thought and he replied that Maximilian must absolutely not accept unless the Mexicans really showed that they wanted him. He could not be an adventurer.

In Vienna the Empress Elizabeth, hating the prison she conceived her position to be, said Maximilian and Charlotte were insane to seek a Throne. Were it in her power, she would gladly give them hers. The Archduchess Sophia was torn between the fear of having her dearest son go to a faraway and perilous land, and the wish that he attain a great place in the world. She seemed unable to make up her mind.

At Miramar the Archduke and Archduchess threw themselves into a sudden new interest, Maximilian dipping into numerous books on Mexico, Charlotte studying them. They received additional reading matter almost every day, lengthy letters from Gutierrez saying that all Mexico prayed for their acceptance of the Throne, that Maximilian and Charlotte held the fate of the country in their hands, that it was given only to them to save Mexico. Gutierrez had not seen Mexico for twenty years but he sent pictures, books, testaments, all directed toward convincing Maximilian that he sail for Vera Cruz.

In London the Convention was signed on October 30, 1861. Nowhere did it mention the idea of setting up a monarchy, still less that Archduke Maximilian become the ruler. With intervention now a certainty, the United States complained against what it saw as an open violation of the Monroe Doctrine. Secretary of State Seward's note got short shrift in Europe, first because earlier in his career he himself had publicly endorsed the idea that the United States should annex either Canada or Mexico or both, and, far more importantly, because his country was engaged in a Civil War and he was in no position to do anything but send futile complaints.

The troopships prepared to sail, the British contingent led by Commodore Hugh Dunlop of the Royal Navy and the French with Admiral Jean Pierre Edmond Jurien de la Gravière commanding. Madrid gave the leadership of its forces, which would consist of troops already stationed in Cuba, to General Juan Prim. Prim had originally opposed the entire project, saying it must fail, but no Spaniard could resist the opportunity, however remote, to be another Cortés. The European powers agreed to rendezvous in Mexican waters at the beginning of the new year of 1862.

The group of men who called themselves the government of the Republic of Mexico possessed a Foreign Service which consisted of two men, one, Matias Romero, presiding over a Washington legation and the other, Juan Antonio de la Fuente, accredited to the whole of Europe. De la Fuente had been named to his post months previous, but President Juarez had been unable to advance him traveling money. Finally De la Fuente supplied it himself and came to Paris just in time to face the European reaction to the debt suspension. He was not consulted in any of the conversations leading to the signing of the London Convention, but when it was done and the world knew that France, England and Spain were going to Mexico, he was permitted an interview with French Foreign Minister de Thouvenel. "Your government will learn," de Thouvenel said, "through our Minister and our Admiral what the demands of France are. Personally, I have nothing against you, and I wish that events permitted me to use more friendly expressions." De la Fuente broke off relations with France and went to England for a frigid interview with Lord John Russell, who refused to promise him anything. He broke off relations with Great Britain. In Washington, Romero presented Mexico's case to an American Government unable to think of anything but the menace of Lee's army. Secretary of State Seward would write more notes. It was impossible to do more. Europe was coming back to the Americas.

The troops of Her Most Catholic Majesty arrived first, sailing over from Havana six thousand strong. The landing was unopposed. Their commander, General Juan Prim, came out from Spain in two minds about his mission. Ambitious and with a great military record in Spanish Morocco, he was well connected in Mexico, his wife's uncle being Minister of Finance in Juarez's cabinet. He had talked at length with the Emperor Napoleon about the intervention and had at least temporarily persuaded himself that the matter would be a simple one. It was said of General Prim that from the moment he agreed to go he hoped to make himself King of Mexico. But one look at

Vera Cruz and the condition of the troops he was to command changed his thinking. He saw a steaming tropical city with an open sewer in every street and no means of sanitation save repulsive buzzards. The buzzards, protected from harm by the law that recognized them as the only cleansing force in the city, perched atop the flat-roofed white houses and stalked through the gutters. Great sand hills blown up by the northers stood on the dreary plains surrounding the city. The sand hills entrapped wretched miasmic odors which penetrated completely the humid atmosphere. It was hard to catch one's breath. Vera Cruz had always been the most deadly city of the Americas for Europeans. There yellow jack or *el vomito negro* and malaria were rampant, and when Prim saw the number of his men who were down with the fever he actually felt his hair stand on end. "Thus an army melts away as if it were made of butter," he thought to himself.

On January 2, 1862, the British and French fleets appeared in the harbor. There were no piers on the windswept sandy beaches and the troops were ferried ashore in lighters. The British had eight hundred Royal Marines. Commander Dunlop, their leader, was uneasy. In charge of largely Protestant troops, he could only believe that he would be entirely unwelcome among the Mexicans. He shared this feeling with Prim, for in the brief time the Spanish general had been in sultry and half-empty Vera Cruz, he had taken note of the sullen hatred the Mexicans felt for Spanish uniforms, for *gachupines*. The official Spanish opinion was that troops would never have to be used, that "moral action" would be sufficient to cause the Mexicans to pay their bills and change their ways. Prim wondered if it were so.

The French troops, twenty-five hundred strong, landed knowing that they had come to secure the payment of their country's debts and perhaps do more. It was common knowledge among them that not all the aims of the expedition had been spelled out in the Convention of London. The name of the Archduke Maximilian was known to every ranking officer.

On January 10, 1862, the Allies issued a proclamation saying they came to help a nation they saw with grief wasting its resources and destroying its vitality. There was no mention of

Juarez and his government and no hint of the intention of the European powers. Juarez gave his answer a few days later. Any Mexican who cooperated with the Europeans was a traitor and would be executed.

Yet there were no hostilities. Nearly ten thousand foreign troops milled about Vera Cruz, sleeping in abandoned churches and monasteries and carousing with the port prostitutes. Within a few weeks an additional three thousand French troops arrived. Paris had decided it was beneath the dignity of France to engage in an expedition where her contribution would be so much less than that of Spain. After that there arrived the illegitimate son of the Father Morelos who with Father Hidalgo had made the Revolution. His name was Almonte—it was said his Indian mother called him that because his father had told her to go to the mountains in times of trouble. He was a Conservative and had served as Miramon's Minister to France. Dislodged from his position by the victory of Juarez, he had remained in Paris, joining with Gutierrez in urging European intervention and the establishment of a monarchy. Now he went to Prim and said the troops should not be simply sitting around, that they should move inland, where the citizens of the country would "rise as one man when they see the monarchial flag raised." All Mexico longed for a ruler. It was only Juarez and his clique who prevented the people from making known their will. "Absurd," replied Prim.

Meanwhile the French and British Ministers to Mexico came down from Mexico City to join their countrymen in Vera Cruz. Pierre Dubois de Saligny presented the claims which he wished made upon the Mexicans: money for wines delivered to Augustin de Iturbide forty years earlier, money to recompense French citizens robbed by bandits, the right for de Saligny or a representative he designated to sit on all criminal trials involving French residents of Mexico and, finally, redemption in full of the fifteen million dollars of the Jecker bonds.

Saligny's claims totaled the complete income of the Mexican Government for years to come. "Extraordinary, if not outrageous," said the British Minister, Sir Charles Wyke. Prim agreed. Were they bound to support this sort of thing? they asked each other. There was no easy answer. Europe was three weeks away and their hearts sank at the prospect of waiting a month and a half in a fever-ridden pesthouse for answers to questions sent to their superiors. The first thing, they decided —and the French Admiral Jurien de la Gravière agreed—was to leave Vera Cruz and march inland. The pestilential city was dropping their men like flies. Already Prim had dispatched eight hundred men to Spanish army hospitals in Cuba. The Allied commanders sent word to the Mexicans they were moving inland to get away from the fever zone.

General José Lopez Uraga and Juarez's close aide Manuel Doblado accepted delivery of the announcement. Uraga met the bearers of the note along the Vera Cruz–Puebla road and promised to send some delicacies to the Allied officers. In return Admiral Jurien de la Gravière sent him French wine and cigars. During the contacts Uraga took a look at the French military equipment and concluded that no Mexican force could stand up to such guns. Beaten already, he hinted that he did not greatly esteem Juarez and that perhaps a monarchy was the best way out of Mexico's troubles. Doblado was also very circumspect in his dealings with the Europeans. He was said to be very ambitious. In the soft and winding Mexican fashion he hinted he might overthrow Juarez, and at the same time asked for a statement to dispel the rumors that the Europeans were going to set up a monarchy. They stalled him and at the steaming tropical village of La Soledad signed a treaty under whose terms the Europeans would march inland to several temperate zone encampments which would be evacuated for Vera Cruz in the event war broke out. On February 25, 1862, at six in the morning, the Allies began their march inland.

By noon the brutal glare of the tropical sun and the windless tropical heat had dropped fully two-thirds of the men into the dust by the side of the road. A shocked Admiral Jurien de la Gravière rode up the line and saw the French Empire's best soldiers, Zouaves, infantry, the heroes of the Heights of the Alma, Africa, Magenta and Solferino lying helpless and gasping. It took eight days for the troops to march twenty-five miles.

At last they staggered into Orizaba and Cordoba, where it was cooler and less humid. Their transport was still strung out along the road to Vera Cruz. A series of conferences was held with the Mexicans, but although the representatives of both sides were very polite to one another they could not agree on how to resolve their differences. The Mexicans simply could not pay their debts. There was no way to get around it.

On March 6, General Ferdinand Latrille, Count of Lorencez, arrived in Vera Cruz to take over from Admiral Jurien de la Gravière, who could not be expected to command land operations. Lorencez was cold in manner, but a dashing French officer relying on impetuosity, courage and French military brilliance to conquer any enemy placed before a French army. Five days after his arrival he wrote to Minister of War Randon in Paris, "The conferences will come to nothing, we shall march ahead and reach Mexico City, and Prince Maximilian will be proclaimed sovereign of Mexico, where his wise and firm government will be easily maintained for the happiness and regeneration of the most demoralized of all peoples."

Commodore Dunlop of the Royal Navy did not see things that way. Devoutly happy to be out of it, he ended his part in the meaningless conferences and ordered his men back to their ships. Prim followed him with the Spanish soldiers. The French Minister de Saligny had told Prim to his face that he wanted to be King Juan the First but that France would not let that happen. With the announcement that the Spanish were leaving, the French let it be known that as soon as the Spaniards passed through their lines they would be moving farther inland to take Mexico City. By the terms of the Treaty of La Soledad they had agreed that if war broke out they would withdraw to their original landing places at Vera Cruz, but General Lorencez decided some sick French soldiers inland at Orizaba were in danger and began moving his entire force in that direction. "Let us march to the relief of our ill comrades to the cry of 'Vive l'Empereur!' " he said to his men, and the French columns headed toward Orizaba.

"Well, Admiral?" Prim said to Jurien de la Gravière as, heading for the sea, he met the French marching in the other direction.

"Well, General?" asked Jurien de la Gravière. Prim knew in that moment that the French were never going back to Vera Cruz, that they were going to begin operations from jumping-off places which they had promised to evacuate if war broke out. He saluted and went to his ships.

The French went up into the temperate zone and fought a minor skirmish with some Mexican cavalry. They interpreted the brief exchange of bullets as a unilateral Mexican declaration commencing hostilities and announced cancellation of the Treaty of La Soledad. The French gathered together and prepared for a second conquest of Mexico. "We are so superior to the Mexicans in race, in organization, in discipline," General Lorencez wrote his Minister of War, "in morality, and in elevation of feeling, that I beg Your Excellency to be so good as to inform the Emperor that, at the head of six thousand soldiers, I am already master of Mexico."

The French soldiers moved out on April 27, 1862, an army that had not known a defeat since Waterloo. They saw no enemy formations as they went up the tortuously winding road into the mountains, only the abandoned and overgrown breastworks and rusted cannons which had failed to stop Winfield Scott when he went along the same road fifteen years previous. Sometimes horsemen could be seen on distant mountain peaks, but when the French attained the peaks the horsemen were gone. Occasionally they came to burning villages. The Indians living in them knew only war and pillage, were utterly passive and beaten down, slow-moving and wretchedly sad. They offered no resistance and said it was the retreating Mexican cavalry which had set the fires.

All the French could learn of the enemy indicated Juarez was having his forces fall back upon Mexico City two hundred miles away. His original commander, Uraga, was gone, having said even in front of his troops that it would be impossible for Mexico to fight France. He had been replaced by Ignacio Zaragoza, the Minister of War.

The French were certain the expedition would be a simple military promenade. The Mexicans would never fight, de Saligny assured General Lorencez; the troops would enter Puebla, the only major city along the Vera Cruz–Mexico City road, to cheers and acclamations. Almonte agreed. But even if there was resistance, Puebla had been taken more than twenty times in the years of war between the Liberals and

Conservatives, always by troops amounting to less than four thousand in number.

The French army swung up the mountain roads through almost perpendicular passes and looping turns and outside of Puebla at a former penitentiary falling into ruins they met the Mexicans. Fire poured from the windows of the building. French military doctrine held that troops must never attack without artillery support, but the big guns that had broken the Austrians at Magenta and Solferino were at the rear of the column, and Lorencez was so contemptuous of the enemy that he ordered his men to go in with no preparation. The Zouaves dropped their knapsacks and charged, and dismounted cavalry followed. They deployed to the right and left of the slopes of the hill on which stood the ruined jail, bugles blaring and drums rolling. They sent the Mexicans flying. The French crossed another mountain range and halted in an empty Indian village. The pigs had been left behind. The French roasted them over their camp fires.

For ten days they marched, never again seeing a sign of the enemy. On the fourth of May, 1862, they halted in the dusty little village of Amozoc and there they learned that the Mexican commander, Ignacio Zaragoza, was in Puebla, fourteen miles on, and that he was going to fight there.

In Puebla that evening Zaragoza met with his officers. It would be shameful, he told them, if Puebla fell to a virtual scouting party without the city's possession being protested in a manner befitting an independent country of eight million people. They could hardly expect a victory, he said, but at least they must do what they could for the honor of the Mexican nation. Slim and bespectacled and looking far more the scholar than the soldier, he said what his officers already believed, that they had no chance at all. One soldier wondered aloud if by the evening of the next day they would not be running for their lives. Another frankly said he wished he had never come to Puebla. Even the most militant officer of the army, the young Indian Brigadier Porfirio Diaz, said to his favorite body of troops, the Morelos Battalion, that the best testimony they could give to the world that they were worthy sons of the patriot priest was that they should leave their dead bodies at Puebla, sheltered in the folds of their flag. A colonel of the battalion responded by getting dead drunk. He was not the only man who did so that night.

In the morning, the fifth of May, the French rose before the sun was up and marched upon Puebla. One of the few settlements in Mexico not erected upon the ruins of former Indian greatness, it had been planned by the Spanish as a fortress town to protect the capital from attack. Puebla sat on a hill overlooking a plain leading off to the mountain. When the first elements of the French column reached the plain they found it completely empty. There was no sign of the enemy. The troops were ordered to halt and see to their uniforms so that they would appear properly appointed for the victory parade. The Zouaves broke out whitening for their gleaming spats. Sitting in a carriage behind the troops, Dubois de Saligny was handed a message brought in by an Indian runner. It was from General Leonardo Marquez, the Tiger of Tacubaya, who was electing to ally himself with the foreign enemies of Juarez's government. Saligny relayed its contents to General Lorencez: "As soon as our troops are in sight of the city, Marquez will appear, all conventional resistance will cease, the barricades will fall as if by magic. You will make your entrance under a rain of flowers."

Then the French army broke upon the Convent of Guadalupe and the Fort of Loretto overlooking the approaches of what until then had been called Puebla of the Angels but which afterward would be Puebla of Zaragoza. The artillery, not knowing if there would be any opposition, tentatively opened fire, but it was strangely ineffective in the thin clear air of the Mexican uplands, and the gunners seemed unable to get the pieces sighted correctly. They consistently overshot their targets or fell short. The expected white flag did not appear.

Lorencez ordered up three waves of infantry, the Zouaves obliquing to the right to turn the hill on which the convent stood, but a sudden blast by the Mexicans drove them back. The Mexicans were fighting, after all. There could be no doubt of it. Zaragoza's artillerymen had no small arms, and when segments of the French infantry reached them, they had only cannon swabs to fight with, which they swung over their heads as clubs. But very few Frenchmen managed to get near enough to close with the defenders, the majority struggled up the slopes of the hill to find death or wounds as they formed squares to hold off the wild and half-organized Mexican counterattacks. The Mexican artillery consisted of pieces whose counterparts were in European museums—some of them had seen service at Waterloo before being sold to forgotten adventurers who served as Presidents of the Republic—but they cut terrible wounds in the ordered ranks of the *pantalons rouges*. Infuriated, Lorencez ordered repeated bayonet attacks but, caught in a crossfire between the convent and fort, he could not make any headway.

As they fought through the long, sultry afternoon, the stormheads which signaled the beginning of the rainy season gathered above them, and at four the downpour began. Water spilled over the neat kepis and down the flashing uniforms which, modeled after those of the First Empire, had carried the day on one hundred battlefields on three other continents, against African tribesmen, Russian Cossacks, Austrian Hussars, but which, on this day, could not win the field against a tattered horde.

Hardly able to stand in the mud, and blinded by the driving rain, the French threw a last charge up the slope, and then, failing, halted as retreat came from their bugles which had never in fifty years sounded that call. They withdrew to stand together and softly sing "La Marseillaise." Silence fell on the slopes leading up to the Convent of Guadalupe and the Fort of Loretto, to be broken only by the rescue parties playing muted regimental marches as a signal for any wounded who would cry out their locations. In the distance from Puebla could be heard bands blaring and men singing. General Porfirio Diaz ventured forth, dazed, not believing it possible that Mexico had actually stopped France: "I wandered over the field that night to assure myself that it was all real."

Lorencez waited a day, hoping the Mexicans would come out onto the slopes which had seen his defeat; but they did not. So he took his depleted army back to Orizaba and wrote the Emperor asking for siege guns—and twenty thousand men.

10

IT WAS ALL THE FAULT of the Empress of France, Lord Cowley said to himself. It was she "who governs the Emperor's decisions on Mexico." Everyone the British ambassador knew agreed with him. But that did not matter now. A French expeditionary force had been humiliated by what the *Times* of London called "cross-bred, demoralized, blood-thirsty castes, which combine the vices of the white man with the savagery of the Indian." The defeat must be avenged.

Seeing them in the first days after the shocking news, Pepe Hidalgo found the Emperor somber and meditative and the Empress trying to keep calm. They received him as always and Eugenie said he must stay for a while, but Hidalgo noticed how they rarely spoke at dinner and how Napoleon kept taking off and putting on his wedding ring. "Such are the fortunes of war," the Emperor wrote General Lorencez, "and occasional reverses sometimes cloud brilliant successes; but do not lose heart; the honor of the country is involved and you will be supported by all the reinforcements you need." Napoleon went to the Legislative Body, which voted money, troops and confidence in the Throne.

But there were discordant voices. Deputy Jules Favre said: "To go on with the war would be to involve ourselves in the most unjust, the most reprehensible of adventures. The worst thing that could happen to us in this enterprise would be to win, for with victory would come responsibility. . . . Having set up a government we would have to maintain it." Other deputies asked what the government saw as the end product of this intervention, and hinted that it was not the business of France to connive at the placing of a foreign Prince upon a foreign throne. Minister of State Auguste Billault answered that it was "a painful commentary upon French patriotism that while French troops were marching upon Mexico City, Frenchmen dared to charge before France and the Legislative Body that these brave men were the mere instruments of an intrigue, and that the war they fought in Mexico was a base and unlawful one."

Why, then, deputies asked, had the English and Spanish dropped the whole thing? The newspaper *Le Constitutionnel* explained: "The reason that France is alone is to be explained by the habit of France never to draw back from any sacrifice that will benefit humanity and civilization."

Deputy Edgar Quinet might sneer that "to cover the initial error has always been called 'saving the flag.'" But orders went out to Chasseur d'Afrique and marine artillery, to fusilier and mountain howitzer battery, to sapper, hospital corps and detachment of gendarmerie, to officer of artillery train and equipment train, to the Foreign Legion for 50 percent of its strength, to the Ninety-ninth of the Line, to the First Battalion of Chasseur à pied, to the Second Regiment of Zouaves, to home regiments and colonial troops, the cream of the army. The troopships sailed from Toulon and from Mers-el-Kebir and came to Martinique, where they refueled and took on tropical gear. In Martinique old comrades from Sebastopol and Sidi-bel-Abbes were reunited for a few nights, drinking and brawling and whoring before going on to redeem French honor and garner promotions and medals.

The soldiers of France went to Vera Cruz to crowd the filthy streets with men in magnificent plumes and sashes and hip-length boots. Others wore the white uniforms of the Nubians of the Egyptian Legion contributed by the Viceroy of that country and press-ganged off the streets of Alexandria, half-naked, most of them, the night before the troopship sailed. They would be able to survive the mosquitoes of the lowland fever zone which dropped Europeans in their tracks.

With the reinforcements came a new commander who fully understood that this time there must not be a repulse for France. General Elie Forey was a veteran of the Crimea and Italy. He was as slow and thorough as Lorencez had been adventurous, as jovial as Lorencez had been cold. His men called him The Bear. He began by issuing a proclamation which spoke of the peaceful intentions of the Emperor of the French and the "love he bore for Mexico and the gallant Mexicans." The French general sent his proclamation to General Jesus Ortega, now commanding in Puebla in place of Zaragoza, who had died of disease brought on by his constant reconnoitering in rainy weather. Ortega returned it, saying, "Such communication, on account of its character and language, could not be allowed to remain among the archives of the Mexican government."

Forey then moved on Puebla with the utmost deliberation. Ten months had passed since the French had attacked there. In Paris the first session of the Chambers was delayed in the hope that on opening day it might be announced that Puebla had fallen. On March 17, 1863, the guns of the divisional commanders Douay and Bazaine opened upon Puebla as Forey sent word to the Emperor that he had marked the birthday of the Prince Imperial—which was the previous day—by beginning the investment of the city.

All around Puebla the French methodically dug trenches while the Mexican defenders looked on. Perhaps they did not know what the diggings were, Captain Henri Loizillon thought to himself. All these elaborate preparations were ridiculous, he wrote to his parents. The general acted as if he were opposing a real army, Russian or Austrian. Loizillon had not been at Puebla the previous year and it was his opinion that the city could not possibly hold out for more than eight or ten days.

But the opening artillery salvos did little to dislodge the defenders, and French infantry went up the slopes to the convent and fort, with each step contested by Mexicans firing from the two buildings. General Forey sent in sappers to dig long tunnels, fill them with explosives and detonate them from a distance. Walls crashed and the French swarmed up the hill. The troops of the Mexican General Leonardo Marquez joined in the assault, their fierce, ragged appearance contrasting with the proud uniforms of the Imperial regiments and their commander, in the eyes of the French officers, looking like a wild brigand.

The charge of the Second Zouaves was led by Colonel the Marquis Alexandre Gaston de Galliffet. His men threw a ladder over a crumpled wall and he gave himself the honor of being the first to climb it, hoisting a Tricolor over his head. Bullets sang around him and clouds of dust rose but he stood waving his flag as his soldiers clambered over the ramparts. They met men with short, squat bodies and dark complexions, typical of those that European armies had always scattered with ease.* The French were applying the fundamental tactic of the Great Emperor, which was to bring the greatest force possible upon one point. Austerlitz, Marengo and Jena had been one-day affairs; it was hoped that Puebla would be no different. But it was. The Mexicans were pushed back into the city, but there in the straight right-angle Spanish colonial streets they had to be routed house by house. The French could not advance more than a block at a time, blowing out the walls of one house to penetrate into the one next to it. It was slow going. "What will the Emperor say?" Captain Loizillon wondered.

There was nothing Napoleon III could say, and in his kind way he did not take occasion to upbraid the emigrés who had promised a military parade for the troops. The siege ground on and cargo vessels came into the port of Vera Cruz past dozens of troopships lying at anchor out in the harbor. There they unloaded cannon and food into lighters for transshipment across the mountains to be given to the army stalled in the ditches and wrecked houses of Puebla. Heavily armed escort parties had to worry the mule convoys up the primitive roads, arriving at their destination with the skin of their faces cracking from the dryness of the high altitudes whose heat opened the pores but did not bring with it lubricating perspiration. All the way from the fever lands of Vera Cruz and to the draining tropical area around Cordoba and then up to where the mountains began, there was not a moment free from concern over the hovering white conical hats, which, spotted here and there, signaled Mexican observation. So ragged were the

---

* In the previous year, 1862, the year of the first battle of Puebla, two French contingents landed in Cochin China, fought a few engagements and, in a peace settlement, were given the three provinces along the Mekong River Delta and a protectorate over Cambodia.

guerrillos that the French contemptuously pitied them. But sometimes the Mexicans did more than merely observe. On the last day of April, 1863—the siege was six weeks old by then —two thousand Mexicans fell upon a company of the Foreign Legion escorting sixty mule-drawn carts filled with three million francs in gold, pay for the troops at Puebla, and killed all but six of the Legionnaires.

At Puebla in that spring Colonel the Marquis de Galliffet went down into the dust and debris with a terrible stomach wound. Of a long heritage, so rich that he said his family was "reduced to working for glory," the Marquis laughed at the infidelities of his blonde wife the Marquise and was capable of telling his staff officers that he had cuckolded them all the previous night, for he had spent it with her. His stomach laid open, he took off the kepi which he had perched on the point of his sword as he led so many charges, and pressed it over the wound from which his intestines were flowing. He put a blanket around his waist and dragged himself to an aid station. In Paris the news came that there was some hope for the Marquis but that because of the lack of ice which might help retard the bleeding, he would likely die. The Empress Eugenie said that henceforth no ice could be employed in the preparation of her food; she would not use ice when she knew that such an officer might die from lack of it.

The French slowly closed the circle and in the heart of Puebla the defenders ate dogs, cats, the leaves of orange trees. Two months had passed and the city lay starving and half-dead, bodies rotting in the stagnant rainwater of the trenches and mine galleries. The Mexican General Ortega sent a messenger to ask the French if his soldiers would be permitted to march out with their baggage and arms, to disperse with the panoplies of the honors of war. The French refused. Mexico, they reasoned, had only one army and it must be broken at the place where it had fought. Ortega was told that his men would be given their parole, but his officers made prisoners.

On the morning of May 17 the sound of detonations was heard in the French positions surrounding the small corner of Puebla still held by the Army of the Republic. Ortega was blowing up his guns and his barricades. The explosions were shortly followed by a messenger who said General Ortega and his officers were waiting in the plaza in front of the cathedral.

The French lined up with the forces of Leonardo Marquez and marched forward through streets lined with white flags. Muted hisses and whistles were heard as the Tiger of Tacubaya rode past.

They found a group of half-naked men. Captain Loizillon was assigned to provide the Mexicans with rations, but found it impossible to control them, for the starving men attacked the food like animals. Rain fell. They ate, their uniforms in tatters, some wearing nothing but underclothing. But some among the officers did not eat. Instead, they slipped quietly away. Porfirio Diaz, as pure a Mixtec Indian as Juarez was a Zapotec, was one. He put on a serape and, posing as a simple peon, went through the French lines and to freedom. Whatever he was to become, Porfirio—so Mexico has always called him—was a fighter. His spirit did not die because Forey and Marquez now possessed Puebla and a French flag was flying from the cathedral tower. Diaz knew the way to Mexico City was now completely open and that the French and indeed the world considered the case a closed one and the second conquest ended, but he sent a telegram from Ayutla, east of the capital: "We may have to wait long for victory, perhaps years, but I promise you that you will yet raise our flag on the National Palace again."

Juarez must have esteemed what Porfirio had said. He sat in the office of the President surrounded by boxes and trunks jammed with papers, some of which spilled out on the floor next to the spurs and drums lying there. Outside in the waiting room were a few loyal Ministers. Juarez had thought of fighting in the passes of Mexico City, but it was impossible. The provincial governors sent word they had no troops, equipment, money, not even faith in his cause. So he must go. In Paris the news of the fall of Puebla came as the Emperor and Empress were at dinner at Fontainebleau. A note was handed to them, and Eugenie exulted—"happy as a child with a new pair of shoes," thought Pepe Hidalgo. Her husband scribbled a few words on a piece of paper—"Puebla is ours"—and threw it to the leader of the band of the Light Infantry of the Guard, which was playing by the table. The band broke into *Queen Hortense,* and the next day the guns of the Invalides fired in tribute to the victory and all the public buildings were illuminated.

In Mexico City the Congress of the Republic met. They gave Juarez a vote of confidence and, at three in the afternoon, cannons sounded to mark the end of the assembly. At sundown, the normal hour for the lowering of the flag in front of the National Palace, the ranks of all the troops which could be collected presented arms. The national anthem was played and drums rolled. Juarez appeared on the balcony overlooking the central plaza, the Zocalo. It was known throughout the city that the government would be leaving that night, and a large crowd had gathered. The lowered flag was handed to Juarez; he raised it to his lips and in a high, clear voice cried out what the crowd instantly echoed: *Viva Mexico!*

That night, May 30, 1862, sixteen-year-old Sara Yorke, an American resident of Mexico City, stood on her balcony over the Calle de San Francisco and saw the thin lines of Juarez's troops heading toward their assembly point in the Zocalo. The moon shone with the bright light of the Mexican uplands and she could see that most of the men wore the baggy white clothing of Indian Mexico and that their women were alongside. They tramped in ragged files and their appearance was so shabby that they seemed in her eyes more like an ancient barbaric horde than a modern army. By the next day they had gone to the north and when evening came Mexico City was a town without government or police. Ignoring the rules and customs of war, Juarez had simply evacuated his capital, leaving no one in authority to run the city until the victorious invaders arrived to take over. Shots sounded in the night and a French resident of the city was caught by a mob and dragged through the streets at the end of a lariat. No one in Miss Yorke's home went to bed that night, and so they were all awake to hear, in the early morning hours, the sound of a French bugle.

In the morning the streets were filled with the *pantalons rouges*. Miss Yorke and the other ladies of the household stepped onto their balcony opposite the Church of La Profesa and looked up the street at a group of French officers standing together. The men turned to regard them with such interest that the ladies said it must be because they had not seen white women in months. One of the staring officers, Captain Charles Blanchot, would marry Miss Yorke's sister.

A few days later, saluting in such fashion that one who saw him thought he looked a perfect Caesar, General Forey formally entered the city. His troops who had taken Puebla surrounded him, and with them marched a pathetic new unit: men who had surrendered when the city fell and had now enlisted themselves in Marquez's forces. As the troops went through the long narrow streets deafening cheers greeted them, nosegays and garlands of flowers fell and church bells rang. Tapestries hung from all the balconies and women, each prettier than the other in Captain Loizillon's eyes, stood at every window. If one glanced quickly at the welcome it had a satisfying appearance, but Captain Loizillon, who had been in the advance guard, knew that it had cost France ninety thousand francs, much of the money being spent by Almonte, who had hired peons to cheer at a rate of three centavos a man plus a drink of pulque, the liquor produced from the maguey plant. General Forey took it all at face value and wrote ecstatically to the Emperor describing how the troops were greeted. He went to the Cathedral where a Te Deum was sung.

Riding in the midst of his soldiers was Colonel François du Barail. He was surrounded by men whose buttons, spurs and swords shone in the sunlight and who marched to the sound of trumpets blaring and clarinets playing. Du Barail thought back to Hernando Cortés and how Cortés must have had the same thought as du Barail: that they had come a long way to serve their countries. As General Forey emerged from the Cathedral the troops shouted *"Vive l'Empereur! Vive l'Impératrice!"* Forey went off to the National Palace, to dream, Colonel du Barail thought to himself, two dreams: one, that he would receive the baton of a marshal of France, and two, that like Cortés he would find the joys of military victory followed by the pleasure of civilizing and helping a people who wanted deliverance.

In the morning Forey went out in a carriage four-in-hand with Hussars in front and an outrider carrying a floating French flag. He rode to the dilapidated Alameda, the central park of the city, and made himself so agreeable that children from then on came running whenever he appeared, shouting, "Here comes Don Forey!" He announced his officers would give a ball for "the ladies of Mexico City," and assessed his officers nearly one hundred francs apiece to pay for it. He was now the supreme power in the capital and ordered that he be given one hundred thousand pesos by the municipality. Then he said he would follow the officers' ball by one of his own. He could afford it, Captain Loizillon thought sourly. Both affairs were great successes. There was a run on French–Spanish dictionaries.

France's army was now the central factor in Mexican affairs. But that army could not stay forever. And it was not equipped to act as a governing body which could put Mexican affairs in order so that the monies owed to France, the original cause of the intervention, could eventually be paid. France had come, after all, the Emperor had said, only to lend a hand. Now Mexico must take up her own affairs. To that end General Forey convened what was called an Assembly of Notables whose duty it would be to stipulate in the name of Mexico what kind of government the country desired. The Notables were embarrassing to look at, really, Colonel du Barail thought to himself—for among them were men practically taken from the street to be outfitted in grand clothing paid for by the French.

The Assembly of Notables met and selected three of their number to act as a junta running the country, under the French, until a new form of government was selected and put into operation. The first of the trio was Almonte, the second a representative of the exiled Archbishop of Mexico, who would shortly be returning from Europe, and the third "a mummy dug up for the occasion" in Loizillon's eyes. Forey had been less than subtle in his handling of the entire matter. He announced the Notables were completely free to choose any form of government they wished—"on condition they choose a monarchy," thought Loizillon. The Notables speaking through their three-man junta duly voted for a monarchy and for a specific ruler—but then, thought Colonel du Barail, they would have voted for the Devil or the Grand Turk if the French had presented either as a candidate. But the nominee was, of course, His Imperial and Royal Highness, Prince Ferdinand Maximilian Joseph, Archduke of Austria.

11

"I SHALL ALWAYS, and in every circumstance of life, be found ready to make every sacrifice, however heavy it may be, for Austria and the power of my House. In the present case the sacrifice to be made would be doubly great both for me and my wife, for it would involve tearing ourselves away from Europe and its life forever. . . ."

Glory beckoned. Yet he could not make up his mind.

"It's a glorious country," wrote Charlotte's brother, the Duke of Brabant, "where much good might be done. If I had a grown-up son I should try to make him King of Mexico. Every brave heart upon earth must love to devote itself to what is good." The Emperor Napoleon wrote, "Never will any achievement have grander results, for the task is to rescue a continent from anarchy and misery," but in London, Foreign Secretary Lord John Russell was saying he could not believe such a position would actually attract the Archduke, and in Madrid the Spanish Minister-President, Calderón Collantes, said the thing was an "absolute impossibility."

Maximilian felt in himself a great desire to go forth as a knight-errant rescuing not a maiden in a castle, but rather an entire people—"I feel that my inherited impulse to rule lives even after centuries"—but the problem was complex. It would have been entirely alien to his character and to the respect he owed his mother to admit what the world whispered was true, that he was not so much a Hapsburg as a Bonaparte. Perhaps in reaction to what the world believed he had always been deeply involved with the honor of his House. That emotion took two forms. One was that he had enormous pride.

The other was that he wished to justify that pride. On the one hand he recoiled from accepting the gift of a Throne from a France whose armies had been at war with Austria only four years before. On the other hand he wanted to do great things in the fashion of an Archduke of Austria in whose veins ran the blood of all those of the great line back to Rudolph I.

The Austrian Minister to Washington wrote to say that surely the brother of the Emperor would not go out to Mexico in the guise of an adventurer, and the United States Consul in Trieste said at Miramar that "anyone aspiring to the Throne of Mexico, if he really attains it, ought to be extraordinarily happy if he escapes with his life." But at the same time the Mexican exiles in Europe wrote that in their country people approached pictures of the Archduke only with their hats in their hands, that they awaited him as a liberator.

Maximilian wanted England to back him and asked King Leopold to use all his influence with Victoria. In response both the Queen and Lord John Russell wrote suggesting he make himself available for the Throne of Greece, just vacated by the deposed King Otto. Maximilian indignantly refused, saying Greece had been "hawked round unsuccessfully to half a dozen princes." England became less receptive. The establishment of a Mexican Empire, combined with a Confederate victory in the Civil War, might cause the United States to recoup its territorial losses by expanding into Canada.

In Paris the Archduke's hesitation was hardly welcome. Minister of War Randon said that now the French flag had been redeemed it was time to go home. It was repeated that one of the two French divisional commanders in Mexico, General Douay, had said the whole expedition was an absurdity "born of a woman's whim." But what would the whole French effort have accomplished if they simply quit now?

King Leopold, having second thoughts, might wonder, if all Mexico wanted Maximilian, "where the defenders of Puebla came from?" And Sir Charles Wyke said one might as well try to drink the ocean as occupy Mexico militarily. A former Mexican correspondent for the *Times* of London came to Miramar to tell the Archduke and Archduchess that Mexican promises were entirely worthless, that there was not a Mexican alive who would not forego his dearest principles if you gave him five hundred dollars.

Despite the opinions of others, the Archduke sent to Paris and London for samples of cloth and buttons which could be used for the livery of his servants if he took the Throne, and in Vienna the American Minister to Austria heard it said he was trying on a pasteboard crown to see how it looked when he faced a mirror.

Meanwhile, in the name of the Assembly of Notables, a delegation of Conservatives from Mexico came to join with the emigrés in Europe in formally offering the Crown. Gutierrez de Estrada was their spokesman.

"Prince: The powerful hand of a generous monarch had hardly restored liberty to the Mexican nation, when he dispatched us to Your Imperial Highness. . . . Without you, Prince—believe it from these lips which have never yet served the purpose of flattery—without you, all our efforts to save the country will be in vain. . . . May it please Your Imperial Highness to fulfill our prayers and accept our choice. May we be enabled to carry the joyous tidings to a country awaiting them in longing anxiety.

"These are the sentiments which in the name of our grateful country we lay at the feet of Your Imperial Highness. We offer them to the worthy scion of that powerful dynasty which planted Christianity on our native soil. On that soil, Prince, we hope to see you fulfill a high task, to mature the choicest fruits of culture, which are order and true liberty. The task is great, but greater is our confidence in Providence."

Maximilian, of course, had known the nature of the offer and had formulated his answer. It was largely based upon the advice of King Leopold, who had said half a dozen times that the Archduke must make the Mexicans want him; that he must not appear to want them. That was what he had done when the Belgians had asked him to rule them thirty years before. And there must be guarantees.

So the Archduke thanked the delegation, but said he could not commit himself merely on the word of the Notables of Mexico City. He must have assurances from the population at large.

Maximilian's response propelled French columns into the countryside seeking signatures on petitions which begged the Archduke to rule over Mexico. The soldiers went to Queretaro, Guadalajara, Morelia, Monterrey, San Luis Potosi, all the chief cities of Mexico, and they destroyed anyone who stood in their way. The opposition did not take the form of serried ranks offering formal battle. Instead, a hundred screaming wild horsemen, some carrying only hatchets, would ride out of a gully. One could never see them until the instant they appeared. Often the Mexicans massed at the base of a mountain, riding forward in great disorder and then rushing back, brandishing their weapons and flinging curses through the air. When the French formed up to charge them they vanished over the mountain trails. They were never able to withstand the French in open-field combat, but they were hard to root out when they took up positions behind walls. Caught, they were instantly shot or hanged. They were bandits or assassins, the French told each other. Many of them were exactly that, living off the little unprotected towns they pillaged.

The harassment of the French did not materially affect the collection of signatures on the petitions. A column would appear outside a town and, if there was any opposition, throw a few shells into it, accept its surrender and be hailed as the liberators of the country. Lines of men and women would cross the plaza on their knees to the church, where they would offer thanks for the coming of the French. Then their signatures, or a statement made on their behalf by someone who could sign his name, would be affixed to the petitions addressed to Maximilian. Then the French would ride away. Hours later a guerrilla band would ride into town to take some hostages whose feet they would slash open before driving them across the open sands. The next day, when the guerrillas had gone, taking whatever plunder they could attach to their saddles, the townspeople would steal out to find the hostages hanging upside down from the trees. Both the dead and those who cut them down were accounted as supporters of the Archduke.

The French reasoned that they could never successfully patrol the immense distances of Mexico. So they had their Conservative allies recruit men for the Mexican army which they would hand over to Maximilian when he came. The commander of this force was Marquez, the Tiger of Tacubaya. His men took their cue from him. In the name of the intervention they christened as a Juarista or a Liberal anyone who opposed their plundering. Marquez's men flung people off the ledges of the mountains onto the rocks below and used living prisoners for bayonet practice. In return the guerrilla bands who called themselves Republicans although they had no contact at all with Juarez buried prisoners, indeed anyone who displeased them, in sand up to their chins. Then horses would be driven at their faces.

The French soldiers themselves became barbarous as they harried a vanishing and unidentifiable enemy up the trails and across the deserts; at the slightest sign of Liberal leanings or unwillingness to sign the petitions they burned towns, destroyed the stone fences of centuries and shot cattle. But the French hated it, hated Mexico, despised Marquez and the guerrilla leaders who arrived in camp bearing self-designated titles of colonel and asking to join Marquez's forces. The guerrilla group might consist of one or two hundred men which the "colonel" inflated to five or six hundred, demanding pay for the greater number. The groups were accepted out of concern that otherwise they would turn against the intervention. The cost of outfitting these bands was borne by the French Treasury. Often, after receiving new rifles and cartridge cases, they deserted. Captain Henri Loizillon had detested France's English allies in the Crimea, but he thought back to them with longing when he looked at Marquez's "bunch of riff-raff on our payroll. . . . Rape and theft" being what made them enlist, "these braves ones."

Juarez, now the President of the Republic only in name, drifted north in front of the French patrols, protected by a few barefoot guards trailing through dust on jaded horses. His last force of any importance was in the south, in Oaxaca. Its commander was Porfirio Diaz and its troops were for the most part boys, some as young as twelve, who had been forcibly recruited. It was not beyond Porfirio to blockade a town, take all the men who could manage to walk, place chains around their necks, and take them away to beat them into recruits. He extorted money from whatever source offered itself. If a so-called battalion rebelled, he shot every tenth man. One battalion quailed at orders; he sabered the officers. Fierce stories were told of him. General Forey said he had it as fact that Diaz slashed open a pregnant woman, cut out her infant and hung it around her neck with her intestines. He was, the French said, only a bandit chief, and no soldier, certainly not the representative of a government that did not really exist, a government with no capital city, no buildings, no power. And for long periods at a time Diaz had no communication with Juarez. At times he was his own supreme commander, wandering the countryside with his men harnessed to the cannons by their belts and scarves.

Like Juarez, Diaz was steadily pushed back by the advances of the petition-carrying French and their Mexican allies who went about seeking Acts of Adhesion. They garnered them by the hundreds of thousands, although very often it was simply one man, generally the intimidated mayor of some little town signing in the name of several hundred Indians who had never heard of the Archduke Maximilian. It did not matter. "Let them send Maximilian immediately," was the only thought in Captain Loizillon's mind. Then the French could leave. "As far as Maximilian's future is concerned, it doesn't interest me in the least." In seeking signatures for the Acts of Adhesion he had traveled at least as far as The Wandering Jew, Loizillon wrote his parents, and he had had quite enough of Mexico. If he stayed after Maximilian came, he would be in line for a promotion; but he did not care, he was going to get out.

But sometimes Captain Loizillon's conscience bothered him when he thought of the Archduke. When Maximilian heard of the millions of francs given to "thieves, brigands, cheats . . . the wretched army" France would turn over to him, the Archduke would "have a tremendous sunstroke. . . . In such a case, what saint should he pray to?"

But it was Loizillon's duty to get Acts of Adhesion for Miramar, and he did his duty. That the French succeeded so swiftly was owing to the fact that the slow and deliberate General Forey had returned home, his recall softened by the baton of a marshal of France. Such a personage, wrote Napoleon, was too important to concern himself with petty details of administration. France's new commander in Mexico, General François Achille Bazaine, had been born fifty-one years earlier in the town just outside the palace and park of Versailles, where upon occasion another infant, five weeks younger, was sometimes to be seen: the King of Rome, who became the Duke of Reichstadt and loved Maximilian's mother. Bazaine joined King Louis Philippe's army at the age of twenty, after having worked as a grocery clerk. He rose from private to corporal to sergeant in a Line regiment and then went to the Foreign Legion and service in Algeria. Next he fought in Spain in support of the French-backed side in the civil wars there. He got a commission and went back to Africa and more expeditions against the natives restless under France's rule. Inscrutable, patient, with heavy-lidded, almost Oriental eyes, Bazaine became an expert in the tortuous matter of dealing with Arab sensibilities.

The Prince-President Louis Napoleon became the Emperor Napoleon III. French troops went to the Crimea and Bazaine was a regimental commander. He fought the Austrians in Italy with a division behind him. He was at home when General Lorencez went to his defeat at First Puebla, but when France sought to redeem the honor of her flag he went along as one of the two divisional commanders. He did very well at Second Puebla, and when the Emperor came to see General Forey as too unsubtle for the situation, the thought of Bazaine was reassuring. He was used to dealing with natives, spoke Spanish from his days in the civil wars in Spain, and he would be at ease in a land where, as with Arabia, one hinted instead of bluntly speaking out.

Expeditions against ill-armed and scattered irregulars were something Bazaine had conducted for years in Algeria. Six weeks after taking command he was able to ship off appeals signed by what he and the Conservatives estimated to be at least three-quarters of the Mexican nation. The petitions arrived at Miramar Castle, where they were accepted as the voice of Mexico. "They want us ardently over there," the Archduchess wrote her grandmother.

But her husband did not say with finality that he would become Emperor of Mexico. In Paris the Deputies were asking where the French involvement would end. It had grown to forty thousand men where once, in the first days under Admiral Jurien de la Gravière, there had been twenty-five hundred.

Napoleon invited Maximilian and Charlotte to Paris for a visit. By mail they discussed it with King Leopold, who told them they must get from Napoleon an official, written statement as to how long the French troops would stay. "Do not allow any phrases to turn you away from this important and indispensably necessary matter, the guarantee which must have the force of a treaty."

The Archduke and Archduchess told Napoleon what Leopold had suggested, adding that there must be a loan to go with the soldiers. Napoleon said they would have to discuss it. The results of their bargaining were that twenty-five thousand French troops would stay in Mexico until a national army could be formed, and that the Foreign Legion would leave eight thousand men behind for eight years. The financial arrangements called for France to be paid 270,000,000 francs for her activities up to July 1, 1864, with additional monies to be paid on a per-soldier basis after that. All French claims, including the Jecker bonds, were to be made good. Additional bond issues would be floated to help get the new Empire started.

The Archduke and Archduchess were welcomed enthusiastically in Paris. They were the guarantee that the French troops would soon be coming home. They were attractive and gay and delighted to be honored with reviews, dinners, balls, performances of a new Alexander Dumas play, a performance of the Comédie Française, a hunting party at Versailles. They were so busy that Charlotte barely found the time to pose for a Winterhalter portrait. When they were due to leave it was clearly understood that the Archduke would accept the proffered post. At the railroad station Eugenie gave him a little gold medallion with an image of the Madonna. "It will bring you luck," she said.

They went to England. The Queen entirely understood their needs—"He has a great wish to distinguish himself and to get out of his present *dolce far niente* [life of sweet nothingness]. . . . She is very venturesome and would go with Max to the end of the world."

They also visited the Archduchess's grandmother, the former Queen of France, Marie Amélie, but at the end of the meeting the old woman became terribly agitated and began to argue with them, saying they should not go to Mexico. Her ladies urged her to calm herself and she half-fainted away. "They will be assassinated! They will be assassinated!" she kept screaming. Looking on, the seven-year-old daughter of the Prince de Nemours thought to herself how curious it was: she had been told that only ladies cry, but Charlotte was quite calm. The tears were coming down Maximilian's cheeks.

The couple returned to Vienna to be received with Imperial honors, a state dinner and a reception. The Austrian Emperor, Francis Joseph, had met with his brother on the first day of the new year, a couple of months earlier, and had discussed the entire matter, saying finally that he had no objections to Maximilian's acceptance of the Mexican offer. Francis Joseph had made no conditions then. But the day after their arrival Foreign Minister Count von Rechberg presented the Archduke with a document drawn up by his brother. A letter to accompany it soon arrived:

> Sir, my dear brother, Archduke Ferdinand Max!
> Since, according to the information I have received, you are disposed to accept the Throne of Mexico which has been offered to you, and to found an Empire there, God helping you, I find myself compelled, as Supreme Head of the House of Austria, and after the most mature and earnest consideration of the duties which are incumbent upon me as sovereign, to notify you that I can grant my consent to this grave and momentous act of state only on condition . . .

And the Emperor ordered his brother to sign the document, which called for his renunciation of any claim on the Throne of Austria, of all his inheritances as an Archduke and a member of the House of Hapsburg. His renunciations would be irrevocable.

Once Maximilian and Francis Joseph had been loving brothers. But the decade and a half since 1848 and Francis Joseph's accession to the throne had changed that. In 1853 a would-be assassin had struck at the Emperor of Austria with a knife; only his high military collar, partially blocking the blow, saved his life. Maximilian had been at Trieste at the time. Francis Joseph was asked by the Court authorities if they should send for his brother. He replied they should not, and they telegraphed Maximilian to stay in Trieste. Instead Maximilian rushed to Vienna. Francis Joseph wondered why. The

Emperor was not mollified when his brother organized a drive to collect funds for the construction of a church, the Votiv-Kirche, to be built where the Emperor had been attacked and dedicated to his safe recovery. Francis Joseph had never forgotten the speed with which his Heir had shown up, coming to a city he had for years before approached in a dallying fashion.

But Francis Joseph was troubled by other things besides his relationship with Maximilian. Lost wars and his unhappy marriage had made of Francis Joseph less the man than the ruler. His thoughts were of the dynasty first, everything else last. Suppose he should die and Maximilian was thousands of miles away? Could Maximilian serve as regent for the young Crown Prince Rudolph? Suppose the Mexican Empire failed? Was Maximilian then to return to Austria to stand in direct line for the Austrian Throne after having been rejected by barbarians? What if Maximilian had children who might one day come from Mexico to claim positions in Austria and possibly dispute such positions with their cousins?

Maximilian saw betrayal and bitterness in his brother's words. "On the advice of Your Majesty," the Archduke wrote, "I pledged my word of honor, which is respected throughout all Europe, to a population of nine million persons which had appealed to me, trusting in a better future and in the hope of seeing an end of the civil war which had been raging for generations past; I did so at a time when I was entirely unaware of any such condition as you have now imposed on me, and could, indeed, have no knowledge of it."

In Vienna the two brothers had a face-to-face meeting, with the Archduchess Sophia trying to calm them. Maximilian shouted at his brother that he would sign nothing and that if necessary he would simply go on a French ship, without any by-your-leave. Francis Joseph replied that if he did, the name Maximilian would be crossed off the list of the House of Hapsburg. They parted, each refusing to budge. Sophia took the Archduke and Archduchess to a suburban railroad station where, with no escort and no honors rendered, they caught the night train south to Trieste.

At Miramar, Maximilian gathered a few friends and told them it was difficult for him to speak about his relatives, but he would do so. His friends said that Francis Joseph's attitude was unbelievably cruel, that he had declared Maximilian civilly dead, that he was holding a knife at his brother's throat. One of the visitors was Pepe Hidalgo. The Empress of the French had given him a special telegraph code to use when communicating with her on delicate matters. Afraid of losing it, he carried it with him everywhere and slept with it under his pillow. He seized it, and telegraphed the Empress in code, ending: SAVE US, MADAME.

The telegram flung Eugenie into an hysterical rage. She wrote a note to the Austrian ambassador, Prince Metternich, and ordered it delivered immediately, although it was nearly two in the morning when she sent for the messenger. Metternich, awakened, could not have looked forward to opening the envelope, for he had grown weary of her excitement on the subject of Mexico, and privately thought of the whole project and everything connected with it as being in the nature of a "grand prostration" on her part. Her letter read as though Metternich himself were to blame for the impasse, but of course she could not use such terms to Francis Joseph: "Appalling scandal . . . no excuse . . . You had time to consider everything and weigh it well, and you cannot, at the very moment when the arrangements for the loan have been concluded and the convention signed, put forward a family matter of no importance compared with the confusion into which you throw the whole world. . . . Believe me yours in a most justifiable bad temper, Eugenie."

The next day Napoleon wrote the Archduke, "It is not my business to enter into the family questions which may have been under discussion between you and your august Brother, but . . . Your Imperial Highness has entered into engagements which you are no longer free to break. What would you really think of me, if, when your Imperial Highness had already reached Mexico, I were suddenly to say that I can no longer fulfill the conditions to which I have set my signature?"

Emissaries went between the two brothers to attempt to settle the differences between them. Francis Joseph relented to the point of saying that if things did not work out he would assure the Archduke, his wife and any future children a place commensurate with their ranks. There was also a warning letter from Foreign Minister Count von Rechberg: "I can only advise that the patience of His Imperial Majesty, which has gone to the utmost limit of concession, should not be too much abused or put to the test by fresh difficulties."

But Maximilian and Charlotte wanted more. The Archduchess entrained for Vienna to press their case that they not be cut off, that there be something concrete to hang onto.

She left behind her husband, whose reaction to the problems facing him took the form of utter weariness. He wanted to be a monarch, to go in ermine and gold before bowing subjects. But the price was terribly high. And Miramar was so beautiful. The Archduke wandered the halls of his castle and sat in the gardens writing a poem: *"Must I be forever separated from my dear native land? . . . You would seduce me with a crown. . . . But must I listen to your sweet siren's song? . . . You speak to me of a scepter and of power. . . . Ah, let me follow in peace my tranquil way! My obscure path among the myrtles! . . . Work and science and the arts are sweeter than the glitter of a diadem."*

In Vienna, Charlotte was so demanding that she tired Francis Joseph. She finally made him promise a certain amount of money as an allowance for the Archduke if he returned from Mexico; that was all. She went at him for three hours straight, harassing and driving him into corners while she thought to herself that he grasped things only with difficulty, but she could not make him yield any more ground. She enlisted the aid of the Archduchess Sophia, who asked her oldest son not to make her second-oldest sign a document which disinherited himself. But Francis Joseph was adamant. Charlotte went back to Miramar.

They turned to King Leopold, who told them: "Give up nothing." The undertaking, the King wrote, was risky and might miscarry "in spite of the greatest courage and talent, because it is impossible. In such a situation, which one was in no way bound to accept, it would be the greatest blindness and imprudence not to keep whatever belongs to one." But he added, "It is no longer possible to withdraw, for matters have gone too far, and it would lead to boundless confusion."

His advice, then, was to combat both Francis Joseph and Napoleon.

Such a task was beyond their strength. Charlotte said to her husband that they were beaten. They must choose one or the other: life in Austria or life in Mexico. They decided it would be Mexico. Maximilian wrote Napoleon he would sign the treaty of renunciation put forward by his brother.

Early the following morning, Francis Joseph's special train pulled into the little private station in the park of the castle of Miramar. He had come for his brother's signature. Maximilian led him to the library. The two were alone for hours. Outside, their younger brothers, the Archdukes Karl Ludwig and Ludwig Viktor, strolled about in company with their relatives, the Archdukes Karl Salvator, William, Joseph, Leopold, Rainier, several Imperial Ministers, the Chancellors of Croatia, Hungary and Transylvania, and the ranking soldiers of the Imperial army, all brought as witnesses. Offshore, on the Austrian warship *Novara,* officers studying the castle through their spyglasses saw the figure of Maximilian suddenly come out on a terrace and run off into the woods. Behind him went Count Karl Bombelles, Maximilian's lifelong friend, in a supplicating attitude, apparently dispatched to bring the Archduke back. Maximilian returned to his waiting brother.

After a while Francis Joseph and Maximilian, both with the marks of tears on their cheeks, came out into the castle salon. Maximilian had signed.

The Imperial train was waiting with steam up and the entire party went to it. All the passengers who would be heading north got on board save for the Emperor. He turned to his brother, gave a military salute, and then hesitated and suddenly reached out to him. "Max!" They kissed. Francis Joseph went to the train.

The next day, April 10, 1864, a group of Mexicans, emigrés all, came to Miramar to offer in Mexico's name the crown of their country. Gutierrez and Hidalgo led them. They formed in the castle square and were led through the dining room and library into the audience chamber where the thirty-one-year-old Archduke and twenty-three-year-old Archduchess sat on a dais beneath a canopy of rose silk embroidered in gold. Maximilian wore the dress uniform of an Austrian vice-admiral and the orders of the Golden Fleece and the Grand Cross of St. Stephen. Charlotte was in crimson silk trimmed with the Brussels lace of her mother, wearing an Archducal crown, collar and ornaments of diamonds, and the black ribbon of the Order of Malta.

Gutierrez read out a speech in French: "High-minded and noble prince . . . unending love and unshakable fidelity . . ." The other Mexicans grouped themselves behind him in a semi-circle. Gutierrez finished. Speaking in Spanish, his voice trembling, Maximilian said that in accordance with the wishes of the Notables and the Mexican nation he might now justly regard himself as their chosen and elected leader. He accepted the proffered monarchy. He would work for the freedom, order, greatness and independence of his country. Gutierrez knelt before him, took his hand and proclaimed him Emperor and cried, "God save His Majesty Maximilian the First! God save Her Majesty Charlotte, Empress of Mexico!" They all echoed him.

Atop the battlements of the castle the Mexican flag rose to the top of the flagstaff; and out in the harbor the Austrian *Novara* and French *Themis* pumped off salutes. The Abbot of Lacroma, wearing his miter and carrying his crosier, administered an oath of allegiance.

Maximilian, Imperial Majesty now, arose from where he knelt before the Abbot and wandered away from the cheering people. He walked into a room where, alone, he sat before a table, stretched out his arms and put his head upon them.

All his life Maximilian had been a dilettante. He had dipped into so many things—sculpture, the writing of poetry and his impressions of foreign places, ancient history. He had dallied with studies of biology, animal life, naval tactics. He had played roles. Now for the first time it came to him that he was going four thousand miles to an unknown land, to duties and difficult decisions. Perhaps he had never thought deeply about it before.

Dr. Jilek, his physician, found him sitting motionless in his library and thought him on the verge of a complete nervous breakdown and physical collapse. It would be impossible for him to preside at the banquet planned for that night. Dr. Jilek took the Emperor to the airy little summer pavilion in Miramar's park and there they remained as Charlotte sat alone at the head of the banquet table, completely in control of herself and showing not the slightest sign of tenseness. Henceforth, she said, she was to be addressed only as Carlota, the Spanish form of her name.*

The Emperor and Empress's departure for Mexico had been planned for the following morning, but it was out of the question. Maximilian could not get hold of himself; and when his wife came to tell him of the congratulatory telegrams Napoleon and Eugenie had sent, he snapped, "I told you that I didn't want anyone to speak to me about Mexico now!" He attempted to write a letter thanking the French rulers, but Carlota thought his effort a poor one and wrote a different version which was sent out over his name. Perhaps Maximilian did not know; certainly he did not care. He wandered through the rooms of his castle and the park, weeping. He saw no one but his doctor. "If someone came to announce that it is all in pieces, I would close myself up in my room and jump for joy," he said. "But Charlotte . . ."

The Emperor and Empress could not put off the trip for very much longer. After four days Maximilian felt he could muster up the strength to go, so the ships were told to be ready for departure. On their final evening, the thirteenth of April, the Austrian Countess Paula Kollonitz, going along as an escorting lady-in-waiting, looked at the *Novara* and *Themis* sitting at anchor in the sunset with, behind them, the snow-covered Alps of northern Italy, and thought to herself it was one of the most beautiful sights she had ever seen. She would never forget it.

In the morning the Emperor walked in the park and returned to the castle by a basement entrance to avoid the people congregating in the halls and rooms of the first floor. The morning was cloudless and warm, with a northeast wind throwing high waves against the crags on which the castle sat. As the day wore on the road that led from Trieste two miles away was jammed with carriages bringing people to see them off. Among the well-wishers was the city's mayor, who handed the Emperor a message of esteem and leave-taking. It was signed by more than

* It had been earlier decided that her husband would reign as the Emperor Maximilian instead of the Emperor Ferdinand because the Spanish form of the latter name was Hernando—which would inevitably remind every Mexican of Cortés.

ten thousand persons—and it had not taken troops to get those signatures. No such testimonial could possibly have been obtained for Francis Joseph, and Maximilian knew it. When the mayor spoke a few words he could not respond.

The bay was filled with boats and the area around the castle crammed with people. The Emperor sat with his wife, his fragile composure returned, and was handed a telegram from his mother:

> "FAREWELL. OUR BLESSINGS—PAPA'S AND MINE—OUR PRAYERS ACCOMPANY YOU; MAY GOD PROTECT AND GUIDE YOU. FAREWELL FOR THE LAST TIME ON YOUR NATIVE SOIL, WHERE ALAS! WE MAY SEE YOU NO MORE. WE BLESS YOU AGAIN AND AGAIN FROM OUR DEEPLY SORROWING HEARTS."

Outside the sound of the newly composed Mexican Imperial anthem was heard. It was time to go. Maximilian staggered out, his wife desperately trying to calm him. He went to the steps leading down to the sea where the two ships bound for Mexico sat at anchor. Nearby were eight other ships that would escort them out of the harbor. Guns sounded from seaward and were answered by the artillery pieces in the park.

Maximilian came to the steps and a crowd rushed forward, throwing flowers and in their Italianate enthusiasm falling on their knees to kiss his hand. His breast was heaving and tears covered his cheeks. He could not speak. A longboat manned by oarsmen was at the foot of the steps leading into the sea; at the landing there was a gold-embroidered red canopy. The nearly one hundred people of their Imperial party got into the longboats, the Empress next to last. Then her husband turned to touch the hands stretched out to him, pressed them for a last moment, and stepped off Austrian territory.

The Countess Zichy-Metternich, an Austrian lady-in-waiting, sat by Carlota, and as the boat pulled away from the dock the Empress of Mexico said to her, "Look at poor Max! How he is weeping!"

They went out into the open sea, the batteries at Trieste saluting them as they passed, and headed south along the Italian coast. The weather was brilliantly clear, and the mountains above Naples and those which showed the Turkish frontier could be plainly seen. The Emperor's spirits revived and he appeared on deck, walking in the rolling sailor's way he had learned on his many trips. They went around the toe of Italy and past Sicily, admiring the green valleys and orange groves and the tip of Mount Etna reaching through the fogs at its base.

The two ships came into the harbor which served Rome, Civita Vecchia, and anchored there. The Pope had invited the Imperial couple to call upon him in Rome, and a special train waited at the station. A yellow-flagged quarantine boat came out with an escorting Cardinal aboard, and they went ashore to the sound of bands and the booming of the cannons on the forts.

In Rome they drove to the Palace Marescotti, Gutierrez de Estrada's European home during all his long years of exile. Then, with the ladies in black gowns and veils, they went to the Pope. Pius IX saw in the Emperor a Catholic who would return all the Church's property expropriated by Juarez. Before giving him Holy Communion the Pope pointedly spoke of how, great as were the rights of nations, the rights of the Church were greater. Afterward, returning their call, the Pope came to the Palace Marescotti in a coach and six. Gutierrez wept for joy when Pius set foot over his threshold. When he left, the Emperor Maximilian saw him to his carriage and then fell upon his knees and remained so until the carriage pulled away.

The Imperial couple went sightseeing in Rome, to the Trevi Fountain and the Borghese Gardens, and then on through the Mediterranean. At Gibraltar, to their delight, the British guns thundered out an Imperial salute. The Spanish cannon followed the English example; Carlota wrote her grandmother that the tribute showed the powers recognized them as rulers. General Sir William Codrington, the Gibraltar commandant, gave them a banquet and received one in return on board the *Novara*. The Emperor and Empress went on shore excursions with the commandant and his daughter, who was his official hostess, and watched horse races in which the jockeys were officers of the garrison. Miss Codrington always remembered how happy the two young monarchs seemed, almost like children.

The *Novara* headed into the Atlantic. After the ship steamed past Madeira the engines were turned off to save coal—the *Novara* could carry only a limited amount—and the sails were hoisted. The passengers were glad to be rid of the soot. The ship's band played every night and when another craft passed, the *Novara*'s crewmen illuminated their ship with Bengal lights. Below decks the new monarchs worked on their coming administration of the Mexican Empire and on perfecting their mastery of the Spanish language.

The ship carrying the new monarchs came into the tropics and docked at Martinique. They were in ecstasy over the red orchids, the pineapples and coconuts and mountain streams, the long, slow sunsets and the glittering luminous insects flying by after dark. On the savannah thousands of Negroes gathered to dance for them to the sound of tambourines. Maximilian and Carlota stood in the midst of the leaping, prancing figures for a long time, while hummingbirds—they were like flying jewels, Countess Kollonitz thought—darted to and fro overhead. Everywhere they could smell the sweet aroma of the mimosa. When they left the dancers shouted, *"Vive l'Empereur,* the embalmed flower!"

They took ship again and the Emperor worked on his regulations for the Ceremonial of the Court. Nearly four hundred pages long, with dozens of charts indicating the proper placings for persons of all classifications at public and private events, it minutely described the duties of the Grand Marshal of the Court and Minister of the Imperial House, what they should wear upon set occasions, what matters they were permitted to bring to the attention of the Emperor and the fashion in which they should address him. The Regulations prescribed four classes of Court mourning, including one for himself, instructions as to when ushers were permitted to be seated in anterooms, the materials which the First Gentleman of the Bedchamber was to place on the night table of the Emperor—snuff, cigarettes, cigars and water—and the fashion in which he was to ring a bell to awaken his master in the morning. There were lists of the order in which people were to walk in Court processions: Princes Imperial, Cardinals, wearers of the Grand Cross of the Imperial and Distinguished Order of the Mexican Eagle, Aides-de-Camp, horse masters, wearers of the Order of Guadalupe, the President of the Academy of Science and the

President of the Academy of Belles Arts, the Librarian and Keeper of the Museum. There were classifications of official dinners, with lists of what liquors would be served, beginning with dinners of the first rank at which would be drunk chablis, sherry, Bordeaux, dry champagne, Rhine wine, foaming champagne, British beer, port and two different liqueurs, and ending with dinners of the lowest rank at which only sherry would be served.

At balls, "the dancers should be careful when they are dancing never to turn their backs on Their Majesties. . . . When the Emperor wishes to dance, the Chamberlain on duty will hold his sword and hat. The Emperor will give his orders to the Chamberlain on duty relative to the persons to whom he is dispensing the honor of dancing with Him, and they will be invited by the same Chamberlain. . . . When the Empress wishes to dance, her Lady-in-Waiting will hold her fan. . . ."

As they went outward bound from Martinique to Vera Cruz they saw the *Tampico* steaming for Europe. On board, invalided home, was Colonel François du Barail. In his eyes the far-off *Novara* and *Themis* seemed as small as flies, and the smoke from their stacks as slight as that of two cigarettes.

Du Barail wrote:

" 'Poor Maximilian,' I thought. 'What are you going to do in this atrocious country which I am leaving without regret, in the middle of these people who have been tearing themselves apart for more than forty years? . . . If you succeed in bringing order in this chaos, fortune into this misery, union into these hearts, you will be the greatest sovereign of modern times.

" 'Go! Poor fool! You may regret your beautiful castle of Miramar!' "

Then the *Themis* pulled ahead to steam into the port of Vera Cruz and sound her guns as a signal that the Emperor of Mexico was coming.

12

THE SOUND OF THE THUDDING SIGNAL GUNS went rolling across the water and up the dingy streets of Vera Cruz. But there was no sign of activity in the harbor or on the coast; and when the *Novara* dropped anchor there was no reaction anywhere. The travelers on deck could see a French military graveyard on a little harbor island, and the melancholy wreck of a French vessel decaying on a coral reef. Off to the right and left were the flat sandy stretches which surrounded the city, dreary waste-lands broken only by a few stranded coconut palms. It was two in the afternoon, May 28, 1864. They waited for someone to come, the Emperor and all the gentlemen in black ties, black waistcoats and white pants.

After a couple of hours passed, Rear-Admiral Bosse of the French navy appeared. They were too early, he told them in what Countess Kollonitz thought was a most arrogant fashion. None of the decorations were in place, and the welcoming com-mittee was inland at Orizaba. General Bazaine was not ready for them and without a generous supply of French troops to escort them to Mexico City they were likely to be captured by Liberal bands. The French admiral left and they were alone in the silent harbor until Almonte of the Assembly of Notables came up in a longboat with the welcoming committee. That its members offered to shake hands with their monarch struck the Austrians as far too familiar.

They must hurry through Vera Cruz, Almonte said. Fever haunted the town, an epidemic was raging. Bells tolled all day for those who had succumbed to yellow jack. He suggested a departure early the next day.

At half past four the next morning Mass was read on the middle deck, and they rowed off, the Empress looking over at Fort San Juan d'Ulúa and thinking of her uncle the Prince de Joinville, who had bombarded it in 1838's Pastry War. They came closer to the city and the dreadful stagnant odor of waters trapped behind the hills tossed up by the northers. The city itself, its flat-roofed stucco houses in monotonous straight lines, struck them as looking like a giant cemetery. At the pier Almonte was waiting with a few shabby representatives of the city government, who shoved forward the keys to Vera Cruz on a silver tray. A French military band played and a few vague explosions from welcoming rockets could be heard.

The heat even at that early morning hour was oppressive. Carriages came to take them to the depot of the railroad the French had built to hurry arriving troops and supplies out of the fever zone. The Empress was put into an open carriage where her companion was the wife of the French officer commanding the district of Vera Cruz. There was not a single Mexican lady to welcome her. As they drove the few blocks to the depot they saw that the torpid streets were empty. Winds came and blew down the few flimsy triumphal arches that had been thrown up during the night. Maximilian wore a set, brooding look and tears came to Carlota's eyes.

They arrived at a wretched little plaza. The whitewashed buildings were flecked with spots made by the northers blowing salt in from the sea. The Imperial couple entered the waiting train and seated themselves on benches of plaited straw. The Venetian blinds were drawn to keep out the glare of the sun. They left Vera Cruz in silence, and within a few minutes the town was behind them as they wound through bare sand hills. They passed over marshes and saw nothing but stunted and scorched little bushes and here and there a cactus. Behind them, on the walls which showed traces of a hundred other ripped-down proclamations, the Emperor's greetings to the nation were pasted up:

"Mexicans! You have desired me! Your noble country, by the spontaneous expression of the wishes of the majority, elected me to watch over the future of its destiny! I respond with happiness to this call. . . . I shall hold the scepter with confidence and the sword of honor with firmness.

". . . Let us unite to attain the common end, let us forget the shadows of the past, let us cover over the hatred of parties, and the dawn of peace and of a happiness so merited will rise radiantly on the new Empire."

The Emperor and Empress went past the hills and into the flat interior, seeing some wild cattle upon whose backs sat white birds plucking out the bugs which rooted there. There was no running water and little shade from the blazing sun. The few thatched-roof huts they saw would not have looked out of place in Tahiti. They came to La Soledad and halted for breakfast in a flimsy wooden building which sat in the middle of grass shacks. A French military band played. They went on and came to the end of the railroad line in Paso del Macho. The streets were like plowed fields. They got into mule-drawn conveyances. Their Majesties taking an English traveling carriage, the ladies-in-waiting a phaeton, and the rest in high, covered diligences. Swaying and rocking over the primitive dusty roads, they left the plains region and began the long ascent into the uplands.

The area was so wild and empty that despite the heavy French cavalry escorts and one of the finest units of the Mexican forces, the *cazadores* commanded by Colonel Miguel Lopez, Carlota looked out and thought to herself that she would not be surprised if Juarez himself suddenly appeared at the head of several hundred guerrillas. But of course the President, with his tattered, barefoot little group, was five hundred miles to the north.

Now in the temperate zone the Imperial party saw brilliant flowers, great vines garlanding giant trees, butterflies and wondrous birds. But they could hardly exchange comments on the changing landscape because of the violent jolting of the coach as it went over the rutted trail. Countess Kollonitz thought to herself that no European could form an idea of what these roads were like without seeing them. Often they were simply the dried-up beds of streams. It took youth and good humor to go on, the Empress thought, and luck to avoid getting seriously injured as heads banged on the ceiling of the coach and arms and shoulders against the sides. The Mexicans escorting them kept apologizing; Their Majesties always responded that it didn't matter at all.

At the remote relay stations garrisoned by French troops they halted so that new teams of mules could be put into the traces. The animals would be urged on by the coachman's whip and the young boys whose duty it was to trot along and throw stones at the lead mules. They ran into rain. The carriages went crashing over rocks and a coach carrying six gentlemen rolled over completely. The travelers got out by climbing up through a window.

Their objective was Cordoba, but they were far behind schedule, and darkness fell. Soldiers with lighted torches were ordered to the tops of the coaches, but rain put out the lights. Then lines of Indians appeared to lead the Emperor and Empress into the city. All along the route to the capital the French had distributed highly colored lithographs of the sovereigns. The Indians had looked at the fair hair and blue eyes and long beard and whispered that the return of Quetzalcoatl foretold by the ancient legends was at hand. Once before, three hundred years earlier, they had thought Hernando Cortés to be their lost god. Their hopes had betrayed them. But their new ruler came to them smiling and nodding, appreciative of all kindnesses. Surely this was Quetzalcoatl. Once he had forbidden war—he had stopped up his ears so as not to hear the word— and the corn had been so magnificent that a man could not carry a single stalk. Under his reign sweet aromas had filled the air and the cotton grew already tinted with a gorgeous dye. He had taught the arts of land cultivation and of working with gold; driven away, he had promised to return. Maximilian and Carlota were aware of what the Indians were thinking, and their hearts went out to them. The Indians' gentle manners attracted the admiration of both the sovereigns and all their party. The Imperial couple saw a people who had time for every courtesy, who spoke in soft voices and used the archaic gentilities of the Spain of two hundred years before. It was enchanting. They began to forget the coldness of Vera Cruz.

Surrounded by dark men in the white cotton dress of the Indian peon of Mexico, Maximilian and Carlota came to Cordoba at two in the morning. They went on the next day through the magnificent acacia, convolvulus, oleander, the trees bending under lilac blossoms and delicious tropical fruits, oranges, lemons; they saw the flocks of bright parrots rising into the air at their approach, the roses, lilies, carnations. There were banana trees, their leaves fluttering in the wind, making a soft rainlike sound, pomegranates, palms. Ahead and behind them were long strings of mules driven by men sitting in the high-backed swaying Mexican saddle and spurring their mounts with roweled spurs dwarfing those of the vanished *gachupines*. Eternal snow sat on the mountains that could be seen shimmering across the long dreamy spaces of tropical growth. And they saw, too, the maguey plant standing grouped like swords thrust into the ground, the plant which provided food and liquor for Indian Mexico. All through the area, grown matted and tangled from neglect, were thousands of acres planted in cotton and coffee in the sixteenth and seventeenth centuries. Lost in them, bullet-riddled, with smashed walls and fallen roofs, were haciendas that reflected what Mexico had undergone since independence.

Through the clouds of dust Their Majesties drove past the old churches and the straight lines of crumbling adobe houses, pink, blue, yellow, green, with here and there a gone-to-seed mansion, beautiful in the Spanish style, with ornate ironwork, heavy balconies and wooden doors. Men carrying trilling birds in wooden cages secured by forehead tumplines jogged by. And they passed other men carrying maguey pulque in goatskin bags, and shepherds driving turkeys and sheep to market. Stray burros and mules with sugar leaves wandered in their path. They heard the music and smelled the odors and listened to the people in the streets hawking mats, honey cakes, cheeses, ducks, sweets, lottery tickets. They saw the people squatting by their coal fires with clay discs to cook tortillas—and Mexico touched them as she had others before and after.

At Orizaba it was raining but they went walking through the crowds that gathered on the plaza to see them. When an official of the city government slipped in the mud and struck his head, the Emperor immediately let go of the Empress's arm and went to the man's aid, speaking to him in so worried a fashion that the people could not believe it. No such display of concern had been seen by the older viewers who remembered the arrogant *gachupines,* and none present had seen Frenchmen act with such compassion. That evening at a ball given the new sovereigns, the Emperor asked after the injured man, and sent **for word** of him in the morning.

Indians came to them with writings in their own tongues, a group of Xocotitlans handing up a parchment: "Cast your eyes on your humble children. . . . Here are flowers. . . . With them the children show that they recognize you as their father." During the quadrilles of the town fiestas Carlota danced with partners who would never have been allowed into a royalty's presence at Vienna or in Paris. Students in white came to give her bouquets, and for the first time they ate the spicy Mexican food, *mole de guajalote* and tortillas with chile, indicating they found it delicious—but that they would not eat too much of it at this first serving. The dark faces silently and impassively staring up at Quetzalcoatl fascinated them, and they always thanked the people for coming. The Emperor did not wear a uniform or even elaborate dress, but simple clothing instead, thinking that thus he would show himself unlike the caudillos and generalissimos of the forty wretched years since independence, the "gorgeous generals" who, as Carlota wrote Eugenie, knew "nothing save how to ride and make war on one another."

Their Majesties continued through the valley road bounded by the giant mountains and saw enormous riverbeds, completely dry, and evergreens, poinsettias, orchids, geraniums and the finest forests. Increasingly they saw arches of triumph and men dressed in *charro* attire with silver coins down the sides of their pants and in their sombreros. They came to Puebla, passing the fort and convent the French siege had shattered. Westward was the gigantic mountain chain which included in its heights Popocatepetl, the Sleeping Warrior, and Ixtacihuatl, the Maiden in White for whose awakening he sat vigil; to the east were the Sierra Madre with the peak of Orizaba, the Mountain of the Star; and, between, the heights named for Malinche. It was wonderfully clear. They had never seen such a transparent sky.

Puebla was in ruins, the destruction caused by the fight whose ending had opened the way for their Empire's existence. As the monarchs appeared, drums beat and trumpets blew and firecrackers blasted. At Cholula, just outside Puebla, they were greeted by fifty thousand Indians who made them a throne and crowned them with flowers. They stood before a pyramid built eons ago in honor of Quetzalcoatl, who had paused there before going onto the sea, leaving behind his promise that one day he would return. Carlota was twenty-four years old on that day, and to commemorate her birthday gave seven thousand pesos to rebuild a ruined shelter for the homeless. Her husband ordered the freeing of prisoners in the city jail.

They went upward to the plateau of the City of Mexico. Lakes gleamed in the distance, and they marveled at how near the perpetually snow-covered mountains seemed. On June 7, 1864, the Emperor and Empress came to the Pastures of Aragon, a short ride from the holiest spot in Mexico, the Shrine of Guadalupe erected on the spot where the Indian Juan Diego had seen the vision of Mary, who bid him say a church must be built there. They had not passed an unpleasant moment in the country since escaping Vera Cruz, and their trip had turned into a triumphal tour. At the Pastures of Aragon they would be met by hundreds of open carriages filled with women, as many men on horseback and thousands of Indians waving green palm branches. The whole assemblage had gathered in the Alameda of Mexico City half a dozen miles away at nine in the morning and had marched in a body to the Pastures, the only flat area for miles around which was large enough to contain them all. The women wore European-style bonnets, a style hurriedly introduced in Mexico in honor of the Empress. The men wore the national costume of the *charro* suit. Pastries and cold drinks were served as the people waited until a few minutes before two in the afternoon when outriders galloped up to say Their Majesties were about to arrive.

Then Maximilian and Carlota appeared and the uproar of cheers was such that no one there that day could ever again think of it without emotion. Thunderous *vivas* were heard and the pealing of bells was lost in the roar of rockets and fireworks and the discharge of a hundred revolvers. It was a welcome which made Carlota seem almost like a little girl in the ecstasy which overcame her. They made for the Shrine of the Virgin where the Archbishop of Mexico waited for them with General Bazaine, and the entire mass of their greeters fell into line behind them. They rode over a solid carpet of flowers thrown under the horses' hooves by people lining the road.

The Emperor and Empress entered the church under a silken canopy and came to a throne that had been provided for them. Mass was said and then, followed by the enormous crowd of shouting people, they went to where an official read out an address saying that now Mexico beheld its beloved sovereigns taking the throne that Mexicans had raised for them. "Words fail me to express at once our gratitude."

Maximilian rose and spoke of how dear this place, the Shrine of Guadalupe, was to him, "as it is to all Mexicans." He saluted the people "with the warmth of one who loves you and has identified his fate with yours." The cheers were deafening and all the ladies waved their handkerchiefs in the air.

In the morning the Emperor and Empress made their entrance into the City of Mexico. At the gates of the city they passed under arches decorated with flags, garlands of flowers, drapery, placards of welcome. Women in mantillas stood on the balconies, and colored strips of paper containing verses of welcome poured down as they drove in a huge state carriage earlier sent on from Miramar. General Bazaine rode on the right in company with the officials of the city government.

The procession passed through the streets, viewed from the balconies of the low, flat-roofed buildings by people who had paid fifteen pesos apiece for their places, and preceded by carriages filled with singing children dressed as angels and by wagons bearing full-sized portraits of the new rulers. They went down the Calle de San Francisco, passing houses more beautifully adorned than ever before in the history of the city, and even in neighborhoods far from the scene of the parade strings of flowers and scarves floated in the wind. The uproar was so riotous that when the Conservative General Tomas Mejia tried to move his horse up to the Imperial carriage to offer his greetings, the frightened animal plunged away from the floods of flowers.

Deeply religious, humble, unambitious, from a tiny village near Queretaro, General Mejia had fought on the Conservative side in the name of the Virgin. All his victories, he said, were under the Virgin's protection and owing to the Virgin's intercession; at her feet he had laid the sword of honor Queretaro gave him. He had not gone over to the French when they first came to Mexico, but waited in his mountain village of Pinal de Amoles while he pondered what to do, looking to religion as his only guide. At the fall of Puebla it had been within his power to block the escape to the north of Benito Juarez, but he had not moved, hoping that Juarez would leave the country without bloodshed. Then Mexico would be ready for a peaceful reinstatement of the Church by whose spirit Mejia lived. General Mejia stayed aloof until he came to the conclusion that he could best serve God by working with the French, and so he had gone to serve under Leonardo Marquez, although the two were complete opposites, Mejia being gentle and forgiving despite his considerable military ability. As Mejia rode in the procession welcoming the new Emperor he looked at him and thought to himself that this man was the answer to the prayers of those who wanted peace in Mexico —that he was a man loving all and deserving of being loved, that it was precisely the absence of such a man which had permitted the despicable Santa Anna and others to gain power so many times. His nationality did not matter, Mejia thought; a single foreigner could not hurt Mexican independence, particularly when that foreigner so obviously wanted to love Mexico as his own country.

The procession halted at the Zocalo, in front of the Cathedral. A Te Deum was sung, and from the great building the sovereigns went on foot over carpets and under canopies to the National Palace. Upon a dais in a long, narrow hall they waited to receive the mass of people pressing forward. Mejia was among them and was asked to say a few words, but, in the presence of the man who might, at last, bring peace, he was unable to do more than stammer, "Majesty . . . Majesty . . ." Smiling that sweet smile which captured all who saw him, Maximilian stepped down from the dais and took Mejia in his arms. "Words mean nothing," the Emperor said, "but I know your heart belongs to me." Mejia never forgot.

The wife of a prominent Conservative came to Carlota and in the Mexican fashion attempted to embrace her. Such a gesture from a subject was unheard of in Europe, and the Empress indignantly drew herself up and stepped back. The Mexican woman burst into tears, but while it was explained to the Empress that she meant no harm, she collected herself and offered Carlota a cigarette. Trying to hide her laughter, the Empress thanked her but declined, saying her doctor had forbidden her to smoke.

That night the Imperial couple heard the shouted cheers of tens of thousands of people gathered in the great Zocalo before the National Palace. For years past the Mexicans had listened to politicians spewing hatred as they harangued the people from the balcony on which the Imperial couple stood. But now Quetzalcoatl was back, he in Mexican uniform and his wife in scarlet velvet. All through the city there were fireworks, some rising to outline in their lights the shape of the castle of Miramar, others with the profiles of the monarchs. In the home of a well-to-do resident was a gigantic picture showing Maximilian on a throne with the figures of Peace and Plenty on his right and left, while Napoleon in the background pointed to a Valley of Mexico where oxen were plowing and a railroad disappeared into the horizon. At the ball in the National Palace, parents held up their children to see the sovereigns, and women fainted in the crush. The Emperor saw a group of Indians and went to two of them and asked them, barefoot as they were, if they would come and sit with him at the table.

On that day, Their Majesties' first in Mexico City, General Bazaine wrote home what Paris most wanted to hear: that with Maximilian in his capital, it would be possible for six battalions of infantry, a company of engineers, a battery of artillery and some support troops to come home.

Another letter came to Mexico City from Monterrey, in the north.

". . . You tell me that, abandoning the succession to a Throne in Europe, forsaking your family, your friends, your fortune, and what is most dear to a man, your country, you have come with your wife, Doña Carlota, to distant and unknown lands to satisfy the summons spontaneously made by a people that rest their felicity and their future in you. I am amazed, on the one hand, by your generosity, and on the other, my surprise has been great to read in your letter the words *spontaneous summons,* for I had already perceived that when the traitors of my country appeared at Miramar as a self-constituted commission to offer you the Crown of Mexico, with several letters from nine or ten towns of the nation, you saw in all this merely a ridiculous farce, unworthy of serious consideration by an honorable and self-respecting man. . . .

Frankly, I have suffered a disappointment: I thought you one of those pure beings whom ambition could not corrupt.

"You invite me to go to Mexico City . . . to hold a conference there in which other Mexican leaders in arms will participate, promising us all the necessary forces to escort us on the way and pledging, as security, your public faith and your word of honor. It is impossible for me to accept your summons, sir; my occupations do not allow it; but if in the exercise of my public functions I were to accept such an invitation, there would not be sufficient guarantee in the public faith and word of honor of an agent of Napoleon and a man who is supported by the Frenchified part of the Mexican nation. . . . You tell me that you have no doubt that the peace and felicity of the Mexican people would come of our conference were I to accept it, and that the Empire would rely on the services of my lights and the support of my patriotism by placing me in some distinguished position. It is true, sir, that contemporary history records the names of great traitors who have broken their oaths and their promises and failed their own party, their antecedents, and all that is most sacred to a man of honor, and that in these betrayals the traitor has been guided by an obscure ambition to rule and a base desire to satisfy his own passions and even his own vices; but the present incumbent of the Presidency of the Republic, who has sprung from the obscure masses of the people, will succumb —if in the designs of Providence it is ordained that he succumb —fulfilling his oath, warranting the hopes of the nation over which he presides, and satisfying the promptings of his own conscience.

"I am forced to conclude for lack of time, and I shall merely add one more remark. It is given to men, sir, to attack the rights of others, to take their property, to attempt the lives of those who defend their liberty, and to make of their virtues a crime and of their own vices a virtue; but there is one thing which is beyond the reach of perversity, and that is the tremendous verdict of history. History will judge us.

"I am your obedient servant,

"Benito Juarez."

13

THE CONSERVATIVES who had worked so long for Maximilian's accession saw the Emperor as a son of the Church who would return all that the Liberals had taken away—the enormous holdings encompassing half the country's wealth. The Archbishop of Mexico, Antonio Pelagio Labastida, returning from bitter years of exile, had demanded that the French make restitution even before the Emperor came. When the French refused he said he would barricade the Cathedral doors. The Archbishop was told that, if necessary, the doors would be blown open by French artillery. He opened the doors, thinking that the advent of the Empire would make things different. Labastida looked upon the battle to reinstate the Church's position as another Crusade. His priests told the tenants of former Church lands not to pay their rents to the new owners; if they did they were authorizing Juarez's actions, which were the work of Satan.

In all that the Archbishop of Mexico did he was endorsed by the Pope. Pius IX knew nothing of Mexico beyond what the exiles told him. As a young man he had been a liberal cleric, but the events of 1848 unsettled him. He had been driven from Rome by the would-be Italian revolutionists who considered him an ally of Prince Metternich. The Pope had wandered in exile and when he returned to Rome, his hold upon even the limits of the Vatican City was tenuous. For years Napoleon III had assigned French troops to help him keep his place. It made Eugenie happy and placated Catholic opinion in France. Otherwise the Romans who booed Pius when he drove through the streets might well have driven him away. The Pope felt the times were out of joint, and in 1864 issued his *Syllabus of Errors,* condemning all the trends of the nineteenth century: "Anathema on him who should ever maintain the Pontiff can and must be reconciled with and compromise with progress, liberalism and modern civilization!" Even the Empress Eugenie was shocked, and publication of the syllabus in France was forbidden by her husband. Widely hated in one Catholic country and prohibited free expression of his thoughts in another, the Pope determined to have his way in a third. There were times when Archbishop Labastida and Gutierrez de Estrada might remind Eugenie of Philip II of Spain and the Inquisition, but the Pope did not feel he could afford another rebuff of any kind. Sometimes in a strangely whimsical way Pius IX wondered aloud if he had the Evil Eye. But he was not going to back down in Mexico.

Maximilian of Hapsburg made Emperor of Mexico arrived in his domain believing it would be a horrendous mistake to turn back to the Church the properties she had lost. It would involve enormous upheavals, and even more important, turn against him all those with Liberal sympathies. He knew he must have their support, for they constituted at least half of those in the country who cared at all about the fashion in which Mexico was to be governed. Otherwise the Conservatives would not have needed the French. But of course he could not be a Liberal, for it was the Conservatives who had helped bring him to power. Therefore he must be a compromiser. It would be his natural position in any event, for he was without a past in Mexico; he was of no party and had no friends or enemies. He could stand above the bitterness and hatred and strife.

The Emperor's whole character fitted him for this role. He disliked, detested, blood and violence. As commander of the Austrian navy he had never seen a shot fired in anger, but once a sailor had died in his presence. It affected him terribly, as did the funeral which left the boy's body in an Albanian shore-town cemetery. Maximilian did not come to Mexico as a conqueror but as a conciliator. And the task as he saw it was not impossible. Mexico was so rich that there could be enough for all. He saw the poverty of the Indians, the beggars whining for alms under the arches of every aqueduct and arcade, the children in rags. His heart went out to them. Let there be peace.

No sooner had Maximilian arrived in Mexico City than Archbishop Labastida demanded that he promulgate orders returning all the Church property and rights. The Emperor turned him away by saying he must first study the situation. The Archbishop was harsh, driving, a destroyer of the infidel. There was no middle way for him. But Maximilian said he would issue no decrees for a while, only order two merciful edicts: one, that the French blockade of the coasts be lifted, for in the name of preventing gun-running to the Liberal bands the blockade made people suffer; and, two, that the officer-prisoners held since Second Puebla be released. Aside from these orders he took no official action beyond entertaining applications for posts in his Court. So many of the Mexicans making overtures alleged themselves to be of the noblest Spanish blood that the Emperor laughingly said it was a pity there was no factory for turning out family trees, for it would be a sure money-maker.

Surrounded by Viennese dandies and French officers, the new monarchs set out to act in such manner that the Mexicans would see them not only as son and daughter of the great world of Europe but also as simple people of the same cloth as their subjects. Maximilian practiced twirling a lariat and disdained an umbrella to protect him from the sun at the *charro* riding exhibitions; at the bullfight he wore a sombrero and shouted along with the crowd. Meeting people, he smiled and joked in the friendliest manner. With Carlota, the Empress came through before the woman. Mostly she wore simple dark-colored gowns with high necks and a bit of lace at the wrists as she visited schools and hospitals. But her chitchat was inferior to his. She was adroit at asking the right questions. But, fundamentally a very serious person, she did not have her husband's quick smile or ability to charm in an instant. She tried her best.

Their own attitude, the monarchs felt, was modern, suited for the New World. King William of Prussia never went out in anything but officers' uniform and the Queen of England was always "We" when she spoke to subjects. The Spanish Viceroys were of that stripe. But Maximilian and Carlota wanted to be loved. In Italy, Francis Joseph had denied them their wish to be liberal. Now there was no one who could command them. Never going anywhere without leaving behind a memento of their visit—largesse in the form of money —the young monarchs set out to seduce even the lowliest of their subjects. When a barefooted, white-cottoned peon told the Emperor of his troubles with the corn crop, an elegantly uniformed aide-de-camp took down his words while Maximilian promised to look into the matter. The rich and Conservative Mexicans who made up "society" were shocked. The French gaped. But Maximilian said it was not like "stuffy old Europe." Here he could be a people's monarch.

But it was precisely their backgrounds and their royal lineage that had given them their position. If simple sweetness was what was wanted, why import an Austrian Archduke and a Princess of Belgium? There was the contradiction. So they must have a Court and be royalty. And of course it was how they had always lived, walking over gleaming parquet floors and under the lights of thousand-candle chandeliers, past gilt furniture in tapestry-hung chambers, to eat off gold plate and drink from cut crystal.

Maximilian might take in stride that an Indian guard at the National Palace had sold for fifteen *reals* per person the right to watch the Emperor getting into bed on His Majesty's first evening in Mexico City. And he could even accept the vermin-filled sheets that had driven him to sleep that night on a billiard table. But soon he had a troop of brilliant Palatine Guards, the corps of gentlemen-at-arms, dressed in sky-blue-and-silver uniforms, standing at attention in the corridors of the palace. The flunkies of his Court wore enormous belt buckles on their lace-embroidered coats and carried silver- or gold-mounted swords; the columns of his official paper carried letters from such correspondents as the Elector of Hesse, who thanked the Emperor for informing the Elector of his ascension to the Throne and who called upon God to bless the new enterprise while supplicating His Majesty's benevolence toward the Ducal House.

Maximilian was the Emperor but in his democratic way he went about in a little leather vest and upon occasion very little escort. Even the Liberals of the city told each other it was impossible to dislike him, he was so open and friendly. Walking his horse one day he saw a man's hat captured by the wind, caught it as it flew by, and smilingly handed it to its owner. The man was a Liberal but he yelled *"Viva el Emperador!"* A friend wrote of the incident to Manuel Romero de Terreros, who when the French arrived in the city dressed his house in mourning and went to live in Europe. Had he been there, the friend wrote, he might have changed his mind about things. "They are beginning to love us," Carlota wrote her grandmother. She set to work sewing nightshirts for the patients in the hospitals.

Eight days after their arrival, the Imperial couple moved into Chapultepec Castle, which was on the site of the summer residence of the Aztec Emperors, a half hour's drive from the Zocalo. Montezuma had walked there in the gardens and bathed in the clear pools as he wondered what to do about the approaching Cortés. His palace had been torn down and in its place a castle was erected which served as a country seat for the Viceroys. With the departure of the Spanish it had fallen into disrepair and sat abandoned and lonely on a hill. It was an enchanting place with butterflies and hummingbirds darting through its great park. Its enormous trees were the most dramatic the Europeans had ever seen. It captured Maximilian's fancy the moment he laid eyes on it, and he set about hiring hundreds of artists, masons, carpenters and painters to make it a castle worthy of a mighty sovereign. Great gilt monograms went up over the windows and doorways, and ornate wallpaper was laid on. The monarchs ordered marble, bronze and silver statues, elaborate murals, great stone walls, terraces and walkways, enormous balconies. Because of the magnitude of the labor involved it was no longer possible for anyone else to obtain the services of skilled workmen in Mexico City, for they were all at work on Chapultepec.

While the vast transformation of Chapultepec went on, Their Majesties entertained at the National Palace, inviting guests of all the varied backgrounds which Mexico provided, including those of the most Liberal stripe. For state dinners the people assembled in the drawing rooms which stretched the length of the building, half a dozen chambers connected with folding doors. Silks and satins brought from Europe draped the doors and windows. The chairs and carpets were all French. Equerries, chamberlains, aides and secretaries—almost all either Austrian or French—came in and then the doors of the last room were flung open and the monarchs entered. They led the way to the banquet hall, where Maximilian conducted Carlota to her place at the center of the oblong table. His seat was opposite hers. A card with the Imperial cipher and the name of each guest sat on the plates.

The banquets, in accordance with the Ceremonial of the Court which he had written on the *Novara*, included fifteen to twenty wines and lasted three hours. After the dinner all rose and filed into the brilliantly illuminated salons where formal presentations to Their Majesties were made. Everyone remained standing as the Emperor and Empress separated and, each accompanied by a chamberlain, walked about the room. Carlota was remarkable at saying the right thing in the right language to each guest, touching upon each individual's interests. It was impossible to speak with the Empress, her face charmingly pink after the large meal—she ate everything—and not go away believing she had a very real involvement in one's problems. What she said was not easy chitchat and a guest could not know what hours of study her quick words represented, the research done on everyone invited.

The servants were handsome Indians outfitted in Imperial livery, but their service was spotty. They stole the linens and silver, the food and plates. One was seen to scratch his head with a fork in front of the guests. But even so the effect of the palace soirees was dazzling. At musical evenings the orchestra played Strauss waltzes, marches by Saverthal. Day by day, as Austrian servants were brought out to replace the Mexicans, the affairs achieved almost the perfection of the older Courts of Europe. The Conservative Ignacio Algara looked at the Grand Marshals and Grand Masters of Ceremonies Intendant of the Imperial Household, at the dames of honor and ladies-in-waiting, at the Imperial coachhouse with sixteen carriages, at the magnificent table service and wine cellar, the brilliant Palatine Guard and superb ceremony. And all that he saw made it impossible for him to believe that Juarez had once lived in the same rooms of the same building.

The French were anxious for the Emperor to take over all

responsibility. By doing so he would set them free from an enterprise which unbalanced their budget and upset the Legislative Body. But Maximilian refused to take any definite steps beyond appointing people to the Court and to his diplomatic corps, including Pepe Hidalgo as Minister to France. (Both Hidalgo and the somber Gutierrez de Estrada had declined to come back to the homeland. Estrada said that with his mission in life successfully concluded, he would retire from all public life.) The Emperor was not throwing off proclamations in the usual bombastic Mexican fashion, Carlota wrote, and so the people, unused to such goodwill and reticence, showed enthusiasm turning "almost into idolatry." Her husband had been respected from the first day, she wrote her grandmother, but now he was "adored." The Liberals, although "not yet monarchists," were "Maximilianists."

The Emperor decided to take a trip. He had always loved travel. Also, it would show Europe that Mexico could now be safely traversed and thus was open for profitable investment. But actually, reflected the recently promoted Major Henri Loizillon, it would require heavy French escorts to prevent some band of kidnapers from capturing the Emperor. A cavalry troop was assembled and the Emperor set out, leaving behind the Empress as regent.

Maximilian went north in a carriage which moved at a trot except for the moments when he wanted to take notes and ordered it to go slower. The notes were largely on historic or scientific matters. He talked of the great museum of natural history he would construct, wherein would be shown every example of wildlife in Mexico.

All around him were the jingling Zouaves and Chasseurs d'Afrique attended by scattered units of the Mexican forces. Sometimes he was held back as the troops went ahead to clear the passes of Liberal, or merely outlaw, riflemen. He was impatient at the pauses and wanted to share the risks the soldiers were taking. That was impossible, of course, but in camp he lived as the men did, laughing at the bedbugs and vermin which infested the shabby village inns, and sleeping on the ground when they were in the open country. He saw a Zouave who had invented a blower for applying insecticide to blankets and bought it from the man, who spent the night drinking to the health of the Emperor and to the death of fleas.

Indians came to see their monarch and he asked them to dinner and gave them gold and silver medallions embossed with his profile. "One is led to the conclusion that he has the intention of governing with sweetness," Major Loizillon wrote home. But what futility, Loizillon thought to himself. What the Mexicans needed was a hand of iron to hit them strongly and regularly.

The Empress would not have agreed with Loizillon's sentiments. Maximilian was doing much good with his cheerful ways and his motto which he endlessly repeated: "Let's forget the shadows of the past." The Emperor went through Queretaro, Morelia, Leon. He came to Dolores on September 16, 1864, which was the fifty-fourth anniversary of the day Father Hidalgo had sounded the call for the revolution which eventually drove the Spaniards out. On that day and in that place Maximilian stood and cried, *"Viva Mexico!"* Then he went on his way, circling back toward Mexico City, past the Indian women washing clothing in the streambeds, past the naked button-eyed dark children wondering who it was that smiled and waved.

Carlota left the capital to meet him at Toluca, fifty miles to the west. She ran to him so swiftly that her legs, bare of pantaloons, could be discreetly observed by Charles Blanchot of the Chasseurs d'Afrique, who thought to himself it was consolation of a sort for all the mud and discomfort of the trip.

On October 30, two and a half months after leaving the capital for his tour, Maximilian returned to Mexico City, there to work some more on the final proofs of the Ceremonial of the Court, which would soon be published. With the conclusion of the rainy season, the city was at its best. Orange trees, sweet mimosas, violets were all in bloom. He sat in the Castle of Chapultepec, wonderfully transformed from the sorry half-ruin it had been, and looked through the clear transparent air at the mountains, the broad, distant fields of corn and maguey surrounded by red-flowered bushes, at the little towns between the castle and the city, and said nothing could be so cheering as that view. From the castle to the Zocalo ran a straight, rutted road with two ovals adorned with bad statuary, and boggy meadows along its sides. He looked down at it and said he would make of it a promenade to surpass the Champs Élysées: The Emperor's Road.

The social season of that fall of 1864 was brilliant, with opera companies performing in the capital and glittering entertainments offered by rich Conservatives and French officers in honor of the Imperial couple. On his trip, Maximilian had met the Spanish poet José Zorrilla. He had appointed him head of what would be a great National Theater, with a resident company of artists and prizes for the best tragedy and the best comedy written during the year. Zorrilla was also named as Imperial Reader and his poems praising Their Majesties were often read at soirees honoring the rulers.

But in Paris, the government kept asking when the country would be pacified so that the troops could come home. General Bazaine decided to make a last sweep. His troops spread out in ever-widening circles from Mexico City, carrying their regimental standards into the arid desert and reptile-infested jungles as they sought the one decisive battle which would crush all opposition. But it seemed to the French army that they were only getting in deeper and deeper. They lost all restraint in their hanging and shooting. Anyone taken with weapons in hand was given half an hour to make his peace with God and then strung to a tree. Victor Hugo wrote:

> We come, we kill, we loot, we pass and, unblenching
> Leave behind us a land scorched and stenching.
> And the things that we do in blood and flame
> Are glorious, or they would be our shame.

The French felt the grossest contempt for the Mexicans, holding them to be thieves and liars all, even as they laid out unthinkable sums to equip the Emperor's army. But the Mexican units were unreliable and would not fight unless driven into battle by the French and by the few Mexican officers who had ability. One such officer was Colonel Miguel Lopez, who had commanded the Mexican troops escorting the Emperor and Empress from Vera Cruz to the capital. With tears in his eyes, laying about him with his sword, he would attempt to check the retreat of his men before the bands who called themselves Liberals, but almost always he would be left by himself, screaming, *"Cabrones!* * Turn and fight!" Another was General Tomas Mejia. He was the best soldier Imperial Mexico produced in those years. Something of his piety and faith in God and God's cause came through to his ragged troops, and they stood and fought when he asked them to.

Marquez remained the man he had always been, hanging Liberal women to trees by their breasts, murderously flogging them and leaving them to die. When recruiting for his force lagged he sent out press gangs with lariats to capture whomever they could. He would send them to units far enough removed from their homes to discourage desertions. As his tattered bands traveled their women went along to cook, curry the horses, do the wash and carry their men's boots. At night officers nailed shut the doors of expropriated houses to keep the soldiers and their women from running off. The French watched with a mixture of horror and amusement.

The fighting and slaughter were such that there were sections of the country where the sounds of rifle shots brought wild pigs running from every direction to devour the corpses. They were joined by crows and dogs and foxes who ripped open the stomachs. If a man was hanged in the higher altitudes he would become black as he mummified, and then dry as parchment.

The Emperor had not wanted to come to Mexico with a sword in his hand. It was against his nature. He ordered that all executions by military courts-martial had to be reviewed by him, and from then on it was possible for the vilest murderers to gain Imperial clemency by declaring that their rapine and theft stemmed from political idealism. Thus he sent to the chain gang man after man who by bribery of the somnolent guards could easily escape to take the field again. Despite Juarez's letter he still believed he could effect a union with those who politically opposed him. Reluctantly, General Bazaine complied with the repeated orders to show leniency, saying privately they were costing the lives of French soldiers. He felt an immense gulf existed between the man who had been an Archduke of Austria and himself. It was difficult for a former private of a nondescript regiment to offer forceful views to someone whose name was von Hapsburg. Meanwhile Paris was

* One who countenances and encourages the seduction of his wife by another.

at Bazaine to wind up an expedition draining France of millions of francs and tens of thousands of her best soldiers. Ill at ease, Bazaine began to press Maximilian to make decisions and put his Empire in order.

In the eyes of the monarchs everything depended upon resolution of the Church question. They thought Archbishop Labastida to be hundreds of years behind the times, a relic of the days when Mexicans in medieval fashion uniformly fell to their knees at the sound of a ringing bell informing them that the Host was being borne to a dying person, or that a high dignitary of the Church was passing. Labastida did not wish to modify the Reform laws of Juarez; he wished to abolish them and return everything without exception to the Church. The Imperial couple placed their hopes in the Papal Nuncio, the Pope's messenger, whose dispatch they had requested of Pius when they visited Rome on their way to Mexico. Through the Nuncio they would bypass the Archbishop and appeal to the Pope himself for an intelligent approach to Mexico's situation. Meanwhile, waiting, the Emperor perfected a point here and a point there of his Ceremonial for the Court, telling those around him that he believed it would be the world's most complete work of its kind. Maximilian also set up a commission to study the formation of an army, financial system and judiciary which would be a credit to a civilized nation. At his weekly public audiences he was charming and approachable, as he was upon his frequent visits to prisons, mines and poorhouses, where he looked at everything, distributed alms and chatted. He stood as godfather to hundreds of Indian children baptized, as he lightheartedly told Bazaine, "with fire pumps."

His Majesty worked to introduce Mexicans into his service, charming those who came with his gossip and risqué jokes. He gave each of his staff an affectionate *abrazo* in the morning when he came to his office, and spent hours with them asking about their home lives, and their sweethearts—were the girls pretty, and exactly what was the relationship? He pushed them to the limit to tell "spicy details," noted his secretary, José Luis Blasio, a young Mexican whom the Emperor nicknamed The Child. Sometimes he would amuse himself with his aides by seeing how far he could separate the ends of his beard.

Those who had similar Dundrearies had to compete. He had little battles with them about keeping his offices warm. "Don't you see," he asked Blasio, "that we are freezing?"

"No, Sire, I see that we are frying."

"These children who have hot blood do not realize that an old man of thirty-two, like me, is as cold as ice."

In the evenings they played billiards together—the losers at the Emperor's order having to crawl under the table as a penalty for poor play.

Some aides were alert to help him, and concerned with his welfare. They told the Emperor his butler was stealing from the Imperial wine cellars and hawking the bottles to whomever had money to pay for them; he replied that we are all of us robbed in this world, and no doubt the butler thought old Hock was bad for the Imperial digestion. Blasio saw that His Majesty never showed anger at anything. He might look displeased or reproachful, but that was all.

On November 29, 1864, half a year after the arrival of the Emperor and Empress, the Papal Nuncio came to Vera Cruz. Dressed in green-and-violet ecclesiastical trappings, Monsignor Pedro Francisco Meglia was rowed ashore from the Royal Mail Ship *Solent* to the sound of artillery salvos and the ringing of bells. The French mustered up what passed for a private railroad car and the Nuncio traveled in it to the end of the line where a gig with long shafts, especially brought from Havana, waited to take him to the capital. He arrived in Mexico City to officiate at the religious services connected with the coming Christmas celebrations, Maximilian and Carlota joining him in washing the feet of the poor.

The Emperor and Empress in all their letters home had consistently sounded happy, optimistic. Here was a representative of the Europe they had left, one who would be sending reports home. They took great pains to show the Nuncio how well they had done—how they had, at the personal expense of the Empress, beautified the Alameda, the central park, so that flowers bloomed on what had been a neglected dusty square; how they had ripped up the crude paving of the Zocalo and put in footpaths, fountains, trees and shrubs, and how The Emperor's Road was on its way to being the first promenade of the New World.

1. Schoenbrunn Palace, the summer residence of the Austrian Imperial family.

ABOVE
2. Young Archduke Maximilian,
   the future Mexican Emperor.

LEFT
3. Maximilian's mother,
   the Archduchess Sophia,
   with Maximilian's brother, the
   future Emperor Francis Joseph.

ABOVE
4. The Belgian Princess Charlotte,
   who was to become
   the Mexican Empress Carlota.

LEFT
5. The Duke of Reichstadt
   with the future Emperor
   Francis Joseph and
   the future Princess
   Caroline of Naples.
   All of Vienna would say
   that the Duke, the son of
   Napoleon the Great,
   was Maximilian's father.

6 & 7. Miramar Castle at Trieste:
   The square (above) and from the guns terrace (below).

8. The Austrian Emperor Francis Joseph.   9. The Austrian Empress Elizabeth.

10. Francis Joseph and Elizabeth at their mountain retreat.

ABOVE 15. Maximilian is offered the crown of Mexico
in Miramar. (*After Cesare Dell'Acqua.*)

BELOW 16. The departure from Miramar for Mexico.
(*After Cesare Dell'Acqua.*)

17. Their Mexican Majesties enter Mexico City.

ABOVE 18. Benito Juarez.

OPPOSITE PAGE:

ABOVE 19. His Imperial Majesty the Emperor of Mexico.

BELOW 20. Her Imperial Majesty the Empress of Mexico.

ABOVE 21. Chapultepec Castle, the Emperor's principal residence in Mexico.

BELOW 22. The National Palace, Mexico City,
as it appeared in Maximilian's time.

ABOVE 23. A French artillery train moves against Mexican guerrillas.

BELOW 24. French cavalrymen clash with Juaristas.

ABOVE
LEFT 25. Porfirio Diaz,
Juarez's best general.

ABOVE
RIGHT 26. The Marshal of France,
François Achille Bazaine.

LEFT 27. Leonardo Marquez,
the Tiger of Tacubaya.

28. Colonel Miguel Lopez:
    "But this is death! Murder!"

29. The Princess Salm-Salm:
    "Isn't the sum enough?"

30. The Convent of the Cross, Queretaro—"La Cruz,"
    where Maximilian made his last fight.

31 & 32. Miramon and Mejia:
"A brave man must be honored even in the face of death."

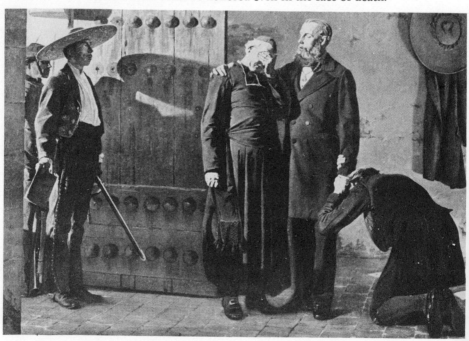

33. Maximilian prepares to leave his cell for the last time.
"Be calm. It is the will of God that I should die."

ABOVE 34. The execution.

BELOW 35. The place of the execution some days later,
      with crosses marking where the three men stood.

ABOVE 36. Maximilian's casket is taken to the *Novara*.

BELOW 37. Arrival in Vienna.

ABOVE 38. The dedication in 1901 of the shrine
atop the exact spot where the execution took place.

BELOW 39. The Castle of Bouchout outside Brussels
where Carlota was to live on, lost in madness.

40. Carlota (middle) in 1925, eighty-five years of age.
    Two years later she was dead.

Still the Nuncio's message from the Pope was: no compromise. The Church must have everything back, every stick of its property. Religious tolerance of any faith but Catholicism must end; the civil power must have no power of any kind over Church officials. Monsignor Meglia was the *Syllabus of Errors* in person.

Maximilian tried to reason with him, saying theirs would be a Catholic state, but also a modern one. Catholicism would be the state religion, but other faiths would be allowed. The state would pay the salaries of the priests and make itself responsible for the upkeep of their religious buildings and orders, but never again could the Church be what it had been. Surely the Nuncio would understand.

The Nuncio left to confer with Archbishop Labastida. For two days nothing was heard from him. An emissary was sent to ask his decision on what Maximilian had requested. He sent back word that all the Emperor's requests were out of the question. Mexico had strayed from God's way and must return to the true path. Indeed, that was what the country's people ardently desired.

Maximilian and Carlota could not believe anyone to be so blindly obstinate. It seemed to the Empress that the man was mad. Perhaps it would be best for Bazaine simply to throw the Nuncio out the window, she remarked to the French commander, who laughed. That the Pope's representative would actually say the country wanted the Church as it had been! It was as if, she said, someone were to come and say in broad daylight that it was night. Carlota sent for the Nuncio and sat with him for two hours explaining that although Mexico carried wax statues of Jesus and the saints, and lit candles, true religion did not characterize the acts, but rather superstition and learned routine. It would be the task of the Empire to bring the people a newer way of looking at God, and a deeper, truer religion. If they failed in that work, the Protestant giant to the north might take over the country and it would be lost to the Church forever. The young Empress was a logical thinker and felt in herself a very great strength and power—she could lead armies if she had to, she believed—but as she expounded her views she felt as if she were having a true picture of what hell must be like: a hopeless impasse. She tried every tone, Carlota wrote Eugenie, serious, playful, grave, prophetic; "he brushed aside my arguments like so much dust and put nothing in their place, but seemed to take pleasure in the nothingness that he created round him." At the end the Empress rose as a sign that the Nuncio should leave her. "If the Church will not help us, we will serve her in spite of herself," she said. Her husband decreed that the vast properties would not be returned. The Nuncio went back to Europe. He did not call to say fare-well. The Imperial couple had been in Mexico hardly more than six months and had lost the Church.

Juarez in his old black carriage jolted north in front of the French. He left Monterrey with the insults of the provincial governor reverberating in his ears. Juarez was finished, the governor said. The governor's son cocked a revolver and or-dered Juarez out of his father's office. The President went on to the state of Durango, through the dusty sagebrush wastes and vast emptiness of cactus and mesquite, the flat abode of the roadrunner, buzzard and rattlesnake. Occasional goatherds or vaqueros—cowboys—watched a file of three or four black car-riages go by through the winds swirling at the dry plants. Perhaps in the little falling-apart towns of the northern Mexico desert a few of the people who saw the closed-windowed vehicles knew that here was The Sick Family—the President of the Republic and his handful of supporters, with a bedraggled little crew of soldiers surrounding the carriages, one of which bore the archives of the Republic.

Juarez bought his wife a new dress and sent her, with the children, north to the United States, standing in the dust and watching her carriage until it disappeared from view. She took with her the wooden rocker used by all their children as some-thing to speak to her of home.

The President went up to Chihuahua. When the carriages rolled through the flat, straight streets not a person raised a cheer for the man wearing as usual a Prince Albert coat with top hat. They found a cave and buried the archives in it. Looking on, Juarez's coachman thought it was enough to make one weep.

Once in the distance they saw a cloud of dust rising and the few Ministers and soldiers thought it must be a French patrol.

The end appeared to have come. Juarez said that if this was their fate they might just as well meet it head on, and so they advanced upon the cloud until they saw it was only a sheep herd. Had he known that? Nobody knew. Juarez lived in a little shack patched with wood and canvas. He ordered that the band that passed for his bodyguard be withdrawn from in front of the shack, and one of his Ministers said the President should be more cautious. "What can they do to me?" Juarez asked.

"But you should be more careful."

"Of whom?"

"Of the enemy."

"Why?" Juarez asked. "If we are going to win? You will see."

The President of the Republic had only the flimsiest communications with the Liberals in the south, who on rare occasions would send a messenger disguised as a wandering religious mendicant. Juarez lived backed up against the border, finally coming to rest in the sleepy border town of Paso del Norte, a few tumbled-down adobe huts in the empty cactus desert. He was helpless, his family was gone, the world seemed leagued against him, but he was at ease. "Don't worry," he said. The wife of one of his Ministers asked what she could do to make him more comfortable—some sewing, some special dishes he might like prepared? He seemed surprised at her question. He lacked nothing, he replied. Rumors drifted south to the capital that he was dead, or in the United States or entirely deserted by his few followers—"Don't worry," he said. His newspapers were weeks old and letters sent to him might or might not be received, and often bad news found him more quickly than good. It did not take him unawares.

He referred to Maximilian as The Foreigner, or, aping Maximilian's first remarks upon arrival at Vera Cruz, The Chosen, but he did not express personal hatred of the man sitting in the National Palace at Mexico City. In fact he showed no emotion at all. Sometimes others did. A blind drummer came to him and spoke in such fashion that at least one of his Ministers felt envy for the man's eloquence. The drummer said: "Never have I so much wanted my sight as now to see the most eminent man of my country. Those who see say that the sun is more beautiful at its setting than at the beginning or in the middle of its course; and so the President of the Republic seems greater to me in this remote state than in Mexico City, commanding those who command. His eminent virtues are well known to me, for there are some things so clear that even the blind can see them." Then he played reveille on his drum.

The Empress had come to gain some understanding of Mexico. At first she had possessed an almost poetic conception of what their life would be like in the great Empire they would erect in the New World, but by January of 1865, after half a year, Carlota saw the reality. She could not go for a ride on her bay mare Isabella unless French cavalry went ahead to clear the road of men who might be simple peons in from the country for market day, but who as likely might be armed and danger-ous. Half an hour out of the capital no diligence was safe from robbers unless attended by strong escorts.

The Emperor involved himself in searching for a country estate, and finally would settle on one in Cuernavaca, not far in miles from the capital but sufficiently below it in elevation so as to be in a semitropical region; but the Empress spent her time studying the problems that confronted them. It seemed to her that Mexico could be made great only by the Indian masses of the countryside. The Europeanized mestizos were too corrupted. So at her instigation her husband passed decrees reducing the amounts of money the Indians could be obliged to owe, ordered that debts could not be passed from father to son, and forbade excessively long working days and corporal punishment. An uproar resulted. The Indians were tractable when downtrodden, the Emperor's advisers said; improve their lot and there would be trouble. Maximilian could have been dissuaded from follow-ing his course but the Empress would not permit it. The de-crees went through, along with an edict saying that forced conscription for the army was to be abolished as unworthy of a humane and civilized nation.

There followed a flood of decrees dealing with public health measures, education, the improvement of cattle, the care of horses, the exploitation of the coal mines and development of the mercury and copper resources, the building of roads, the extension of the railroad all the way from Vera Cruz and the installation of trolley lines in the capital itself. It was the Em-press who wrote most of them. The Emperor more willingly devoted himself to the finding and then the refurbishing of his country place in Cuernavaca. It had been the property of the immensely wealthy silver-mine magnate Joseph Borda in colonial days. Borda had set out to create a home surrounded by gardens which would equal those of the palaces of Europe. Terraces, stone works, ponds, great lanes of trees had all gone to ruin in the chaos following the Revolution. To bring the place to its former glory was a task which appealed to Maximilian.

Carlota's zeal for frenzied work stemmed in part from a personality and mind which detested idleness and frivolity. Also there were the incessant urgings of Napoleon which, unlike her husband, she could not forget: "Settle those questions which concern the actual organization of Mexico as speedily as possible. . . . There should be an end to uncertainty. . . . Anything is better than uncertainty." Eugenie also wrote warning that the French Legislative Body was becoming increasingly impatient and that her husband absolutely must have something to offer it, must "be able to say what has been done for the reform and organization of your beautiful country."

In Paris there was no lack of stimuli to make the French monarchs anxious to justify their role in Mexico. The earlier optimistic statements were coming back to plague them. "Since Maximilian is established," said Deputy Jules Favre, "since Maximilian is the Messiah announced in all time past; since he is really the man both for the Indians and the Spanish, who receive him with acclamation; since he meets on his passage only with bouquets from the señoritas—let our soldiers return. What have they to do in Mexico? They are not needed, and can only be an obstacle in the way of that entire unanimity of feeling that exists between the prince and the nation."

The heavy irony aroused Maximilian; that and the incessant drumming by his wife upon the theme that they commence serious work. He fitfully threw himself into the writing of dozens of laws. But of financial matters he knew nothing—"The Archduke Maximilian never knew how to count. . . . The Emperor of Mexico knew how to count even less, if that is possible," said a Frenchman who served the Mexican Empire. And so, as he drew up law after law—and in the end the edicts filled ten large beautifully bound octavo volumes—Maximilian designated the spending of gigantic sums for their enforcement. The government did not have the money, or anything like it, and so new loans were floated in the European markets, with the greater percentage of what was raised being taken up in commissions for the French backers. The Emperor did not take notice of an entirely unbalanced financial situation, but set up a budget calling for the government to expend fifty million pesos a year. The income of a government of Mexico had never reached fifteen million.

For a time the Emperor had thought the Indians would be his officials. But slowly he was forced to realize what could happen if Mexico was ruled by men who had never had responsibility and did not understand it. There was what he and the Empress came to call "a nothingness" about the masses of the Mexicans, which found them passive in the face of bandit raids against their villages and made difficult the procurement of men willing to do anything for the Empire or for anything else. The French said it was because Mexico was a half-breed and mongrel country, lazy, debased, unambitious; but the Emperor and Empress were able to reach beyond that and say the problem was the result of the people's subjugation by the Spanish and by the Church. Yet there was that cursed willingness to sit in the plaza, back to crumbling wall, to sleep in the sun. Maximilian might order free schools to be established in each community, but teachers were hard to find. Appointed, they decamped with the money given them to buy equipment or simply took it and did nothing in return.

Maximilian was more able than Carlota to accept the dreamy philosophy that everything could be done tomorrow. He could devote himself to projects that interested him and were far more pleasant to contemplate than the sloth and monstrous inefficiency of his army, the great majority of whose members would not fight the guerrillas despite their willingness to shout *"Viva el Emperador"* even as they fled. The Emperor announced that many had wished to erect a marble column with his statue surmounting it in the capital, but that he was declining in preference for one which would have upon it the heroes of Mexico's Revolution—Hidalgo, Allende, Morelos; then he spent his time overseeing the plans for the monument.

Carlota, by contrast, found it impossible to look the other way. "In civilized nations," she wrote Eugenie, "there is an organ which responds to every pressure from authority, one can touch it like a keyboard and produce the desired sound, but here one might go on strumming on it all day, for it is like a voiceless piano, and the effect of a measure is hardly felt beyond the paper on which it is recorded."

That was not what the Empress of the French wanted to hear. The letters of the French officers in Mexico hinted that the project was unfeasible, and Jules Favre was asking: "Why this discrepancy between the official statements as to the pacification of Mexico, to the unanimous consent to Maximilian's elevation to the throne and the facts: the country under martial law, and the French army marching, torch in hand, protecting one party and punishing the other by the wholesale destruction of life and property?" Favre ended by remarking that in 1814 the Senate deposed the Great Emperor for violating that provision of the French constitution which said "declaration of war must be proposed, discussed and promulgated like laws." The implication for a sovereign whose armies fought in Mexico without a declaration of war was not pleasant.

Yet the French could not do otherwise than sink deeper into Mexico. They had invested so much blood and treasure that the great adventure had to work. So along with the shipments of troops went French experts on government and finance. They probed and suggested, and Maximilian and Carlota listened, but always with the knowledge that the primary loyalties of these experts were to France, not Mexico. This extended also to the French soldiers, who almost alone supported the Empire. Recruiting booths for Mexican service had been set up in Brussels and Vienna, and the Austrian and Belgian officers were always welcome at the National Palace and at Chapultepec. But it was not the same for the French. Carlota asked every French officer she met for a photograph of himself which she could put into an album, and of course they were all flattered, but after having given the picture most of them were never invited back. The French soldiers were walking reminders that everything in Mexico was done at the behest of the Emperor of the French. They knew it and the sovereigns of Mexico knew it too. Hating the fact, the sovereigns had reiterated that hard truth in every letter to Paris. "The Austrians and Belgians are good only in times of calm, but let a storm arise and there is nothing like the red trousers," Carlota wrote Eugenie.

The Imperial couple were in the strangest of positions. They could not order the red trousers to do anything, only make requests. Inevitably they found it galling. Guerrilla bands led by Liberals or outlaw chiefs circulated through the countryside, pursued by French squadrons, and the sovereigns alternated between thinking the harshness of the French was all that stood between them and their subjects, and deciding that the French were not stringent enough. Eventually they decided on the former view even as Bazaine raged at what his men underwent so that an Austrian could "play at clemency." A coldness arose between the commander and the Mexican monarchs.

With the new year of 1865 Maximilian conferred the highest class of the Order of the Mexican Eagle, that of Grand Cross with Collar, upon Napoleon, and also sent to Paris some oyster shells: "I should be happy to know that they were placed on your writing-table to receive the ashes of those pleasant cigarettes which incline one so agreeably toward business and meditation." But what were such things to the Emperor of the French? At fifty-seven he was not feeling well, the result, perhaps, of those excesses which after more than twelve years of marriage infuriated his wife as much as ever.

Increasingly Eugenie berated him in front of other people, even to the point of rasping that her husband spoke like "an idiot." She went, alone and enraged, to Scotland and to German spas and left him to his women and the sluggishness which more and more characterized him. He had never wielded power until quite late in life, and it did not agree with him physically. He seemed half-asleep most of the time, and withdrew into his dreamy self to write a definitive life of Julius Caesar. Immersed in his books and notes, the nephew of the Great Emperor seemed far more interested in the Rome of Caesar's day than the Paris of his own. When the pressure of state affairs intruded upon him it was always in the form of bad news. Italy had proved to be not at all grateful for the French participation in the war of 1859. Prussia was growing into a powerful and threatening country, constantly rattling its sword and, in collusion with Austria, sweeping into the Danish provinces of Schleswig-Holstein to appropriate them for itself. There was constant sniping in the Legislative Body about everything. In his world gone somewhat sour, thoughts of Mexico were less than welcome.

Maximilian and Carlota, in the Mexican highlands, did not think of Napoleon III that way. There he was regarded as power personified. Their letters never dealt with any other problems he might have, but solely with their own. The attitude they took was akin to that of children to the teacher whose personal life does not exist and who lives only in the form of mentor and guardian. Sometimes they could not escape seeing Napoleon's desire to have done with his role in Mexico; and they answered that longing with letters speaking of French glory and French honor, of the French greatness which could not permit her troops to leave a job half done.

Yet in the first months of 1865 the Empire of Mexico appeared to be getting stronger. Or at least a case could be made for its success. Money was coming in from Europe, dispatched by investors who took faith from the optimistic stories planted in Paris papers filled with details of the vast Mexican riches awaiting exploitation. In the capital a trolley line was built to run out into the suburbs despite universal fear of the marauders who had taken over the outlying villas abandoned by owners afraid of being murdered in their beds.

At the inauguration ceremonies the Emperor and Empress declined to sit on a special dais but remained with the rest of the people on little stools, he smoking a companionable cigar with the other men. That they had put through a trolley line made Mexico City more European. In the spruced-up Alameda Austrian or French bands played each morning; and in the evening the equipages of the city drove there, the women inside flirting with the men passing by on horseback. It was possible in those months to find in Mexico City a way of life very much akin to that which the Europeans had left behind. The officers found romance. Two daughters of the highest echelon of the capital's society shocked everybody by fighting each other in the Alameda for the love of a French captain. But outside the city gates one heard, sometimes, the thunder of shrapnel fired to break up the charge of a couple of hundred machete-swinging men; and one guerrilla band prided itself on its possession of the head of a French officer with pomaded hair which gave off, they said, the scent of the finest eau de cologne.

"Bands seem to spring up out of the ground," Carlota wrote Eugenie. "Why must evil passions take possession of men?"

Napoleon wrote back, "It is necessary to redouble your resolution. . . . I greatly regret the local insurrections which still impede pacification of the country. . . . I once more recommend to Your Majesty to display energy."

14

BAZAINE'S WIFE WAS twenty years younger than he. While the
French commander soldiered through Mexico she entertained
herself in Paris. She was not discreet. Some of her letters came
into the hands of the wife of a gentleman friend. This lady
sent them to Madame Bazaine's husband and then told Madame Bazaine what she had done. Terrified, Marie Bazaine
went to Napoleon and confessed everything to him. Could he
somehow get back the letters before they reached Mexico City?
Napoleon understood the situation—who could understand it
better?—but it was too late. The mail packet had sailed.
Bazaine's wife went home and, so it is said, took poison. She
was dead when the letters arrived in Mexico City, to be destroyed by one of Bazaine's aides. The French commander
never knew, but perhaps rumors reached him, for he managed
to forget his wife. He first saw Señorita Pepita Peña at a ball,
sitting with her mother. He made inquiries. She was of a good
Mexican family. He was fifty-four to her seventeen, but still
virile and possessed of a great position, for he was a marshal
of France now. Pepita became the marshal's wife in the private
chapel of the National Palace. For a wedding present the Emperor gave them a large sum of money and the Buenavista
Palace.

Bazaine in Mexico remained as he had always been, a calmly
competent field soldier, deeply aware of the social gulf between himself and titled officers who had begun their careers
from a more elegant base than that of private in Louis Philippe's army. But he had a Mexican wife now, spoke better
Spanish than the Emperor, and could not help but be aware

191

of the gossip which said he was really the first man in the country, with the Emperor being in the marshal's service, not the other way round. The marshal's wife busily went around matchmaking for her young friends and the officers of her husband's forces, and they led a pleasant life together. Even as the Spanish General Prim had been considered an aspirant to the title of King Juan the First, so Bazaine was looked upon as possible governor-general of a Mexico become the protectorate of France. Where would that leave the Emperor and Empress? Their letters to Bazaine's monarchs sometimes praised individual French officers, but never the marshal. Bazaine knew it and fought back. Bazaine wrote Napoleon: "There has been no indication on the part of the government that the Emperor has taken any step with regard to the grave questions by which the country is disturbed. Nothing is done, and there is no indication that anything serious is going to be done."

The gulf between the Mexican monarchs and the French commander widened. The Belgian Minister remarked, "To eat priest for breakfast and Frenchman for dinner when one has been called to the throne by the clergy and must rely upon France for sole support may be regarded as a dangerous policy."

In Paris, the Empress Eugenie, born Señorita de Montijo, grew angry at Empress Carlota, born a Princess of Belgium whose grandfather was a King of France and who now presumed to criticize a French marshal. She wrote Carlota that Bazaine was one of the finest officers France had to offer, and when Carlota wrote asking the recall of Bazaine's chief aide —his face and manners were displeasing, she said—Eugenie replied that it could not be done. A very great uneasiness came over Eugenie when she thought about Mexico.

Knowing what his government in Paris most wished to hear, and being human, Bazaine permitted himself to sound optimistic when he wrote of his military operations. At the same time Carlota was writing letters on "Mexican nothingness"— "It is made of granite, it is more powerful than the spirit of man, and God alone can bend it. It was less hard to erect the pyramids of Egypt than to vanquish Mexican nothingness." Could not the French send out more troops? "It is now a question of making a last effort which shall crown the work. . . .

France will applaud you, for France has always been true to success, magnanimity and glory."

Glory, yes, but in Paris they had counted upon the accession of the Mexican rulers to bring a flow of money west to east and it was not working out that way. Month after month expenses mounted in keeping an army of forty thousand Frenchmen and unnumbered Mexican allies pounding across the vast country in pursuit of a foe which could never be brought to bay. The questions in the French Legislative Body became more brutal, and Napoleon's Ministers, most of whom had always been skeptical of the expedition, used every stratagem known to accounting to conceal the actual expenditures, masking them in the budgets of departments which had nothing to do with Mexico.

In Cuernavaca Maximilian went ahead with his rejuvenation of the gardens of Joseph Borda's former home. Carlota hated it, the discussions over decorations and flowers. Often he was there without her. The Emperor's bedroom opened upon a section of the garden and a sentry stood by, but the guard faced in a direction that made it difficult for him to see and identify those visitors who entered. They were ladies of his Court, and the wives of Mexican officials and, more regularly than the others, the wife of the chief gardener. Carlota knew. Her husband's secretary, José Luis Blasio, The Child, noticed how a sadness came into her face when gallant flirtations by various people were delicately mentioned. Away from her presence the Emperor was indiscreet in his conversations, mentioning various women of the Court to his aides and saying he could see the ardor in their eyes—"They ought to be formidable women to love." He always had an eye open for good-looking women and was choosy, saying of one officer's wife that he didn't see how anyone could marry such a mummy made of nothing but bones and parchment.

Yet Maximilian's relations with his own wife were strange. For her bed companion was, literally, the book containing the codified laws of Mexico. Her husband was never with her. On their mutual trips to outlying districts they were as a matter of course offered a room with a double bed. They did not share it. Maximilian never traveled with his wife without bringing along a little cot. Shown to a bedroom selected for

the Imperial couple, he would offer thanks; but when the host
had retired, the Emperor's servants would find a place where
the cot could be set up. It was impossible to conceal from all
the world that this was so, and a rumor arose—and found its
way into print in a booklet—that he had contracted venereal
disease on his trip to Brazil before taking the throne, and
that it had destroyed the possibility of normal married life
between them. The rumor and booklet could not have told
the truth, but may have come close to it. For the estrangement
had begun before Maximilian went to Brazil. They had lived
in what is called a normal fashion up until he had made a
certain trip from Miramar to Vienna. After that, his valet
Antonio Grill noticed, things were different. Had he, as it
was said of his brother Francis Joseph, infected his wife with
what was called a social disease? And had she, as was said of her
sister-in-law the Empress Elizabeth, turned away forever in
Victorian Era disgust from the physical side of marriage? Or
had Carlota merely thought herself infected? Or, putting aside
the question of infection, had some proof of infidelity struck
at her more than perhaps it would most women?

The booklet enraged the Emperor; on her part the Empress
worked harder at their job. She gave up her horseback riding, for
it was depressing to have to ride behind a French escort in the
streets and suburbs of her own capital, and for relaxation she
took to drifting through the soft twilight in a little Indian
canoe in the lake near Chapultepec, alone.

The Europeans who had come to Mexico as escorts returned
home. The Countess Zichy-Metternich went to Paris, and to
Vienna to introduce the captivating Mexican dances. She declared that the country was charming and that she could not
dislike the bandits because they were so picturesque.* Several
of the Europeans had come to Mexico anticipating great riches
from their positions close to the Emperor; these soon took the
diligence to the coast and sailed from Vera Cruz, saying they
had not contracted to live among barbarians. The others began
to squabble among themselves. There were three who rose to
the highest prominence. One was Count Karl Bombelles, the

* Years earlier, in Greece, the Austrian Archduke Ferdinand Maximilian had
felt the same way about Grecian marauders.

Austrian who commanded the Palatine Guards in their rearing-
eagle helmets and flaring thigh boots. His father before him
had spent his life in the employ of the Court of Vienna. The
other two were Sebastian Schertzenlechner and Felix Eloin.
The first had been a lackey in the employ of the Archduke,
but had gradually risen to be his master's private secretary.
The second was a Belgian diplomat recommended for the post
of head of the Imperial civil cabinet by the King of the Belgians. Eloin and Schertzenlechner detested each other. The
French disliked both of them and were joined in this attitude
by most of the members of the Court who, however, found
Eloin more palatable. By early 1865 the two men spent much
of their time slandering one another to the Emperor. On February 20 they lost their tempers before him and, in the eyes of
a listening officer of the Austrian Legion, abused each other
"like pickpockets."

Maximilian sided with the Belgian, Felix Eloin. "Don't tell
lies!" the Emperor snapped at Schertzenlechner, who offered to
resign his position and said he would never again wear his
Order of Guadalupe. The next day he told the French officer
commanding the military units of Mexico City that seven
thousand Indians, displeased at the way he had been treated,
would march on the capital to protest the unjust charges made
against him. Maximilian was told and appointed a commission
led by Bombelles to look into the wild claim. In the end Schertzenlechner went back to Europe, taking his red-haired mistress
along. He was denounced by all at the Court, but he also left
with a pension provided by the Emperor. Eloin became the
most influential of the Imperial advisers, a position he attempted to strengthen by his constant tirades against the
French. Those at Court looked upon the French as villains. If
Paris so wished, they told each other, everything could be made
right. "If I may venture to tell Your Majesty all that I think,"
Carlota wrote Eugenie, "I believe it will be very difficult to
weather these first crises, which affect our very existence, unless
the country is occupied in greater force than at present. . . . It
seems to me that it would be easy to send us some reinforcements from Algeria."

The situation infuriated Napoleon, whose closest associates
now told him to his face that he should never have listened to

his wife. He sent clear instructions to Marshal Bazaine as to what should be said to Maximilian about the course things were taking: "Let him know very well that it is much easier to abandon a government that does nothing to stay alive than it is to support him in spite of himself." There followed a flock of French financial experts with orders to get from the Mexicans, not give to them. Accountants and clerks traveled throughout Mexico to collect taxes and control the customs with the aim of sending money back to Paris. They immediately became embroiled in arguments with officials of the Imperial government. These disagreements were settled by threats backed up by French bayonets. Even so, the drain on the French Treasury went on. Couriers, road repairs, money for spies, the payroll of the Mexican army—there was no end to the expenses. Even a genius could do nothing about the situation they found themselves in, Major Loizillon wrote home.

The French became unpleasant. Mexican officers disliked going about the streets of Mexico City because of the likelihood of insults being thrown at them by enlisted personnel of the French army. On a different level Marshal Bazaine's relations with the monarchs grew ever more frigid. They found Bazaine slow and unwilling to do anything; the French marshal spoke of Maximilian as "the German dreamer."

The Imperial couple's own officials and soldiers were fortunate to receive 20 percent of their salaries each month, and so no Mexican wanted to take an Imperial position. The Emperor had to make it a penal offense to refuse appointments to minor jobs. The army conditions were such that when an English traveler saw a contingent of Marquez's lancers he refused to believe that such slovenly specimens could make a pretense of belonging to any army of the world. Rarely paid, the soldiers doubled as brigands vying for plunder with the bandits and Liberals they were supposed to be putting down. Their officers could not trust them, and at large-scale operations French Zouaves had to be brought in to make sure the men obeyed orders. Looking at the Emperor's Mexican soldiers the Belgian officer Modeste Loiseau reflected that as they lacked the slightest love of country, one could not expect too much of them, and so they had to be permitted their women, the "vultures" and "harpies" who stripped dead or wounded men of their belongings. Forced conscription was brought back as Maximilian reluctantly came to see that otherwise he would have no army at all.

At the same time the Emperor who had once been a sailor Prince busied himself with his program for a magnificent navy. He drew up elaborate plans, designed insignia and appointed a future commander for a fleet which consisted of exactly three small coastal vessels. That he thought in terms of admirals and flotillas amused the jokesters who floated a great fleet of paper boats down the open gutter before the home of the commander-designate.

As Maximilian toyed with his plans for a future world navy, reality crushed his National Theater. For months his director, the poet José Zorrilla, had advanced funds to put together a repertory company which would elevate the theater in Mexico. He had hoped to make it something people would want to be associated with. It hurt Zorrilla to think that people would know the Emperor was doing nothing for the theater, so he told nobody that the money was his own. When one of the actresses suffered the loss of her mother, Zorrilla paid for the funeral himself, saying the Emperor wanted his theater people to be taken care of. Somehow the Emperor found out and asked Zorrilla about the matter. The director told him that he had done it because the girl was a part of the National Theater and the mother of such should have a Christian funeral. "These things are no longer done, except by poets," the Emperor said, and authorized a small sum for the theater. Zorrilla was touched, but the National Theater was becoming a farce, and people made fun of it. Nothing could be done. There was no money. Zorrilla resigned as director and as Imperial Reader also.

Zorrilla was not the only official to go. General Leonardo Marquez affronted the concept of a liberal and humane Empire. It was made clear to the Emperor by a dozen people who might have rallied to him that the Tiger of Tacubaya was a horrendous liability, but the Emperor could not force himself to discharge the general out of hand. Instead he contrived a mission for Marquez; that he should go to Jerusalem to study the Chapel of the Holy Sepulchre with a view to reproducing it in Mexico. Marquez sailed for Europe with the former President, Miguel Miramon, who had returned from exile, unasked, to serve the Mexican Empire. Miramon was ultra-Conservative. It was he who had made the disastrous agreement by which Jecker and Napoleon's half-brother de Morny were now pressing for redemption of the fifteen million dollars in bonds given by Miramon in exchange for seven hundred fifty thousand in cash. Miramon was an embarrassment. The Emperor sent him off to Berlin to study Prussian artillery tactics.

The Emperor and Empress, thousands of miles from home, drifted along; and to the north the Union army came to Appomattox. Five days after Lee's surrender, Booth shot Lincoln. President Andrew Johnson was an unknown quantity in Mexico as in Europe, but perhaps there was hope he might reverse Lincoln's policy of nonrecognition. Maximilian wrote to him.

"Far be it from me to give way to petty considerations when my duties as a ruler are involved, and not for a moment do I hesitate to take the first steps toward the restoration of the friendly relations that formerly existed between the United States and Mexico. . . . The state which I am erecting is not intended to be an Empire on the European model, but a state of freedom and progress and the home of the most liberal institutions. . . . Hoping, President, that our correspondence will not end with this letter and that I shall, in the very near future, have an opportunity to confer with you, in writing or orally . . ."

President Johnson refused to accept the letter. Like Lincoln he was from a modest background; like Lincoln he saw the American continent as the harborer of a way of life in which one rose by one's own merits. There was no room there for an aristocracy based on birth, no home there for a monarchism founded upon the European past. Johnson invited Señora Juarez, in exile in New York, to call upon him in Washington. She went wearing the dress her husband had bought her on the day he put her on the road north before he went off to Paso del Norte. Johnson had kept the Secretary of State he inherited from Lincoln, William Henry Seward. For years Seward had been writing notes to France complaining about the transgression of the Monroe Doctrine. Now he was in position to deploy an experienced army of hundreds of thousands of battle-tested men.

Even before the collapse of the South, the Confederate Vice-President, Alexander Stephens, let it be known to Lincoln, an old friend from their days in the prewar Congress, that perhaps the way to unify the two warring parties was to mount a joint expedition against the French in Mexico and the Emperor the French supported. The Confederate President, Jefferson Davis, a veteran of the Mexican War of the 1840's and a former U. S. Secretary of War, was mentioned as the prospective commander. The project foundered on the Confederate insistence that they be rated as equal partners with the Union. Lincoln thought of nothing but the unification of his country, and refused any cooperation with the separatist Confederacy.

But with Lincoln's death and the end of the war, the leadership of the victorious Union army recalled Stephens's offer and agreed among themselves to do something about Mexico. Ulysses Grant indicated he thought it as important to displace the French as it had been to crush the Confederacy, and sent Philip Sheridan to the Texas border with orders to give U. S. army rifles to Juarez for distribution to the Juarista bands. Sheridan was instructed to do so covertly, but he went beyond his formal orders and made clear the fact that it was his hope to lead an army to Mexico City. In Washington, General John Schofield hoped to obtain the command. He was a fire-breather. Seward dampened Schofield's request for an immediate crossing of the frontier with two hundred thousand Union and Confederate veterans, and sent him instead to Paris. "I want you," Seward said, "to get your legs under Napoleon's mahogany and tell him to get out of Mexico." General Schofield went to France. From that moment the dangerous Sheridan maneuvering along the Texas border with his fifty-thousand-man "Army of Observation" was seen in Paris as a sword of Damocles hanging over France's head. In Mexico City, Marshal Bazaine quailed at the idea of having to fight the United States; in France a panic seized those who realized what war with America would mean.

The Empress of Mexico's active intelligence found in the collapse of the Confederacy a wonderful opportunity to obtain desirable immigrants for Mexico. The South had been a civilization unto itself. Now it was ended but there remained former warriors who saw themselves as "Chivalrics," those who kept to the old southern ways and who saw themselves as the heirs of those medieval knights and their ladies found in the books of Sir Walter Scott. Such a man was Matthew Fontaine Maury, the founder of the science of oceanography and the world authority on ocean charts and currents. His was perhaps the most brilliant scientific mind ever at the disposal of the United States Navy, which he had left to serve the Confederacy. During his U. S. Navy days Maury had corresponded with Admiral the Archduke Maximilian, who arranged for him to receive a medal from Francis Joseph and who sent him detailed accounts of the currents in the European waters which were the maneuver grounds for the Austrian fleet.

Now Jefferson Davis was manacled to a casement at Fortress Monroe, and Maury—whose invention of the electric torpedo had lost the Union more ships than any other cause—wondered if he would suffer a similar fate if he fell into Union hands. He asked Maximilian's permission to organize an immigration to Mexico of former Confederates. Such a movement of talented and capable people, Maury said, would be comparable to the flight of the Huguenots from France in the seventeenth century. He saw himself as another Joseph of Egypt.

Maximilian sent word that Maury was welcome to come and discuss the matter. Maury arrived and submitted a plan by which liberty of worship would be guaranteed to the largely Protestant former Confederates, plus free land for settlement. He found Maximilian gracious and the Empress an impressive personality as she discussed land offices, salaries, the appointment of agents to sign up immigrants in the South. "She is very clever, practical and businesslike," Maury wrote his wife. He was quickly made to grow accustomed to the usual somnolence of Imperial officials and he told the Empress that she could do more business in a day than all the Ministers put together could do in a week. "I believe I could," she replied.

As the result of their conversations Maury received the title of Imperial Commissioner of Immigration. Over his signature tens of thousands of fliers were distributed throughout the South. "Ho for Mexico!" The leaflets promised the former Confederates they would find free land and fortunes.

General Jubal Early, one of the premier Confederate generals, joined Maury in Mexico. So did General Edmund Kirby-Smith, former Confederate commander of the Trans-Mississippi Department, which embraced an area larger than France; General John Magruder, who commanded in the Peninsular Campaign before Richmond; and the former governors of Louisiana and Missouri. The Chivalrics came by boat from New Orleans or across northern Mexico with its organ cacti and prickly pear, wilderness plains and upland sheep pastures. All of them ended in the ornate velvet-covered chairs of the lobby of what had been the Emperor Iturbide's palace, but which had become the Iturbide Hotel. There they dreamed away the hot afternoons talking of the old days. With money contributed by the Imperial government the Chivalrics started an English-language newspaper filled with reminiscences of the battles of The Lost Cause.

Maximilian saw himself as giving succor to political exiles and had the former Confederates in for teas, musicals and receptions. Their courtly ways appealed to him and he particularly admired the handsome General John Magruder, who wore a cutaway suit of salt and pepper, a tall dove-colored hat and patent-leather boots. Magruder told his fellow southerners to wear similar attire if they wished to catch the attention of the Emperor. Soon there was a coterie of similarly dressed gentlemen in the capital, joined by Maximilian now blossomed out in the fashion dictated by Magruder.

The immigration matter was largely in the hands of the Empress, but her husband made double use of Maury, appointing him director of what Maximilian decided to call the Imperial Astronomical Observatory. The proposed observatory took up a good deal of the Emperor's time, and he made elaborate plans for observation points throughout Mexico. They would coordinate their work with the Mexican Society of Geography and Statistics, whose creation he also announced. Both would work with the Imperial Mexican Academy of Sciences.

After a time the former Confederates went off to a five-hundred-thousand-acre tract near Cordoba consisting of lands originally taken from the Church by Juarez. There they set up the Carlota Colony. They planted cotton, sugar cane and coffee, plowing with their old cavalry horses. The Confederate Hotel in Cordoba was their social center, where they held cotillions, gambled and drank juleps at the bar tended by a former mess boy who had served Stonewall Jackson. The farming did not go well. Liberals and bandits fired at them as they worked in the fields. Maury and the Empress planned colonies in half a dozen localities, and their agents in the American South continued to speak of New Virginia, but the whole idea irritated Washington. Suppose someday the Confederate exiles came back in force with a Mexican army at their side? Immigration from New Orleans was ordered stopped, and Sheridan's patrols made crossing the Rio Grande a hazardous matter. The flow of immigrants began to dry up and, foreigners far from home, their money gone, the Confederates in Mexico grew lonely. They had not thought it would turn out in quite this fashion.

Maximilian was thirty-three and Carlota twenty-five. They had been married nearly ten years and it was certain now that she would remain childless. But an Empire needs an Heir. In an offhand way, hardly even informing the Empress beforehand, Maximilian took the grandson of the executed Emperor Iturbide under his wing. The boy was two years old, named Augustin for his grandfather. His mother was an American and hesitant about separating herself from him, but the rest of Iturbide's family convinced her to give him up. They were all accorded the style of Imperial Highness and given generous allowances, along with the hope that the boy would succeed Maximilian as ruler. The child as Crown Prince and Heir Apparent would solidify his position, Maximilian said. But in a Latin nation where to have many children was a sign of manliness there were those who mocked an Emperor whose wife was barren. And it went against *machismo* to see a woman so active in the running of the government.

Essentially it was Carlota who was now the Empire. Her husband spent his time in reworking laws to eliminate poverty, encourage cultural activities and make Mexico Paradise. But when the day-to-day financial or military problems were presented to him he sighed and retreated to the writing of such bulletins as the one on how Independence Day should be celebrated—and made the French snort by referring to their participation in the events as one reserved for "the Auxiliary Army." The Empress could work away at her desk for hours, but the Emperor drifted from his to walk Chapultepec's terraces and admire the flowing streams of roses and poinsettia. When he returned to his labors he was likely to push away such reports as the one dealing with the Imperial army commander whose hundreds of men ran away from an enemy band leaving the commander and only four others to offer battle. (The commander hanged himself, saying he was the only one to do his duty.) Maximilian preferred to outline a course of studies for the country's children emphasizing the importance of classical languages and philosophy, and he worked on his plans for the National Museum, petitioning the keeper of the Imperial Collection in Vienna for return of certain objects which, originally the property of the Aztec rulers, had found their way to Austria. He became interested in the pearl fisheries of Lower California and found money to contribute to their development, asking in return only that he and Carlota be provided with fine pearls which they could give as presents.

That there were cracks in his Empire did not appear to touch him. "Only one person is calm, the Emperor," Major Loizillon wrote home. Maximilian retained the little vanities which made one observer class him as half-gentleman and half-dandy; every morning he had in a barber to divide his hair from the middle of the neck upward in order to hide the growing bald spot, and he allocated generous amounts of time for the grooming of his flowing beard. He installed a hydrotherapeutic bath in his room, and often went to bathing establishments in the city.

Sometimes in the romantic tradition of the Prince who goes incognito among his people the Emperor went out with only an aide-de-camp. Someone told him that the bakers of the city frequently enslaved impoverished Indians, and so one night he appeared before the closed shutters of a shop in whose basement men were chained to the ovens. The proprietor refused to open the door and shouted out curses. Maximilian smiled and sent for guards who opened the door to reveal a hellish place filled with vile fumes. He ordered the Indians freed at once and went home to write an edict forbidding such practices. One more edict to be ignored.

The ruler of Mexico went to a jail and was shocked at the sight of the half-dressed and starving prisoners. He ordered an immediate investigation of their conditions and an expansion of the prison so that they would be more comfortable. When he left he emptied his purse into the hands of one of the shabbiest of the men. Perhaps it helped the one prisoner—if the others did not murder him for the money—but there was no follow-up. The condition of the prisons, the one he visited and the others he did not, remained unchanged.

While the Empress read reports, seated at a table covered with political, social, economic and administrative treatises, the Emperor went about in the Mexican fashion with his big sombrero, red vest and pantaloons with buttons up the side, always affable and approachable. He liked making his visits and taking his tours of inspection, and sent word to the remote province of Yucatan that he intended to meet his subjects there. But by late 1865 when it came time to make the trip, his enthusiasm had waned. His health was not good. He suffered steadily from what the former Confederates called "the Aztec curse," dysentery, and the journey would be extremely long and tiring. The Empress volunteered to go in his stead.

All around them were signs of a military situation that was far from stabilized, but word came from the north that Juarez had fled the country. The report was untrue. Advised by the Republic's governor of the state of Chihuahua to flee to the United States, Juarez had said: "Don Luis, no one knows this state better than you. Show me the highest, most inaccessible, and driest mountain, and I will go to the top of it and die there of hunger and thirst, wrapped in the flag of the Republic, but without leaving the national territory. That never!" Upon occasion the President of the Republic escorted members of his little suite to the southern side of the Rio Grande to see them off for festivities offered by Sheridan's officers at Fort Bliss. But he never went with them. Instead, Juarez remained in the village of Paso del Norte, just south of the United States border, where, amidst the naked hillsides hemming in the goat herds and the droning buzz of the insects attending them, he sat as the President of the Republic. There he was alone except for a handful of the faithful, still in his black broadcloth coat, white linen vest, white gloves and polished boots.

But Maximilian believed he had gone, and so, bestirring himself to display a sudden fitful energy, he promulgated what was called the Black Decree. On October 3, 1865, the Imperial government announced that as Juarez had left the country the political basis for the various bands was ended, and they were now simple criminals outside the bounds of civilized warfare. Anyone taken with arms would be executed. There would be no appeals. Once, a year and a half earlier, in the first days in Mexico, the Emperor had said there was no question of granting pardon to those who carried arms against him—for they were not criminals, they only misunderstood the situation. That was when the French looked upon him as the son of the Duke of Reichstadt—they all thought him so—and as such the grandson of the Great Emperor and therefore a ruler who would set things right. Time had proved him otherwise. Now at their urging, reproached with their charges that he was weak—"poor ghost of a sovereign," Loizillon wrote home—he signed the decree which would show them he was strong.

From that moment on the French and the Imperial armies were implacably murderous in a different guise than before, for what they did was done now in the name of the Emperor. In each of the roaming irregular cavalry bands of the Republic— the Chinakos, they called themselves, the Poor Ones—there was carried now, so it was said, a thin gold cord. It would fit the neck of an Imperial Majesty.

In late 1865 the Empress went to Yucatan to give thousands of pesos from her private fortune to schools, hospitals, the poor, for work on cathedrals. She went to cotton-spinning factories and farms, dressing simply in a little bonnet and wearing no jewels, asking questions and taking notes. She was there for two months—while her husband and the gardener's wife were together almost constantly in Cuernavaca. During Maximilian's absence from his work, his officials, following the Emperor's lead, idled or played their time away. Out in the deserts and mountains the French continued on their endless patrols, men and pack mules falling into ravines as the troops went up the narrow trails—the bodies were shredded by the rocks as they fell—and finding towns supposedly conquered blossoming with new resistance a week later. "We scuff our feet around and end up by doing nothing," Loizillon wrote to his family in France, adding that he and his men longed for home. It had been, he said, long enough.

The Empress came back from Yucatan on January 6, 1866, Mexico's Day of the Three Kings. Her husband came to her in tears to say her father was dead. She had loved and admired King Leopold, and her reaction to his death was strange. She permitted herself to show no emotion, saying it was "her duty" to stifle her feelings. Six weeks later a mission came from the new King of the Belgians, her brother Leopold II, to give them the official announcement of the death and of the accession to the throne.

It was of the utmost importance that the members of the mission return with a happy impression of Mexico. What they said would be listened to. Nothing was spared to make them believe Mexico City was another Paris. The night before their early-morning departure for Vera Cruz they were the guests of honor at a ball where to the music of an Austrian band they waltzed with the capital's ladies and played baccarat with the gentlemen. The Austrian Baron von Malortie, an aide-de-camp to the commander of the Austrian Legion serving the Emperor, always remembered the beauty of the scene, the Emperor's officers, "sons of Mars" in dress uniform, the iced champagne, the mass procession at five in the morning to the Hotel Iturbide where a twenty-mule carriage waited to take the Belgian mission away.

There was no escort. It was a calculated risk. To send a powerful body of soldiers along would indicate that perhaps the Empire was not as peaceful as the Belgians had been told. One Mexican officer sat on the seat by the driver.

That afternoon, as Baron von Malortie rode through the massed landaus, victorias and phaetons of the Mexican women who came to the Alameda each afternoon, he received word that the Belgians had been attacked in the pass of the Rio Frio, one day's ride from the capital. A telegram had just been received. Malortie ordered out a squadron of the Austrian Legion's Hungarian Hussars and rode with them toward the pass. Before they got there they saw a group of galloping horsemen. It was the Emperor, Count Bombelles and two other officers. They escorted the Emperor into the pass, joined also by fifty Chasseurs d'Afrique, their white mantles floating behind them in the moonlight. At the pass they found wounded men and the dead body of the young Baron d'Huart, an aide-de-camp and special favorite of the Empress's brother, the Count of Flanders. The Belgians had fought with their revolvers when a band swooped down upon them. The Mexican officer had hidden under the driver's seat of the coach.

Maximilian stood for a long while before the young Baron's body, which lay in a small chapel by the road. The effect on European opinion would be horrible. That night, back in the capital, the Empress talked with Malortie. "And where are the guilty?" she asked. He replied that it was a political outrage —there had been no attempt at robbery. "No doubt," she said. "I fear the guilty one is standing behind me." Malortie looked and saw the figure of the marshal of France. Tears were in the Empress's eyes, but she turned around and at dinner showed no emotion. Malortie thought of Marie Antoinette smiling at the men taking her throne away from her.

In the Hofburg the Emperor's family must have received the news with incredulity, for in every letter home Maximilian tried to show them that he had done the right thing in going to Mexico. He did not write to Francis Joseph. In fact he had sent to all the Courts of Europe a statement saying his brother had despoiled him of his rights by making him sign the abrogation of all his rights as an Archduke. But he kept up a steady correspondence with his brother Karl Ludwig and his mother. It was all working, he wrote. Mexico was a wonder, he was a success and happy to be free from "old Europe," straitlaced, tired and restrictive as opposed to the "fresh, free life" of the New World. "I am able to do something for the good of my fellowmen, and often receive tokens of true gratitude, a consolation which I never knew in old Europe. I love strenuous work, but I want to know that it is recognized, I want to see results, and all this is lacking on your side of the ocean, whereas I find it here to an increasing extent. My last tour and the celebration of our national festival were a great comfort to me in this respect. . . . This is better than to molder in inactivity in old Europe."

What Maximilian wrote in his letters home found a reflection in what he said in his speeches to his people. "My heart, my soul, my work, and all my faithful endeavors belong to you and to our beloved country. No power on earth shall turn me aside from the accomplishment of my task; henceforth every drop of my blood is Mexican, and if God permits new dangers to menace our beloved country, you shall see me fight side by side with you for your independence and integrity. I may die, but I shall fall at the feet of our glorious flag, for no human power could avail to force me to leave the place to which your trust has summoned me."

But sometimes it came to him that the situation was becoming desperate. One evening he sat with his aides and officers, chatting and gossiping as he loved to do, and the talk turned to Italy. He spoke of the country with vivacity and longing. His eyes sparkled. He moved his graceful hands as he spoke of the beauties of the lakes and mountains, the charm of the Italian countryside. Then suddenly those hands came up to cover his face, and as his people watched in silence, they heard from behind his palms a long, hoarse groan.

Far to the North, Juarez received from his son-in-law in the United States an equivocal letter indicating that all was not well with the President's favorite son. Juarez understood and wrote back, "Really my little Pepe is no longer alive, no longer alive, isn't that so?" The son-in-law's next letter was edged in black. Juarez went to a fifty-ninth-birthday banquet offered him by a few people and arose to propose a toast.

"I drink to the independence of the nation, Citizens. That on invoking that sacred name everything may yield to the Fatherland. That we may make it triumph or perish. That the sentiments of independence may be the bond of all Mexicans." The people applauded his slow, deliberate words. "I repeat that as men we are nothing, that principles are everything. That, greater than all despots and their power and their armies, our cause will soon triumph."

"*Viva Juarez!*" they shouted.

The health of his family was proposed. He got up, his voice suddenly turning ragged, and said, "I see the country here and I say to it solemnly that my sacrifice is nothing, that the sacrifice of my family would be much, would be infinite for me; but if need be, so be it." The short, square figure sank down into the chair.

15

WHEN FRENCH OFFICERS home on rotation or convalescent leave were received by the Emperor Napoleon, they found him uninterested in their adventures in Mexico. They went prepared with extensive reports, but he asked only a few vague questions. How did they deal with the fierce rays of the Mexican sun? They attached handkerchiefs to the backs of their kepis. And the health of Their Mexican Majesties? It seemed good. The Empress Eugenie appeared. The weather was so fine. Would her husband wish to walk with her in the garden? The veterans were dismissed with thanks.

It had only been four years but half a lifetime seemed to have passed since Admiral Jurien de la Gravière had first gone to Vera Cruz. The French public had long ago written off the expedition as a failure. It was in their memory that it had taken the Great Emperor less time to conquer all Europe. Napoleon studied the reports of his police spies, and they uniformly said the people wanted to get out of Mexico. His advisers, the Legislative Body, his War and Finance Ministers, the relatives of soldiers in Mexico—they all urged evacuation. Even the Empress Eugenie was beginning to understand the cause was lost. She cried when people talked about withdrawal, but she offered no objections.

Yet the Emperor did not want to throw in his hand. His uncle had closed accounts in Egypt with his army shattered by battle and disease, and, leaving orders to poison the hopelessly ill, he had taken ship for France to explain away the disaster; he had left the remnants of the Grand Army staggering home from Moscow and rushed home to recoup his fortunes with hardly a backward glance. But Napoleon III was not Napoleon I. Softer, less precipitate, he inched toward the final decision to give up Mexico. Through his Foreign Minister he asked the United States one last time to recognize Maximilian's Empire. France had come to the rescue of the Americans with Lafayette and Rochambeau during the American Revolution; could not France similarly be permitted to help Mexico in this fashion? The answer was no. Europe had stealthily attempted to come back to the American continent while the United States was racked with civil war. Now the war was over. Europe must go home with its Imperial Highnesses. If necessary, the Union army would send them home. Napoleon's thoughts turned to Austria. Perhaps Austria would step in when France had left off. A shipment of four thousand men was said to be about to embark from Trieste to go to the aid of their hard-pressed former Archduke; Napoleon permitted himself to believe that the Americans would not object. He was wrong. The figure was found to be two thousand, but it was still too much for Secretary of State Seward. He instructed his Minister to Vienna, John Lothrop Motley, to inform the Hofburg that if the volunteers sailed the United States would consider Austria at war with the Republic of Mexico—and that its powerful navy would not remain neutral. The would-be Austrian contingent was disbanded.

By early 1866 it was time to call it quits. Napoleon knew it now. He broke the news to Maximilian. "Sir my Brother: It is not without pain that I write to Your Majesty . . ." and he told him that France must go home. "Evacuate as soon as possible," he wrote to Bazaine, "but do everything required of us to see that our work does not fall into ruins the day after we leave." He gave the marshal a year, eighteen months at the very most, and then the troops must be home. Stammering and mumbling, the Emperor of the French went before the Legislative Body to say the troops would come home in three contingents.

Napoleon's letter reached Maximilian in Cuernavaca where he disported with the gardener's wife amid the blue-flowered jacaranda and the larkspurs, where he spent hours watching the darting hummingbirds. He flung back a proud answer:

"Your Majesty believes that sudden pressure makes it impossible for you to observe the solemn treaties which you signed with me less than two years ago, and you inform me of this with a frankness which cannot but do you honor.

"I am too much your friend to wish to be a cause of peril to Your Majesty or your dynasty, either directly or indirectly. I therefore propose to you with a cordiality equal to your own that you should immediately withdraw your troops from the American continent.

"For my part, guided by my honor, I shall try to make arrangements with my fellow-countrymen in a straightforward manner worthy of a Hapsburg."

Napoleon winced. He ignored the scornful permission to take his leave at once, but in Mexico the French garrisons, spread in a giant circle with Mexico City as the center, began to contract their perimeter. One by one orders went out to the outlying stations. The military bands which played three times a week in the Alameda of every principal town of Mexico packed their instruments, and the infantrymen threw away their excess equipment. Officers who had come out to Mexico with two or three personally owned horses tried to sell them off. Then the soldiers marched out of the towns, headed for Mexico City. Behind them the Juaristas came on, to be met by citizens averring they had always been against the intervention and the Empire, that all cooperative acts had been forced by fear of bayonets. Everywhere printed pronunciamentos went up on the peeling whitewash of the plastered adobe walls: "Death to Maximilian." "*Viva la República.*" "*Viva la Libertad.*"

As they slowly converged on Mexico City the French withdrew from the fighting. If attacked, they returned fire, but they did not intervene when units of the Imperial army or the Belgian or Austrian Legions ran into trouble. Near San Luis Potosi a group of Austrians came under Liberal fire. The commander of a passing French column refused requests for aid, saying to his men, "Soldiers, eat your breakfast. I have my orders; you must not touch those men." The Austrians were decimated as the French looked the other way.

Porfirio Diaz advanced from the south, gaining new adherents with each step he took on his way back to the central highlands on which stood the City of Mexico. The bishop of Oaxaca sent a messenger to ask what guarantees of safety he might expect from Diaz when the French left and the Liberals took over. The bishop had been an ardent interventionist. Porfirio sent word that he would have him shot in his golden robe. That would lend éclat to the procedure. The bishop fled. As Diaz moved north, Juarez left Paso del Norte to go due south to Chihuahua and from there south again to Durango.

The net was tightening. In America former Secretary of the Navy Bancroft, speaking at a memorial meeting on Lincoln's birthday, referred to Maximilian as an "Austrian adventurer." The Austrian Minister, Baron Wydenbruck, was in the audience. He felt himself turning hot and cold. He wondered if he ought to walk out. But his orders from Vienna were to remain neutral in all things regarding Francis Joseph's brother, so he stayed seated as Bancroft used the word *adventurer* several more times. When Wydenbruck complained to Seward he was told the Secretary of State saw nothing wrong with Bancroft's phraseology.

Maximilian in his letters let nothing touch him; everything was going well. "Life on this continent is much pleasanter," he wrote his friend the Count Hadik in Vienna; "it is free and untrammeled. One does not find here the old stuff and rubbish of a weak and senile Europe. . . . You would be surprised to see how the Empress and I have become regular Mexicans, and live at ease among this people. I find it quite natural that the European newspapers cannot understand it, for they have no standard to judge by; we children of the New World care not a rap about them; we cry *'adelante!'* [onward!] and cast a backward glance at old, narrow-minded, outworn Europe. . . . If you were to see your old friend the emigrant, my good Hadik, you would laugh; your Archduke stronger and more able-bodied than before . . . working from ten to twelve hours a day, now at the Ministerial Council, now at the Council of State, now at army organization, now at ecclesiastical meetings, taking the chair in the most flowing and elegant Spanish, occupied for the rest of the time with audiences, or rushing off on wild horses like a regular *ranchero;* the mistress of the house fresh, gay, faithful and loyal, sharing all her husband's toils and dangers."

It was all sham, of course, particularly his words about Carlota. There was nothing between them now. As the political and military situations worsened by the moment, he developed a sudden willful, almost childish, insistence that all affairs of state be placed in his hands. No one must interfere. Maximilian saw his wife as a threat to his authority, and he took to gesturing her out of the room in lordly manner when he held conferences with the officials or soldiers. The Emperor and Empress met only at mealtimes, and when she sought him out in his quarters she had almost to solicit audiences. He received her, thought the courtier Adrian Marx, in exactly the same fashion as he received the rest of the world. But nothing more.

Carlota's father was dead and her grandmother, the former Queen Marie Amelie, followed shortly afterward. At twenty-six her roots were gone. She had nothing left but her husband and their work together—there would never be children. Their life together had begun to disintegrate even during Miramar days; and now in the collapsing situation which surrounded them, her husband closed her out and slipped away into the arms of the girl in Cuernavaca, the gardener's wife. And with that betrayal came his insistence that he conduct the Empire alone. The Empress had been, reflected the French officer Charles Blanchot, a reader, a chartist, a doer; but now suddenly she seemed caught in long, melancholy reveries. In the early days Carlota had gone to hear the singer Concha Mendez— normally she did not care for the theater, saying that after half an hour she had to pinch herself so as not to fall asleep—and had loved the singer's rendition of "La Paloma." She sent Señorita Mendez a bracelet, had her in for musicals and often went about humming the tune herself. But in early 1866 her humming entirely ceased, to be replaced by a perpetual set-lips appearance. Often she stuck a handkerchief between her lips and tore at it. She did so more and more. One could not help but notice.

The Empress's ladies-in-waiting, with the best will in the world, were of little help. Kindly, gracious, polite, in awe of her, they were totally uneducated, as Latin American women were. They knew Paris as the home of their dress designs and Rome as the seat of their religion, but nothing else of Europe. They had experienced difficulty in understanding what the word *Austria* meant and did not comprehend that in Vienna the people did not speak French. They did not read and so could not reach out to her intellectually, and her rank did not permit emotional intimacy with them. She was alone. Her husband drank more and more heavily. He took twenty glasses of champagne a day and constant sips of wine; "Very healthy effect in this climate, where the human organism has need of tonics," he said. Sometimes he simply failed to appear at luncheons or dinners where numerous guests were invited. At the head of the elaborately decorated table, looking down at the elegant meal—the tone of the Court must be preserved—Carlota tended, as time went by, to sit in a deeper and deeper dull and brooding silence. "Like a funeral," thought the French officer Charles Mismer after such a meal.

Her husband's demeanor and dress grew increasingly sloppy. The Emperor would receive visitors while wearing what Adrian Marx thought were flashy, vulgar bedroom slippers and badly done coats. His four dogs would sit growling and yapping in the corners of the exquisitely decorated rooms of Chapultepec and the National Palace. But Carlota did not seem to notice as she withdrew more and more into herself. When she spoke at all to the people around her, it was of banalities utterly un-revealing of anything important. Her husband worked inter-mittently upon the dictionary of the ancient nobility of Europe which he had begun in idle moments while coming over on the *Novara*, and he put her ladies-in-waiting to chasing rare butter-fly specimens and searching for different types of mushrooms. Carlota hated his procrastination and the gossip about him, and the lengthy drafting of the meaningless laws and regulations concerning Orders and ceremonies. But there was nothing she could do. Her handkerchiefs were ripped through within an hour or two after she put one in her sleeve or her pocket.

On July 6, 1866, Maximilian's thirty-fourth birthday, a Te Deum was sung for him at the Cathedral of Mexico City. He did not attend; Carlota did. For a long time she knelt on the floor of the church with her head in her hands. At last, when those around her were wondering what to do, she arose and said to the people, "It is agreeable to me to receive your wishes in the name of the prince who has consecrated his entire exis-tence to you and to assure you that his life and mine have no other goal but your happiness." By then all of official Mexico knew that the girl from Cuernavaca was pregnant by Carlota's husband.

For hundreds of years Germany had been a welter of petty princedoms, duchies, city-states and two major powers, Austria and Prussia. In 1864 the two cooperated in a short campaign against a hopelessly outgunned Denmark, but the world knew that one of them had to be the chief German power. In the summer of 1866 Francis Joseph of Austria and William of Prussia went to war to dispute the leadership of the German world.

As soon as the declarations of war were handed down from Vienna and Berlin, United Italy entered the field against Austria. Count Cavour was dead, but Victor Emmanuel's government saw the possibility of expanding its territory at the expense of Austria. The prospects for Austria under any circumstances against Prussia were not good, but to fight a two-front war was entirely beyond her abilities. The fleet planned and constructed by the Archduke now Emperor of Mexico was ordered to sea in Italian waters. At the same time the bulk of Austria's land forces advanced into the mountains of Bohemia as Prussia's army came south to meet them.

On July 3, 1866, Prussian Uhlans cantered to the Bistritz River and came under Austrian artillery fire. The Austrian commander was Ludwig August von Benedek, who had done well against the French and Sardinian forces at Solferino in 1859's Italian battles. He had not wanted this command, saying he did not know the Bohemian terrain, but Francis Joseph had insisted he take it. His opponent was Helmuth von Moltke, who, looking more like a scientist or mathematician than a soldier, was perhaps the most brilliant officer in German history. He rivaled in his genius King William's Chancellor, Bismarck. Together the three sat their horses and looked on as the forces clashed at the village of Sadowa.

The Prussian plan depended upon the superiority of their breech-loading rifle, the "needle gun," and on the arrival of additional forces scheduled to come up at a crucial moment determined long before by von Moltke. The needle gun was frightfully effective against the Whitecoats, but the Prussian reserves appeared to be late. It rained all that day, as it had the previous night, and transport was difficult. But in time the artfully delayed punch of the Prussians landed as the reserves came on. Their uniformly gray-green tunics and trousers went through a celebrated fog to take the Heights of Chlum, a vital position. Looking on through a telescope, Moltke saw the artillery of the Austrian right wing was preparing to move back. All day he had been using a red handkerchief; now he put it away with a flourish and moved his horse next to King William and said, "The campaign is decided."

A nervous William looked at him with annoyance and said he did not know what Moltke was talking about. Better, he added, that they should keep their minds on what was happening and not speak of the future. "No," Moltke said. "The success is complete. Vienna lies at Your Majesty's feet." He was correct. That night the broken Austrians staggered back across the River Elbe. Sadowa * in one day had determined that Germany would be unified under Prussian rule.

Paris at first received the news of the battle with rejoicing. It meant Austria was finished as a major power. But within a few hours the feeling of elation vanished. Austria's fall could only be attended by Prussia's rise to the head of a new and fearsome united Germany. On the night following the battle the French Council of State met, the Emperor presiding and the Empress sitting in. Napoleon seemed paralyzed, almost in a torpor. In one day's fighting the world's scheme of things had been entirely upset and France was now the neighbor of a Prussia no longer seen as the home of nearsighted professors and gloomy musicians but as the awesome military machine it had been in the days of Frederick the Great. Napoleon's numbness seemed indicative of an almost complete nervous breakdown.

But the Empress Eugenie was in command of herself. She passionately urged a French military demonstration along the Rhine to exact Prussian guarantees that the numerous armies of the German states would not be merged with that of Prussia, and that France would be given other concessions to insure her future safety. Now was the moment, she cried. Prussia's

---

* The day's occurrences are also known as the Battle of Konniggratz.

army was far away in Bohemia and the road to Berlin was open, if things came to that. It was, she always remembered, a great moment in her life as she carried her feeble husband and the confused Ministers along with her. They agreed to dispatch eighty thousand French troops to the Rhine, summon the Legislative Body into special session so that credits for additional mobilization could be asked, and publish a stern warning to Prussia. It would all be announced in the official paper the next day. The State Council adjourned.

In the night the dazed Emperor reconsidered. France's arsenals were depleted by the Mexican expedition, and France's best troops were tied down there. It was his wife who had done that. Now she was vehemently urging a new adventure along the Rhine. He retracted the orders agreed upon, and sank deeper into apathy.

In Bohemia, King William and his officers happily planned their victory march through Vienna. Bismarck opposed the idea, saying it would be sufficient simply to arrange matters so that Austria was excluded from all future activities involving the German states. Prussia must consolidate its gains and not at the moment seek new conquests. The officers demanded their victory march and further advances, possibly into Hungary; and Bismarck sarcastically suggested they slash on into the Balkans and then to Constantinople. He bent them to his will. The Prussian columns turned and made for home. The moment when France might have intervened had passed, and the road to Berlin was closed.

Five days passed while France and France's ruler absorbed the meaning of what it meant when the Prussian Guards burst through the Fog of Chlum. "It is we who were defeated at Sadowa," was heard everywhere. Napoleon and Eugenie went to St. Cloud to wander the gardens together, he numb and voiceless, she sobbing. He spent much of his time in bed although he could not sleep, and only pulled himself together to practice laboriously with a new Chassepot army rifle while his wife looked on. "Never before have I seen the Emperor to be so completely nothing," said the Austrian ambassador, Prince Richard Metternich. The Empress asked her husband to abdicate in favor of the Prince Imperial, with herself acting as regent. He refused. Meanwhile, at Bismarck's insistence King William kept his entire army of more than one million men in a state of full mobilization.

Entirely befuddled and dull, Napoleon went to Vichy to take the cure in the waters there. His strength only slightly revived. He returned to St. Cloud and took to his bed. That was on August 7. The next day there came a telegram from the port of St. Nazaire. The Empress Carlota of Mexico had arrived in France and wanted to see him immediately.

16

CARLOTA HAD BEEN TO SEE Señora Bazaine the day before she left and had said nothing about going. The Court did not announce her departure in the newspapers. But suddenly she was on the highroad to Vera Cruz with a suite of less than a dozen persons. Her husband accompanied her to the Shrine of the Virgin of Guadalupe and they prayed there together. Then in the dawn of July 9, six days after the Prussians and Austrians met at Sadowa, Maximilian returned to Mexico City and Carlota headed east. She carried with her for expenses thirty thousand dollars taken from the special funds set aside to fight flooding in the capital. It was the last substantial sum the Empire owned.

She was in a frightful hurry, urging speed on her people in a passionate manner, so anxious to get on that occasionally her words stumbled over themselves and drifted almost into incoherency. The party arrived at Puebla. Carlota went to bed, to arise at midnight, insisting that she see an official of the town whom she had met before. She was told he was not in the city but refused to believe it. Torches were lit and she was driven to the man's home. It was entirely dark. Carlota demanded the right to search the house. Keys were found and the doors opened, and she stalked through the empty rooms. Nobody was there. She went back to the private home where she was staying. The next morning she offered no explanation as her group hurried on.

The Empress and her small party rode through the torrential rains of the Mexican summer, one of the carriages overturning in the mud. She excitedly said they were going too slowly; they must leave the carriages, leave the luggage and continue on horseback. She was talked out of it. Near Paso del Macho a band of armed men swooped down, cut the traces of the mule teams and drove the animals off, screaming "Good-bye, Mama Carlota!"—the term which some of the Empire's enemies cruelly used for her. Soaked, the travelers made their way on foot to where the little railroad from Vera Cruz had its terminus. The French sent new animals to drag in the carriages.

In the steaming lowland jungles of the torrid zone the travelers came to a hamlet filled with French troops awaiting embarkation home. They were joyously singing "La Marseillaise," which away from France was always accepted as the country's national anthem but which in Paris indicated impending disorders and, perhaps, the specter of Revolution. The Empress listened. Her face contracted and her eyes became fixed in an intense gaze. Her grandfather King Louis Philippe had fled the Tuileries in a horsecab to the sound of mobs singing that song.

The Empress and her party arrived in Vera Cruz, the port stifling and fever-ridden. They hurried to the docks. The French mail steamer *Empress Eugenie* lay in the bay. Arrangements had been made for the party to board. But when Carlota walked toward the French lighter which would carry them out to the ship she suddenly flew into a rage. She demanded that the lighter lower the French flag and raise in its stead the flag of Mexico. Her position was incomprehensible to the French captain. It went against the grain to lower his country's flag from the mast of one of his country's boats. An impatient foghorn blew from the *Empress Eugenie* and, reluctantly, the Frenchman ordered the Mexican colors raised on the lighter. The party took the boat out to the steamer whose French flag waving at the flagstaff Carlota entirely ignored. As soon as Carlota entered her cabin she sent for the captain of the ship and asked if the pounding of the engines could not be stopped. Mystified, he said this was of course impossible. She insisted that every time the pistons throbbed they resounded in her head "to the point of making me crazy." She ordered him to have mattresses nailed to the walls and floors in an attempt to deaden the noise. It did not work well. For the first time in her life she was violently seasick, and her nerves were on edge for the entire trip. The heat was awful.

The steamer stopped at Havana to take on coal and supplies, and the Spanish warships in the harbor pumped off Imperial salutes, but the Empress of Mexico refused to go ashore. The ship sailed on past the West Indies and into the open sea, the heat and the pounding of the engines continually distracting her. Carlota found it impossible to sleep, and hardly spoke to the members of her entourage when they saw her. Most of the time she remained alone in the cabin with her mattresses nailed about her.

The steamer reached St. Nazaire, signaled Carlota's arrival. The Empress came ashore to find no official reception other than the presence of the mayor of the town, who did not have a Mexican flag to display in her honor. A resident of the town possessed a flag of Peru, and for a moment it had been thought to fly that, but the Prefect, hearing of the plan, advised against it.

The mayor saluted her and began to stutter excuses for the lack of a more seemly demonstration. He pointed out that St. Nazaire was a raw city just recently built—partially to serve as a staging point for French troop and supply shipments to Mexico—and began pointing out new streets and houses to her.

"Mr. Mayor, I thank you," Carlota said. "But how is it that the Prefect is not here to wish us welcome? The troops have not presented arms; therefore the Court of Mexico is going to have to cross your city without escort. I order you to have us immediately conducted to the railroad station. I wish to see the Emperor tomorrow!"

They went to the station and from there Carlota sent a telegram to Napoleon. "I have today arrived at St. Nazaire, charged by the Emperor with the mission of discussing with Your Majesty various matters concerning Mexico. I beg you to assure Her Majesty of my friendship and to believe what a pleasure it will be to me to see Your Majesty again."

The train came to Nantes. A telegram from Napoleon was handed to her. "Your Majesty's wire has just reached us. Since I returned from Vichy quite ill, I am obliged to stay in bed and can therefore not see you. But if, as I assume, Your Majesty will first visit Belgium, I shall find time to recover."

Carlota was horrified. He was putting her off. It was a diplomatic illness, a barely concealed Not At Home. She did not care. She was not going to Brussels but to Paris. Her suite tried to calm her. Surely the next day in Paris there would be Imperial honors, red carpets, troops, a Sovereign's Escort. "Perhaps not," the Empress muttered.

At the Gare Montparnasse no one came to greet her. Carlota and her party went into the street to hail a horsecab. They drove to the Grand Hotel, new and imposing. Weeping, she locked herself in her room. General Waubert de Genlis, Napoleon's chief aide-de-camp, appeared, saying he had expected to greet her at the Gare d'Orléans. He was not subtle—or perhaps he had his orders. He blurted out, "How long does Your Majesty plan to stay in France?"

The Empress replied that she had no family or other interests in Europe that would call her from Paris. Count Cossé-Brissac, who accompanied Waubert de Genlis, asked if it would be agreeable to her, then, if the Empress Eugenie called upon her at two the next afternoon. "Quite agreeable," she said.

Eugenie drove up looking solemn, accompanied by two ladies-in-waiting and two aides-de-camp of her husband. Carlota's chief gentleman-in-waiting and one lady-in-waiting greeted Eugenie at the bottom of the main staircase of the hotel and escorted her up to the first landing where the Empress of Mexico waited. Carlota descended one step to meet her guest. They embraced and kissed as other guests and members of the hotel staff looked on. They sat together and Carlota excitedly began to speak of their troubles in Mexico. They had not been able to send money to France as payments against their debts because Marshal Bazaine's incapacity prevented retention of all the customhouses save those of Vera Cruz; their domain had never been truly secured although France had pledged it would be; and finally, it was impossible that France would now withdraw her troops, for to do so would be to dishonor her flag. Eugenie listened in silence but it seemed, Carlota later wrote Maximilian, as though tears were rising in the French Empress's heart. But after a time Eugenie began to talk of lighter subjects, their ceremonies in Mexico, their entertainments and parties—what were they like? And Chapultepec? Would not Carlota describe it all? The Empress replied in the liveliest way that Mexico was a wonderful country, but then she switched to serious matters again. Eugenie evaded her. Eugenie had grown much older since last they met, Carlota observed to herself. The throne had aged her. And she knew absolutely nothing of Mexico. I know more of China, Carlota thought.

Finally Carlota asked when she could return Eugenie's call.

"The day after tomorrow, if Your Majesty so wishes."

"And the Emperor? Shall I not be able to see him too?"

"Oh, the Emperor is still unwell."

They cannot endure pressure anymore, Carlota thought. "I shall break in," she said.

Eugenie was taken aback, and chose to treat the remark as a jest. But Carlota might come the next day, she said. Eugenie went back to St. Cloud, to learn to her horror that Bismarck had coldly told the French Ambassador to Berlin that if France voiced a single objection to any of the gains which Prussia sought from victory at Sadowa, he would fling his more than one million mobilized and victorious men across the Rhine in the direction of Paris.

On the following day an Imperial Stables carriage came to bring Carlota to the palace at St. Cloud. She wore a black dress imperfectly pressed, and a white hat her lady-in-waiting Señora Manuela del Barrio had bought her that morning in the Faubourg St. Honoré. The hat and dress did not go well together. From the hat's rim hung a mantilla. Carlota's face was very red and her excitement such that for a moment in the carriage Señora del Barrio thought of telling the coachman to return to the hotel. But at the entrance to the palace grounds the Empress pulled herself together and from the carriage bowed gracefully to the Tricolor hanging from the flagpole. The drums of the turned-out guard rattled in her honor.

The carriage came to the entrance. A detachment of the Imperial Guard in First Empire bearskins presented arms as Carlota stepped out to be met by the ten-year-old Prince Imperial wearing his Order of the Mexican Eagle. The boy offered his hand. She took it and he led her up the staircase past a double row of the Cent Gardes standing rigidly at attention. At the head of the staircase stood the Emperor and Empress of the French. Brief ceremonies of welcome were held and the suites were introduced to each other, the French women thinking to themselves that the Mexican ladies were small and ugly. The monarchs adjourned to the study of the Emperor.

"Sire," the Empress of Mexico said, "I have come to save a cause which is your own." She offered the familiar arguments: they had not been given enough money or time, the situation was not as it had been represented, Bazaine was incompetent. But as she spoke she took note of how lost and weak Napoleon seemed, how helpless. Leeches had been applied to him the previous day in an attempt to pull him out of his funk; he was even more pale than usual. Carlota spoke of Napoleon's promises to them when they went out to Mexico, of French honor. Tears came into the Emperor's eyes. He looked beseechingly at Eugenie. Finally he said he could do nothing. It was beyond him to help.

Carlota grew excited, saying it could not be that the ruler of a nation of forty millions, disposing of enormous capital, possessing the highest credit resources of the world, could say something was impossible. She spoke with logic and with flawless command of the facts, and Napoleon listened. But his look was haunted. Fear of what he had done mingled with fear of the more than a million mobilized Prussian soldiers, of the Legislative Body, of the crowds of Paris who had driven other French rulers from their thrones.

Carlota, Eugenie and Napoleon argued for an hour and a half. Eugenie's face and the face of her husband were streaked with tears. Napoleon was in agony. Above all things he hated scenes and to be unkind. He had always been that way. But the Empress of Mexico would not let him be. Introducing new lines and approaches, she refused to let him pronounce the final fatal words that the intervention must end. When Napoleon appeared ready to tell her the truth, Carlota broke in so that he could not get out a firm statement that the intervention was finished. Anguish clouded her face, but the trend of her arguments continued logical and clear.

It was terribly hot. Outside Señora del Barrio remarked to the French lady-in-waiting Madame Carette that Carlota often drank orangeade in hot weather. Madame Carette called a butler and told him to take some in. He returned with a filled crystal carafe on a silver tray and knocked on the door.

Eugenie told the butler to enter. The French Empress looked

at him and fuzzily asked why he had brought the orangeade. The butler replied he had done it at Madame Carette's order. It passed through Eugenie's mind that they should not have been interrupted, but she took some orangeade and suggested to Carlota that she should also refresh herself. Carlota said she did not wish any. Eugenie persevered. Carlota drew back. At length, very reluctantly, she drank a little. Terrible thoughts, frightful things, rushed through her mind, and from that moment something hung in the air between the three of them.

They concluded their talk, Carlota saying with the Emperor's permission that she would speak to his principal advisers; the advisers would see she was correct in arguing that the French could not leave Mexico, and that they would back up their chief when he announced compliance with her wishes. Napoleon would have agreed to anything to be free of her presence, and gladly told her that she could talk to his people the next day.

Carlota left them and went downstairs. The driver and footman of the carriage had wandered off into the park surrounding the palace and so for a time, her face twisted, she paced through the salons she had known as a little girl visiting her grandfather and grandmother. The servants grew progressively more nervous as they looked at the frantic visitor with the unseeing eyes.

Finally the carriage arrived. An aide-de-camp to Napoleon stepped forward and offered the Empress his hand so he could assist her as she went up the lowered steps. She silently declined. She sat down, pale and exhausted, and fell back against the cushions. They went down the driveway and when they again passed the French flag at the entrance Carlota appeared not to see it, for she did not bow. That night Eugenie had trouble sleeping. She dreamed of Mexico and Maximilian.

In the morning Carlota received the chief Ministers, the Minister for Foreign Affairs, the Minister of War, the Minister of Finance. They came to her in the Grand Hotel, heard her arguments and appeals and turned her down. Yet she was brilliant in her marshaling of the facts and the presentation of her case. Achille Fould, the Minister of Finance, left saying that if he stayed any longer she would talk him around.

That was on August 12. On the thirteenth, unannounced,

she went again to St. Cloud. There was no way to prevent her being received by the Emperor. She told him she had something to show him, and put before him the letters he had written the Archduke Ferdinand Maximilian in Miramar: *"I beg you always to count upon my friendship. . . . You may be sure that my support will not fail you in the fulfillment of your task."* And, when Maximilian had hesitated to accept the Crown, *"What would you think of me if, when Your Imperial Highness was once in Mexico, I were suddenly to say to you that I cannot fulfill the conditions to which I have set my signature?"* It was agonizing for Napoleon and Eugenie. The worst experience they have ever been through, Carlota thought to herself. The French Emperor and Empress wept, and Napoleon twisted away by saying he would not make a final decision until his Ministerial Council met. Eugenie drew Carlota out of the Emperor's study. They went into the Empress's apartments. Minister of War Randon and Minister of Finance Fould were there. At the sight of them Carlota again began pleading her case, but with the difference that now she accused more than she reasoned, charging avarice and dishonesty upon the part of the French. "Where are the persons," she cried, "whose pockets are filled with gold at Mexico's expense?"

Fould lost his composure and lashed back, using the words *ingratitude* and *sharp practices.* Carlota completely lost all restraint and began to rage at them. Eugenie stood up crying, and then fell back into an armchair, apparently in a swoon.

The next day the Ministerial Council, unanimously, voted to wind up France's affairs in Mexico. They attempted to inform Carlota this was the end of her hopes, but she refused to accept what the Council said, saying to their messenger, Minister-President Rouher, "I take my answers only from the Emperor himself."

So Napoleon would have to tell her finally that it was over. He dreaded the interview. It took place on August 18 at four in the afternoon in her rooms at the hotel. Nervous and ill, he listened in miserable silence as she said he should dissolve the Legislative Body and go to the French people. He nerved himself to say, finally, that he had done his best by Maximilian, but they must think now only of extricating him safely from Mexico. She interrupted him so as not to hear. He forced her to listen. It was over. She must not indulge in illusions. "Your Majesty," she snarled, "ought not to indulge in any either." He arose, bowed coldly and silently walked out.

Napoleon left behind him a woman whose composure and control were completely gone. She was unable to relax and her words became increasingly violent. "Charlatan!" she rasped to Señora del Barrio. "Hypocrite! I ought to have remembered that the blood of the Bourbons flows through my veins—I, a daughter of the race of Orléans—and not have disgraced myself by humiliating myself before a Bonaparte, and negotiating with an adventurer!" She thought back to the orangeade. The drink had been poisoned. They had tried to kill her. "Assassins!" Sleepless for two nights running, she wandered her rooms in the hotel, saying that Napoleon was Satan and his entourage was Hell. Long ago her father had owned copies of Albrecht Dürer's wood engravings of the Revelation of St. John, and they came flooding back before her eyes as if in a vision, the Four Horsemen of the Apocalypse; and it seemed to her that each had the face of Napoleon.

Occasionally, by surreptitiously giving her drugs, her suite managed to get her to sleep for a brief period. Once they took her on a brief shopping trip. But the moments of calmness grew less frequent as she thrashed about in her frenzy. Distracted, she said Maximilian must be told, must be warned against the Devil.

"Dearly beloved treasure: . . . No power can aid us, for He has hell on his side, and I have not. *It is not the opposition, He chooses the legislative bodies; still less is it anxiety about the United States, He means to commit a long premeditated evil deed; not out of cowardice or discouragement or for any reason whatsoever, but because He is the evil principle on earth and wants to get rid of the good, only humanity does not see that his deeds are evil and they adore him.* . . . He is the Devil in person, and at our last interview He had an expression that would make one's hair stand on end, He was hideous, and this was the expression of his soul. . . . He has never loved you from beginning to end, for he neither loves nor is capable of loving; He fascinated you like the serpent, his tears were as false as his words, all his deeds are treachery.

". . . Maintain yourself as long as possible, for if hell is thrown out, it would be in the interest of France and the whole of Europe to make a great empire in Mexico, and we can do this. Things in the Old World are sickening and depressing. *He* is so near and one smells him in all the bloodshed. . . . Bismarck and Prim are his agents; he makes propaganda in every country and laughs at the victims who have fallen. On the other side of the ocean one can defy him.

". . . You cannot exist in the same hemisphere as He, he would burn you to ashes. . . . Do not trust the French, one never knows whether it is not *He* who is bringing them. . . . So soon as you send for me, I shall be overjoyed, but I think that you cannot exist in Europe with *him* and that *He* fills the whole atmosphere from the North Cape to Cape Matapan. . . . I embrace you with all my heart; your ever faithful Charlotte."

Her face flushed and her eyes shining feverishly, Carlota said she would go to Rome and appeal to the Pope for help. Satan would not dare follow her there. Her people persuaded her to go via Miramar. She left Paris, which she detested now, on August 23, two weeks after landing at St. Nazaire. She traveled on a special train put at her disposal by Napoleon. Perhaps she did not know who provided her transportation. At Mâcon, north of Lyons, the garrison troops and populace cheered her, but she turned away, saying it was "contemptible." The train went through Savoy and into the wild mountains bordering Italy; she said the rain and landscape pleased her because they were like Mexico. At the Italian frontier she sighed with relief; now she was away from *His* country.

They came to the Italian regions where Carlota had been Vicereine and Maximilian Viceroy in the distant days when she was a bride in love with her young Archduke. They had tried in their time to protect the Italians from the Whitecoats. The Italians had not forgotten. In Milan and at the Lake of Como people cheered the twenty-six-year-old Empress who had aged so since last they saw her. She softened.

Dearly loved Max:
. . . Everything here breathes of you, *your* Lake of Como, of which you were so fond, lies before my eyes in all its blue calm; all is the same, only you are over there, far, far away, and nearly ten years have passed by! And yet I remembered it all as if it were yesterday,

and Nature here speaks to me of nothing but untarnished happiness, not of difficulties and disappointments. All the names, all that happened, come forth from some long unused corner of my brain, and I live once more in our Lombardy as if we had never left it; in two days I have lived over again the two years which were so dear to us.

Only I should like to see you here, the people are so friendly. Early yesterday I heard mass at the tomb of San Carlo and visited the cathedral, which was filled with people in a moment; it was not curiosity, but grateful affection; and here in my bedroom I found your youthful portrait, probably put there on purpose, with the inscription *Governatore Generale del Regno Lombardo-Veneto.* . . . And now I am hoping, dear treasure, that you will be satisfied with me, for I have worked incessantly for the object which you set before me.

. . . The moon is shining now, and there has been singing; it is beautiful beyond words.

In Mexico the wife of the gardener prepared to give birth. Carlota knew of that accouchement, as did the Court circles of Paris, Vienna, Brussels. The Empress did not even mention it, nor criticize her husband. She was never known, then or later, to say a single word against him. He became again for her the young, charming and gentle Prince whom she had loved almost from the first day she met him at her father's Court when she was sixteen. He remained that way. For her the love affair lasted forever.

In those days as she rested by the waters of Lake Como, Max was constantly in her thoughts. She became again the intelligent, appealing Princess and Empress. Yet it was Carlota who had sent him to Mexico and it was Carlota who might yet save him. So she must be off to Miramar and from there to Rome and the Holy Father. The Empress entrained and went through Italian towns where the ladies waved embroidered Mexican flags, and King Victor Emmanuel came to meet her at Padua and said Maximilian was kind and good. Carlota wrote her husband, "He asked me to tell you how much he loved you, for, he added, 'He has such good ideas. . . .' "

It was remarkable that the ruler of United Italy should express such sentiments to the sister-in-law of Francis Joseph, for while Prussia had triumphed in that summer of war against Austria, Italy had lost. The battles in the south had been in the waters bordering the Italian Peninsula off Lissa. There the Austrian fleet planned and constructed by Maximilian had scored a great victory under Maximilian's protégé, Admiral Wilhelm von Tegetthoff. The climax of Lissa, the greatest sea battle of the era, came when Tegetthoff's flagship, *Archduke Ferdinand Max*, sent to the bottom the enemy's *King of Italy*. Four thousand miles away a lonely and worried ruler of whom the French troops never spoke without using the words *puppet* or *Arch-dupe* exulted; and when days later Francis Joseph drove from the Hofburg to Vienna's Prater, a murderous cry rose from the crowds who watched him: *Long live Maximilian!* It was not long before word of that cry reached Mexico City. There followed affirmations that a great Austrian destiny might yet await a ruler who had engineered what was Austria's greatest triumph in a summer of despair.

Carlota took leave of Victor Emmanuel for a homecoming to Miramar, where the victors of the Battle of Lissa lay at anchor. Tegetthoff accompanied her as she sailed in a pouring rain past the assembled squadrons with their cheering sailors and thumping naval batteries.

Carlota came ashore at Miramar, tears flowing as she walked the rooms Max had designed and furnished. For the first time, she said, she saw it clearly. She wrote her husband that the ivy bower by the summerhouse had become in the years of their absence a wonder of the world, and the fan-palms, weeping willows, cedars and pines had grown to a marvelous size. It was all magnificent. And out in the water lay his creation, the Austrian fleet. Everyone praised him, she told her Max; he was the holder of the honor of the House of Hapsburg; it had crossed the Atlantic with him. It was sinking in Europe; with the sun it would rise again in the Western Hemisphere. "Charles the Fifth showed the way. You have followed him. Do not regret it. God was with him." She pressed his picture to her lips, weeping.

Carlota knew Napoleon would have written Maximilian by then—and he had, saying, "It is henceforth impossible for me to give Mexico another *écu* or another man." But she wrote encouraging him to remain, saying that the abdication of France's throne had destroyed her grandfather Louis Philippe, that Max was still young and virile and would yet triumph, that it was his duty to save Mexico. "You should say plainly to all: 'I am Emperor.' . . . They must bow before you. . . . We shall get money from all quarters . . . and there you will stand before the world, supported by your own people. . . . *The finest empire in the world, for Mexico must and will inherit the power of France. . . . Then we shall be able to alter states and appoint kings at our will!"*

Carlota stayed in Miramar to celebrate Mexico's independence day. A glittering diadem in her hair, she presided at the banquet in the castle. The guns thundered in honor of Father Hidalgo's cry from his church in Dolores in the desert: *Viva Mexico!* The next day she took a train for Rome.

At Botzen she saw an organ grinder and drew back, saying it was Colonel Paulino Lamadrid of the Imperial Mexican army in disguise. But he was far away, her suite reminded her. She refused to believe them and began to speak wildly of the Devil and assassins. They had poisoned her, she cried, her servants, the ladies-in-waiting. They tried to calm her. The Empress ordered that they return her to Miramar. Perhaps she would be safe there. They telegraphed ahead to Rome that she would not be coming. Then she changed her mind. They went on, the Austrian army contingents along the way firing off salutes of a hundred and one guns, and the Italians, when they reached Italian territory, doing the same thing. As they progressed south the trip took on the aspect of a triumphal tour, with local authorities offering parades, music, salvos of artillery, flowers; the notables in Reggio attired in full dress uniform giving a ceremonial luncheon; the garrison at Bologna accompanied by the Bersaglieri providing a state reception and march-past, with the city illuminated by blazing lights when darkness came.

It was all for a woman now almost completely insane. Sometimes she was able to pull herself together and say to Señora del Barrio, "I have been sick and if it overtakes me again say to me 'Botzen' to make me get hold of myself." But the trick did not always work. Violently trembling, shuddering, her heart beating wildly, crying out against the Devil and the Four Horsemen of the Apocalypse, Death, Famine, War and Pestilence, and always with the underlying theme of death by poison, she was beyond all help. They came to Rome. By orders of the Pope, Cardinals waited and the Guarda Nobile and Papal gendarmes stood with an escort of Cuirassiers. Rain poured down. Dressed in black, terribly pale, she entered a carriage and drove to the Grand Hotel by torchlight.

The next day Cardinal Giacomo Antonelli, the Pope's closest adviser, came to call upon the Empress of Mexico. As Eugenie had come to the Grand Hotel in Paris to spare Napoleon a painful duty, so Antonelli came to Rome's Grand Hotel to spare Pius IX. He stayed an hour, listing the ills Maximilian had done the Church, ignoring the staring mad eyes and replying to her appeals for help that he did not see what could be done. Carlota refused to accept such a decision from him and asked to see the Pope. An audience was arranged for September 27 at eleven in the morning. In the intervening days, unable to remain still, unable to sleep, she wandered Rome. The heat was stifling but she could not force herself to remain in the hotel, and so, bathed in perspiration, she walked or drove in the streets.

The Empress went to the Pope in a Papal coach pulled by four horses and manned by a coachman and postilions in livery, knee breeches, three-cornered hats and powdered wigs. Crowds gathered to see her go by. She came to the Vatican throne room where Pius IX awaited her, and stooped to kiss his foot. He raised her and extended his hand; she kissed his ring. He blessed her and her suite, and her people and his retainers withdrew, leaving the two of them alone.

Carlota began to speak. Poisoners! The people who accompanied her, her suite, they were all in the employment of The Dark One. For an hour and a half she raved. There was no part of her conversation that was anything other than mad. At the end she silently went to her carriage. Her people walked with her into the salon of her hotel apartment. She bowed to them there. "You may retire." They left her alone. She sent out orders to take away the guards and to quiet the military band sent to play in the street.

The Pope returned the Empress's call, blessed her suite, left.

At dinner she ate only oranges and nuts, inspecting the peels and shells to make sure they were intact, that nothing had been injected into them. She drank no liquids of any kind. In the morning—the heat of the Roman September was intense even at eight o'clock—she called Señora del Barrio and ordered a cab. Carlota was dressed in deep mourning, with a cloak of black velvet and black silk ribbons tied under her chin. Her face was haggard, the eyes sunken and the cheeks blazing. She ordered the cab driver to go to the Trevi Fountain, and, parched with thirst, she drank from it. They got back into the cab and ordered the driver to Vatican City. The Empress told the guards there that she demanded to see the Pope. They hesitated. She implored them. Finally they took Carlota to him and she flung herself at his feet, begging him to save her from the poisoners. The Pope tried to soothe her and suggested they have breakfast together. Some hot chocolate was served. "This at least is not poisoned," she said. She plunged her fingers into the cup of chocolate and licked them. "Everything they give me is drugged and I am starving, literally starving," she said. The Pope rang for more, but she shrieked, "No, no, they could poison it, knowing it was for me. No, thank you! I prefer sharing Your Holiness's cup." She thrust her fingers into his bowl. Then she said it was poison, that it was better to die of hunger than fall into a trap. Another cup was brought and she put her fingers into it and then licked them, saying, "Your Holiness cannot imagine how good it was. A real treat to feel one is safe, and that there is no poison." She began speaking quite naturally about Mexican affairs.

Time was passing. The Pope indicated he had work to attend to and asked Carlota if she would wish to pray in the royal pew at St. Peter's. "How could I go to St. Peter's, a public place of worship?" she asked him. "I should be a dead woman before the service was over; there would be one of those scoundrels behind each pillar." She refused to leave the Pope's presence for fear of the murderers lying in wait outside. He suggested that perhaps she would like to visit the Vatican library. She agreed and he managed to slip away, leaving Señora del Barrio and Colonel Bossi of the Papal gendarmes with her. Carlota gave the colonel a card on which she wrote the names of several of her attendants, begging him to have them arrested.

The colonel agreed to do so, and sent word to the Grand Hotel that they should be kept out of their mistress's sight when she returned.

At noon luncheon was served to the colonel, Cardinal Antonelli, Señora del Barrio and the Empress, who ate from her lady-in-waiting's plate. The afternoon passed. She said she would not go to the hotel—"It would be madness to throw myself into the arms of those hired assassins"—and begged to be allowed to sleep in the Vatican. It was one of the oldest traditions that no woman could stay the night under that roof, and the Papal attendants were appalled. But Carlota would not listen, and cried that she would sleep on the stone floor of the corridor if she could not have a room. The Pope ordered that two beds be arranged in the library. She slept well while her lady-in-waiting kept watch over her. When she awoke she appeared much refreshed but certain she was about to die. The Empress asked for note paper and wrote her husband.

> Dearly beloved treasure:
>
> I bid you farewell. God is calling me to him. I thank you for the happiness which you have always given me.
>
> May God bless you and help you to win eternal bliss.
>
> Your faithful
Charlotte.

The Empress of Mexico spent that day in the Vatican, refusing to go. Cardinal Antonelli sent word to the Mother Superior of the Convent of St. Vincent, asking her to come and see if she could help. The Mother Superior was ushered in and invited Carlota to visit the convent orphanage, promising that no harm would come to her. They went, the Empress hiding her face in a handkerchief in the carriage and repeatedly asking if anybody was following them or if people were looking. At the orphanage she greeted the five hundred orphans with a perfectly lucid and appropriate little speech. The Mother Superior asked if she would like a complete tour, and she said she would. They went through the rooms and came to the kitchen. The nun in charge asked if she would like some food, and gave her some stew and silverware. Carlota saw some tiny specks on them.

"The knife and fork are poisoned!" she cried, and fell on her knees to thank God for having let her see the danger. She arose, and her eyes lighted upon a pot where beef was simmering in water. She ran to it and plunged in her arms up to the elbow to seize a piece of meat. Badly scalded, she fainted. They bound up her hands and arms and bundled her into a carriage and made for the Grand Hotel. She was still unconscious when they arrived there, but then she awoke and began to call for help. People gathered as she fought to prevent being taken inside. Screaming and kicking, she was carried through the crowd, up the stairs and into her room.

Once there Carlota refused to eat anything. Her people said they would taste the food first. "You make that offer because you have an antidote," she replied. The Empress ended by having chickens brought into a room where the large wooden bed had a silk canopy, the armchairs were of brocade and the toilet necessities were of silver. She tied the chickens to a table and waited for them to lay their eggs and then gave the eggs to her lady-in-waiting Señora del Barrio or her maid, Mathilde Doblinger. She watched every move as the eggs were cooked over an iron-stove charcoal fire. By her orders her maid killed and dressed and then cooked chickens over the fire as she stood by. Yet, Carlota said, she still was not safe. She ordered that they get a cat to test the food. A kitten was brought in.

The Empress refused to touch the water her servants offered, but went out each day to a different public fountain and drank from it, using a cup taken from the Vatican. She could not sleep, saying that if she relaxed her vigilance she might be murdered. Instead she paced up and down, talking to herself and looking wildly about from eyes now sunken deeply into their sockets. She refused to permit her women to see to her hair; the teeth of the comb suddenly seemed daggers to her.

On the night of October 7 her brother, the Count of Flanders —"my big Philippe"—arrived in Rome from Brussels. He had been told of her condition but seemed to think it ridiculous that his sister could not pull herself together. His illusions vanished when they sat down to eat in her room. "Be careful," she warned him. "The dose is strong, don't eat any of that." There was strychnine on his knife, she told him. He wired her financial agents saying they should disregard any instructions they received from her. Then her brother suggested they should go to Miramar.

On October 9 the Empress and the Count of Flanders left the hotel arm in arm for the railroad station. The King and Queen of Naples came to see them off and tried to calm her, saying she should not be afraid to eat or drink. She replied that they should be careful; the poisoners were everywhere; they had poisoned her mother and father, Albert Prince Consort, Lord Palmerston, many others. They arrived at Miramar, where Carlota turned on her brother, screaming that he wanted to kill her. He hid himself from her sight, but sent for all the mementos their grandmother had left her, hoping the remembrances and pictures would calm her. But Carlota could not find peace. She said she wanted to go to Vienna or Brussels. Told that she could not she ran out into the park, hatless and coatless, and had to be brought back by force. A prisoner now, she tried to escape and was finally confined to the garden pavilion in a room whose door was sealed off and over whose windows iron bars were put in place. She stayed there, the Revelation of St. John always in her mind. The Horsemen of the Apocalypse rode before her eyes day and night. And finally in the end the cruelest madness of all came to her: Maximilian had ordered them all to kill her because she had not borne him an heir.

17

CHRISTMAS OF 1866 CAME to Vienna. The Archduchess Sophia had invited the family, the Emperor and Empress with the Heir and his little sister and the Archduke Karl Ludwig with his wife and their two children. The Emperor could be very good with children, and he rocked Karl Ludwig's son Otto in a sleigh and then gave it to the Heir, the Archduke Rudolph, who filled it with the younger children and pulled it along.

The Empress Elizabeth was wrapped in her normal gloom. She was not the mistress of her household or of her life. Her children were in the care of her mother-in-law, the Archduchess Sophia, who had never ceased to think of Sisi as a dangerously neurotic woman who could not be trusted to bring up a family. Sisi had rebelled once, taking her first-born, named Sophia, to Budapest in defiance of her mother-in-law's opinion that a child should not undertake such a trip. Sisi had always loved Budapest and the Hungarians. Her attempt at independence of the Archduchess Sophia had had a disastrous result. The child became ill and died despite all the Hungarian doctors could do.

That confirmed Sophia's opinion of her daughter-in-law. Sisi agreed with her mother-in-law. Each year she hovered closer to the Wittelsbach madness which she had always feared. Once, asked by the Emperor what she most desired for Christmas, Sisi replied that she wanted a fully equipped lunatic asylum; and often on her endless travels she visited, fascinated, the Bedlams of the world. She gave lavishly of her money to help doctors doing research into the origins of insanity. Alone of the Imperial family, she understood what had overtaken her sister-in-law the Empress of Mexico. Her husband the Emperor put the whole thing away from him and never discussed what had happened to Carlota, but Sisi wrote her at Miramar in a kind way. She hoped for an answer but none ever came.

Now they sat *en famille* and Karl Ludwig's son, the three-year-old Francis Ferdinand, climbed up onto the sofa to sit with his aunt the Empress. Looking on, the Archduchess Sophia thought to herself that beauty was a magnet for little boys as well as big men. (She had never denied the sublime appearance of her daughter-in-law.) Little girls were different—they did not notice.

On the Sunday following Christmas, after luncheon they were all together when the clock struck the hour. The works of that clock, from Olmütz, had been given as a present to the Archduchess Sophia by the son now in Mexico. The metallic banging seemed to Sophia to be a greeting from Maximilian, chiming in the family circle from afar; and suddenly tears came to her eyes. The Emperor Francis Joseph glanced at her, guessed the reason why and quickly looked away.

Maximilian's wife had gone saying she would see Napoleon and the Pope and set things right. Her departure had been followed by disordered letters. Then came a telegram on the new interoceanic cable, the wonder of the age, suggesting in a vague way that Carlota was ill, that she had been returned to Miramar, that Dr. Riedel of Vienna had been consulted. Maximilian sent for his physician, Dr. Samuel Basch, a Prussian Jew, and asked if Basch knew a Dr. Riedel.

"He is the director of the lunatic asylum," Basch replied.

Maximilian's immediate thought was to abdicate. "My wife is mad," he said. "These people are killing me by inches. I am thoroughly worn out. I am going away." He forgot the infant in Cuernavaca—it was a boy—whose birth had so enraptured him that it was freely said by the French that he had lost all interest in official business, forgot the child's mother. He ordered his treasures and objets d'art packed and sent with his archives to the port of Vera Cruz for shipment to the Imperial Intendant, Castle of Miramar, Trieste. Packed in boxes, they were loaded onto the Austrian frigate *Dandolo*.

On October 20, 1866, at two in the morning, with no warning and no announcement, the Emperor left Mexico City and headed for Vera Cruz. The finances of his Empire were such that the servants left behind were told to sell off the horses in the stables and the plate from the table to pay bills. Even so there was not enough realized to make good some of the pettiest debts. The proprietor of a hot-baths establishment was left wondering when he would get his fees for the Emperor's ablutions. He never did.

In the morning when news of his departure became known, Maximilian left behind him a capital filled with the wildest rumors. Mariano Riva Palacio, perhaps the most famous lawyer in Mexico, thought the disorder was the most terrible known since the conclusion of Spanish rule nearly half a century before. "In the morning we are told that Maximilian is going to leave and end the Empire; in the afternoon we are told he is coming back to Mexico City and will be supported by the French." People spoke of a blood bath by Diaz's troops, of anarchy, of the possibility that the United States would end its race question by sending a Negro army to take over the country and make it a black colony ruled from Washington.

In the Valley of Mexico there was not a single inch of territory considered safe. To the south, guerrillas blasted open and sacked the Emperor's villa at Cuernavaca, and when Colonel Paulino Lamadrid went with some Austrian Hussars to try to avenge the insult, he was ambushed and shot down, along with his escort. French cavalry patrols circled about trying to maintain some kind of elemental order, but rapists and arsonists sprang up everywhere. They called themselves Liberals with the instinct of those who bet on the winning side. Their victims were anyone who happened to be in their path. No sane man ventured out without a saber or revolver, and those without such weapons carried knives or machetes. Murder was nothing, robbery less.

In the Carlota Colony near Córdoba the refugees from the former Confederacy found themselves surrounded by masses of wild men slashing at them with sabers and running them through with lances. Mexicans who had worked for the colonists were stoned; and those southerners who escaped death were chased from their town and their Confederate Hotel. Their animals were slaughtered or driven away. Their suitcases and their valuables were left lying in the streets or in the ruins of the burned houses. Five thousand people staggered off to beg transport back to New Orleans or New York or any port that was not Mexican. Back in the United States, Thomas Reynolds, the former governor of Missouri, found he could not forget the rawhide whippings, the prisoners made to kneel between their coffins and their graves before they were slain, and particularly the sight of a sixteen-year-old boy shot by a dozen executioners who hit him in fifty places as his blood went dribbling through the Mexican dust past the crouching figure of a priest whispering prayers over other bodies.

In a gray cloak and his sombrero, the Emperor headed east toward the ocean. He came to the Hacienda Zoquiapa, where he spent the night and from where he sent word to Marshal Bazaine to revoke the Black Decree which authorized the shooting of prisoners. He had had enough of killing. Maximilian continued on foot down the zigzag trail. (The roads were in such poor repair that it was likely that at any moment the wheeled vehicle would go crashing off a cliff.) Finally he came to the town of Aculcingo. In the night the perfectly matched white mules in Castilian harness which pulled his carriage were stolen. He had loved their chic appearance.

In his entourage, among whom Mexicans were a rarity, there was no doubt that he would board the *Dandolo* and sail for Europe. Nothing he said or did encouraged his people to believe that he was not on the verge of abdicating; and he was preparing the drafts of dozens of letters beginning: "On the eve of leaving our beloved motherland . . ."

One man opposed the Emperor's abdication and departure. He was Father Augustin Fischer. Father Fischer had been born a Lutheran in Germany and had emigrated to the United States where he worked as a cowboy, gold panner and notary public before taking Catholic orders. Intelligent, persuasive, fluent in many languages, he was an adventurer who, accompanied by a lady, had drifted to Mexico only a few months previously. An impressive personality, Father Fischer had found his way into the Emperor's circle. He became another of those advisers who, as Bazaine lamented, were able to catch the Emperor's full attention and faith for a limited time, during which they could make him change his mind about anything. Count Karl Bombelles was off with the Empress in Europe, and Eloin, his influence much diminished, had been sent to Brussels, and Almonte was back in Paris. Into their shoes stepped Augustin Fischer. He saw the possibility of securing a great position for himself in the once-rich Church of Mexico and set out to convince the Emperor to give the Empire one more try. Far too clever not to mask his intention, he told the Emperor he agreed the time for abdication had come, and then sent word to the most Conservative and reactionary circles in Orizaba to stage a great welcome for the monarch. The final word, after all, had not yet been said. So when the depressed Emperor came to the outskirts of Orizaba he saw to his astonishment a throng of men and women deliriously welcoming him and proclaiming their undying loyalty to his cause.

Still not speaking of the immediate future, Fischer told the Emperor the French escort should be sent to the rear so that the ruler and his subjects might be together. Reluctant now even to speak the French language, Maximilian ordered the *pantalons rouges* to leave him and went with Fischer and the cheering people to Xonaca in the countryside outside Orizaba. Suddenly Fischer dominated the Imperial entourage. The new generation of young Mexicans would understand the need for a monarchy, he hinted in a subtle way. Once the detested French left, all parties would rally to a monarch who stayed. And what of Hapsburg honor? Had not the Emperor said he would never desert his post? What would be the fate of his loyal supporters if he left them in the lurch and took flight? *Flight* was the word Fischer always used. In any event, there was no need to hurry away. The Emperor was ill with dysentery and a sore throat. In the lovely area around Orizaba he might relax and take stock of the situation.

Maximilian listened. He took long walks and said he was worried because in his swift departure from Mexico City he had forgotten the baton and Court apparel of his Master of Ceremonies. He took note of the magnificent butterfly specimens native to the tropical region and, equipped with a net, began collecting one of each type. Fischer went with him on his out-of-doors expeditions, along with Professor Dr. Bilimek of Vienna, the curator-designate of the proposed Imperial Museum. Dr. Bilimek had always been a good diversion for the Emperor. He talked of nothing but reptiles and insects, whom he termed "little creatures of the good God." As he spoke almost no Spanish, he tended to lapse into Latin in an attempt to get the Mexicans to understand him. He terrified them, for he kept poisonous snakes and scorpions in his room. There was always the possibility that one might escape and come slithering along the corridors. Wearing immense cork helmets, Dr. Bilimek and the Emperor went bobbing through the fields seeking butterflies which, caught, were pinned to the professor's headgear.

Tentatively, the Emperor began asking those around him if he should stay. Stephen Herzfeld, a friend of his youth and of his travels as Archduke, told him it was madness. Fischer said that perhaps Herzfeld was correct, and perhaps the Emperor's friend should go on ahead to Europe to "prepare the way." At Maximilian's order Herzfeld sailed. From Havana he sent an appeal to Fischer:

"I hope that this letter will find you no longer upon Mexican soil—every hour's delay involves the greatest danger—the pretexts upon which the Emperor is staying are idle. *Away, away from this country, which in a few weeks' time will be the scene of the bloodiest of civil wars.* . . . Do you save our poor, noble master —Austria, Europe, the Imperial House, will owe you their gratitude. . . . Do you now fulfill your duties of religion, save the Emperor, the man."

Fischer put the letter away and again spoke to Maximilian of Hapsburg honor. Soon he had allies. Generals Leonardo Marquez and Miguel Miramon arrived home from Europe and their trumped-up missions—Marquez had gone to look into religious shrines in Palestine and Miramon to study artillery tactics at Berlin. Both were long veterans of Mexican civil strife. Their destinies were in Mexico. The Emperor was valuable to them. They spoke in support of all Fischer had said. The Empire could yet be reestablished on a more solid, purely Mexican, base.

Meanwhile, more and more towns surrendered to the Liberals or to mere rampaging bands. Over all of them hung billowing smoke from the burning homes of the Empire's supporters. The enemy kept advancing. The Conservative General Tomas Mejia, without money for reinforcement for many months past, surrendered Matamoros to the capable Liberal General Mariano

Escobedo. Escobedo swept south, even as Porfirio Diaz came north, securing the surrender of everything in his path by announcing that any place which did not submit to "the lawful government" would be given over "to the pillage of my soldiers." In Orizaba the Emperor began to speak of himself as a sentinel holding his post, as an officer who could not run away from the battlefield. Yet he could not make up his mind whether to go or to stay. "Three or four times in a week he made up his mind to abdicate, and as often altered it the following day," a courtier wrote.

A personal aide to Napoleon, General Count Francis de Castelnau, came out to Mexico, hoping to persuade the Emperor that he must leave with the departing French. Maximilian would not receive him. Distracted, his Empire shrinking day by day as Tampico, Monterrey, Mazatlan, Saltillo, Guaymas capitulated to the Juaristas, he listened to Fischer and spoke of a counterstroke that would yet win the day. Marquez and Miramon promised miracles, Conservatives appeared to say money would be forthcoming. Again the Emperor let it be known that he would stay, and three days later ordered up a special train to take him from Paso del Macho to Vera Cruz to the *Dandolo*. Then for the last time he changed his mind and gave himself over to those he had shunned in his early days, the most reactionary Conservatives, the men of the Inquisition who rejected everything even faintly smacking of reform, who mingled religious fervor and hatred of the Liberals with the hope of recouping their own fortunes. Fischer was their spokesman. He was so palpably an adventurer that it seemed impossible that anyone could fail to see through him. In that moment he had become the Gray Eminence of Mexico. Under his tutelage the Emperor left Orizaba and vaguely turned in the direction of Mexico City. He wandered to Puebla and dallied there in the Episcopal Palace for ten days. Word came of the fall of Guadalajara. Maximilian drifted on toward the capital. He passed through the mountains where Colonel van der Smissen, the commander of the Belgian Legion, saw him and was reminded of what prisoners looked like on their way to execution. The Emperor was in a little carriage pulled by four white mules not as good as those which had been stolen.

General de Castelnau and Marshal Bazaine thrashed about

trying to pull an abdication out of him, but their written references to the expected "new form of government in Mexico" hurt him terribly. Maximilian refused to see them. A letter came from his mother in Vienna. His position in Europe would be "ridiculous" if he abdicated, she wrote. She knew him. She knew what it meant that his wife was no longer by his side to stiffen him; and believing all his cheerful letters she tried to bolster him. She was doing the right thing, his mother thought to herself in faraway Vienna. He was her most beloved son. She wanted him to be happy. Better that he "bury" himself in Mexico than come home a failure, she wrote, not knowing what it was she was saying. But his mother had spoken. And Maximilian thought of Francis Joseph—saw himself coming back as the Emperor manqué contrasted with his brother's unbending Imperial Majesty. The last leg of the trip back to Mexico City was covered at a gallop.

Once back Maximilian's fears possessed him again, and he said he would not live at Chapultepec, he would not be in a place where he might have to leave by one door while Juarez came in through another. So Fischer arranged for him to stay at the Hacienda de la Teja, the summer residence of a Swiss inhabitant of the capital. The house, a modest one, was located in the countryside which lay between Mexico City and Chapultepec. Able to see the belltowers and cupolas of the city, the Emperor was almost a prisoner, with Fischer his jailer.

There came a time when he could not deny Bazaine's pleas to see him. "My opinion today is that Your Majesty should retire spontaneously," the marshal said.

"I will stay," the Emperor replied, "because I do not wish to look like a soldier who throws down his gun in order to run more quickly from the battlefield."

But there was no hope at all left, Bazaine said. He had his orders and must take away the French army in the next few days. When he was gone Maximilian would be helpless. Did not His Majesty see that?

Thinking to himself that he would not go with the French as part of their baggage, Maximilian replied that he had no illusions and that perhaps the marshal was correct. Would the marshal come to a meeting of his supporters and give his views? Bazaine did as he was asked, said the thing was hopeless, and saw the assembly, deep-dyed Conservatives all, vote that the Emperor should remain. Fischer had won.

Marshal Bazaine would not accept it. He wrote to Maximilian to say once again that it was all madness, that the game was up and the Empire lost. Fischer wrote back saying he would not permit the officer delivering the letter to enter His Majesty's presence, that "His Majesty orders me to make it known to Your Excellency that . . . he no longer wishes in the future to have any direct relationship with Your Excellency."

From Louis XIV, reflected Charles Blanchot of Bazaine's staff, such a reply would mean something. But Fischer? There was nothing more to be done. After five years the French would go home. Already they were late in the eyes of the French residents of Mexico City. Once the soldiers had seemed deliverers from chaos, but now they took the form of debts which Juarez would pay. The opera company packed up to the last singer and musician and fled to Havana; all over the city French merchants closed their shops and made for Vera Cruz, traveling in convoys to minimize the dangers from Liberals or bandits.

There remained in those last days no relationship at all between Maximilian and the French. Bazaine sent a routine memorandum naming several French officers he believed worthy of Mexican medals, as he had done many times before over the years, and Fischer replied he would not submit the letter to the Emperor—"It would only augment the displeasure of His Majesty." If some other officer signed a request, Fischer added, he would try to get the medals awarded. In reaction to such an insult to a marshal of France, the French began blowing up ammunition originally intended for distribution to the Imperial army. With Fischer and the sinister Leonardo Marquez in charge, there was no guarantee that the shells and bullets might not be directed at the French rear as they made for the sea.

As the French prepared to leave, large numbers of Austrian and Belgian troops let it be known that they would be departing too. Many of them had accepted bounties for enlisting in the Emperor's service and thus were legally bound to him. But Maximilian said he scorned to hold men against their will. Let them follow their destinies as they saw fit. Others said they would honor their oaths, and these, mostly professional soldiers of fortune, formed the majority of the officer corps which would serve under his three Mexican chieftains, Generals Marquez, Miramon and Mejia.

On February 5, 1867, reveille blew in all the cantonments of the French army in Mexico, and the Tricolor went up to the tops of all the flagstaffs, hung there a moment, and then slowly came down. The troops formed up. In Mexico City they converged in the Zocalo, in front of the National Palace and the Cathedral. The marshal came out from his headquarters and his troops saluted as the Mexican civilians looking on slowly took off their sombreros. It was remarkably silent, tens of thousands of people, troops and onlookers, saying nothing as Marshal Bazaine turned to the crowd and saluted. He mounted his horse, which stood in front of the first contingent of troops, Spahis carrying their rifles on the outside of their thighs. He signaled the beginning of the march and the drums began to beat and French trumpets sounded for the last time in that place almost six thousand miles from Paris.

The marshal led them down the Calle de San Francisco, past the Iturbide Hotel, whose balconies were crammed with people who had come to see the final march-past. The Mexican women wore rebozos tossed over their heads and left shoulders, their faces creased with contemptuous smiles. Almost a perfect silence prevailed save for the sound of thousands of marching feet and the military bands, until the troops passed a balcony filled with Frenchwomen remaining in the city. They waved handkerchiefs and burst into encouraging cries: "What a brilliant army! With such soldiers the world may be conquered, and that they will do. Let them only return to France, and they will march against Berlin and take it at the point of a bayonet." Listening, Prince Felix zu Salm-Salm, a Prussian soldier recently attached to the Emperor's service, grimly said to himself that it would be his dearest wish that he be there to meet them.

The French continued through the city's San Antonio Gate. As they marched past a nearby French military cemetery they uncovered and the flags dipped. It seemed to Captain Blanchot appropriate that this place found itself on the way to France. But we are returning without honor, Major Loizillon thought to himself, one could not dissimulate it. He had been feeling very depressed for some months past, writing his parents that he begged them to excuse him to his friends for not writing to wish them a happy new year, but that he was not up to it. It was Mexico which depressed him, he explained. Failure there, combined with the Battle of Sadowa and the previous year's poor harvest, made him wonder if the luck of the French Empire had not begun to run out. The troops marched on.

Behind them, from the roof of a closed and shuttered National Palace, a tall figure in a gray cloak waited until the last soldier was out of sight before turning away from the now empty Zocalo. "Now I am free," Maximilian said.

No one bothered the long columns as they marched to the sea, and Porfirio Diaz, coming up to besiege the Imperial army units holding Puebla, sent in the sword of a fallen French officer with the request that it be returned to his family. In the night the French saw the campfires belonging to the Liberals' patrols but Marshal Bazaine withdrew more than twenty-three thousand men without a single casualty. Loizillon, on duty as a transport officer at the railhead in Paso del Macho, often saw the Liberal soldiers on the other side of the river. "They look at us, we look at them, and that's where it stays," he wrote home.

In those days while the French moved east the Emperor gave a banquet. "You will see Mexico in twenty years, gentlemen," he said. "I will pierce a boulevard in this place, put a plaza in this other, a park here, a barracks there. . . . The Mexican Empire will be, I swear it, one of the most flourishing of the globe, and its capital will scarcely have any rival in the world for the splendor of its buildings and the majesty of its monuments." Diaz laid siege to Puebla, and when he took it, lined up three hundred members of Maximilian's army. "Since you haven't learned to live like a man, at least learn how to die like one," Diaz said to the prisoners before he had them shot down.

Within a week of the French departure from the capital, the Emperor also left. He rode at the head of nine thousand men walking in irregularly spaced straggling groups unprotected by any kind of flank guard save for the women, children and stray barking dogs tagging along. It was the Imperial Mexican army going forward to meet its enemies upon the field of honor. Its artillery struggled along behind badly teamed half-trained mounts. Half the men were raw recruits press-ganged off the streets of the capital. They were shepherded by fourteen- and fifteen-year-old lieutenants and elegantly turned out officers of higher rank resplendent in gold lace and stiff tunic collars. In its long, thin, straggling line the army stretched for miles, with men continually dropping out to fry tortillas and tamales on roadside fires fed with dry cacti. The column took the road north carrying pikes, hatchets, swords from Spanish times, old Enfields, battered muskets which had found their way south from the battlefields of the American Civil War, discarded French pieces and Austrian pistols.

The Emperor, its leader, rode a piebald horse with a Mexican high-backed saddle, wearing the coat of a Mexican general minus the epaulettes, dark trousers and kneeboots, a sombrero and two revolvers and a saber. "You must assert yourself, then Jules Favre will not call you Don Quixote anymore," Carlota had written.

Flanking him was Leonardo Marquez. The Mexican general was so deeply lost in thought that he had to be spoken to at least twice before he heard what was said. But he was fawningly attentive whenever he addressed the Emperor. Maximilian was also accompanied by the dashing and handsome Miguel Miramon, who, once President of Mexico, had freely said to many people that the Empire was doomed but that he would rise to power upon its ruins; and by Colonel Miguel Lopez, tall and blond, who had commanded the Mexican escort during the Imperial entrance procession from Vera Cruz. Colonel Lopez looked more German than Mexican in a red Hussar jacket trimmed with black. He was wearing the Officer's Cross of the French Legion of Honor given to him by Marshal Bazaine. The Prussian Prince Felix zu Salm-Salm was also at the head of the column.

Prince Salm-Salm was new to Mexico, having arrived only a couple of months before. He was a younger son of the reign-

ing Prince of Anholt and had been a soldier all his life. He
had seen his first action during the Prussian and Austrian
attack on Denmark, when he earned the honor of a sword
awarded by King William with *For Courage* engraved on it.
He had no money despite his high rank, and his creditors made
Europe uncomfortable for him, so he had drifted to America
and the Union army, where he rose to the rank of brigadier
general. Peace and the military occupation of the South were
not for him; he dreaded the idea of a dreary, idle life in some
garrison town. With his American wife, a very pretty, blond,
former circus rider from Vermont, he went to Mexico to seek
adventure. It had been only one month earlier that they had
first seen the Emperor. They found him enormously attractive.
The Prince was taken by Maximilian's charming smile and
his gracious, kind ways remindful of that other lost life among
the aristocracy of Europe. In the case of the Princess it was
that she was a strong and determined woman with a weakness
for good-looking, romantic men who, like her husband, needed
direction because they were imperfectly suited for modern
times.

Salm-Salm—whom everybody called simply "Salm"—was one
of the few European soldiers who went with the Emperor. All
the others had been ordered to remain in Mexico City so that
it might not be said the Emperor was tainted by foreign support as he went to seek his fate. The only other Europeans in
the long, straggling column were Dr. Basch, the Emperor's
Hungarian cook, Josef Tudos, and his Austrian valet, Antonio
Grill. Salm had rushed after the army saying he could not bear
to be in safety when there would be fighting to the north. He
presented himself and Maximilian took him to his heart, the
final and perhaps most loyal of the Emperor's advisers. Father
Fischer remained in Mexico City.

Sitting in the high-backed and swaying saddle, the Emperor
led his men to the city of Queretaro, one hundred miles north
of the capital. The Liberals were deploying around it. If the
enemy could be stopped there the Emperor and his army
might force them back. In Mexico City the reactionaries and
ultra-Conservatives exulted to see him go, for they feared the
possibility that in the capital he might decide to seek terms

with Juarez. If he remained in the field as a military chieftain the Emperor was not likely to do that. Perhaps he understood their plot which sent him out to fight Conservatism's battle while most of them stayed behind in safety, but it did not matter. Honor mattered. Like Charlemagne, like Richard the Lion-Hearted, like the Holy Roman Emperor Maximilian of medieval times, like Alexander of Macedonia, like Gustavus Adolphus, like Napoleon the Great, indeed, like Cortés, and in the fashion which had been the dream of the Duke of Reichstadt, he sallied forth at the head of his troops to do battle. Too many had died for him to run away without hearing a shot fired. He remained the fickle dilettante who was yet sending to Europe for two thousand songbirds to fill Chapultepec's forests; he was still capable of writing Fischer to send him burgundy wine and songsheets. But there was suddenly something about him that made even those who classed him as an adventurer among adventurers take pause. He was a man the madness of whose wife meant his domestic happiness was over; he had broken with the most important of his blood relatives, whose antagonism for him must infect relations with all the family; he was at the best an unlikely candidate for victory in his fight against his enemies—in short, he did not have much to lose. But something about him caught at men who did.

Perhaps he sought death. Certainly he dreaded a return to Europe, not least of all because it meant seeing Carlota's madness. Too introspective and too intelligent not to know that if he sought the cause of that madness he must look at himself, he winced at the thought of what she had become. Yet his was a situation which could yet be redeemed. Not least of all by his behavior. So Maximilian went forward, as has been said, less the Prince and more the man, in such fashion as later to make him be called the last knight of the nineteenth century.

Lord Acton, the British historian, has lived in memory because of what he once said about the nature of power. Maximilian of Hapsburg become Emperor of Mexico never had the opportunity to test the belief that absolute power corrupts absolutely. But Lord Acton, who knew him, had something to say about him, later, when he was gone:

"I think he was well-nigh the noblest of his race, and fulfilled the promise of his words, 'The fame of my ancestors will not degenerate in me.' "

THE EMPEROR TO THE MEXICAN ARMY: Today places me in the front and I take command of our army. . . . This is the day I have long and ardently desired to see. Obstacles have hindered me against my will. Today, free from all compromise, I can follow simply my sentiments of good and loyal patriotism. Our duty as loyal citizens commands us to fight for the two principles most sacred to the country: for her independence . . . and for internal peace. Our actions being free from all influence, from all external pressure, we shall defend and maintain the honor of our glorious national banner.

I hope the generals will give to their officers, and they to their troops, a worthy example of the most strict obedience, and the most rigid discipline, such as is due from an army which realizes the national dignity. Of valor and pride there is no necessity to speak, for they are the birthright of every Mexican.

Our trust is in God, who protects, and will protect, Mexico; and we will fight bravely and tenaciously with our sacred invocation—"Viva la Independencia!"

At San Miguel Calpulalpam, where the roads wound between two hills, the column came under Liberal fire from the heights. The Emperor refused to take cover and insisted on going forward with the skirmishers feeling out the enemy positions. "What do you want me to do, run away the first chance I get?" he demanded of the officers who urged him to be careful. "I am a soldier now and must go with my own men." They took the hills and captured some wretched conscripts of Juarez's forces whom Marquez immediately wanted to shoot. But the Emperor remonstrated. One did not shoot prisoners. "Very good, Your Majesty," Marquez said, and had the men taken to the rear. Soon afterward it was found they were gone. They must have escaped, Marquez said.

The Emperor's army came to a little mud hamlet and found there one of their soldiers who must have been captured in the skirmish. He was hanging in the plaza upside-down, slashed to ribbons. They went on, coming under frequent running attack. A ball took the Hungarian cook Tudos in the mouth; he spat it out along with several teeth. The Emperor proved to be a coolly efficient field soldier, attempting by disciplined example to moderate the savageness of his troops, who routinely lanced dead enemies a dozen times.

The army wound through the dark red-earth foothills that edged the desert. They passed through the one-street towns with the dusty walls and the heavily barred openings which passed for windows. The soldiers marched across the brown land for six days, and finally reached Queretaro. It was a religious town, Conservative in the better sense; not reactionary, and very much devoted to General Tomas Mejia, whose home was not far away. He was there, having been permitted to escape the Liberal army after his surrender of Matamoros because Mariano Escobedo, who was now approaching Queretaro, had once been permitted to escape the Conservative army by Mejia. "You freed him today, tomorrow he will hang you," Marquez had raged when Mejia had allowed General Escobedo his freedom. But Mejia was not the man to kill enemies who had surrendered.

The first European-built aqueduct in the New World brought water from the mountains to Queretaro; the arches were fifty feet high. The highway went under one. As the Imperial army approached, its members saw that the aqueduct was garlanded with flags and ribbons. They heard the sound of welcoming petards going off, and church bells ringing. Flowers rained down as they went into the town, through the plaza and past the cathedral. The population was almost purely Indian, and to them it was still Quetzalcoatl who had come; it was almost like the early days now so far in the past. The crowd closed in, shouting and touching the Emperor's horse. In that moment the people of Queretaro wanted and esteemed him. His smile lit up his face. "Oh, he had such a kind, benevolent smile!" Prince Salm-Salm said, later.

18

QUERETARO LAY in an almost straight line between two low ridges of desert mountains. With enough soldiers to occupy the tops of the mountains the Emperor's army could hold the city forever. But they did not have those soldiers, and so, in range of the cannons which the Liberals mounted upon the heights, the Imperial army waited. It is a mousetrap, Prince Salm-Salm said to himself. The Liberals began gathering from all over. One saw them from the bottom of the cup which was Queretaro; the Liberals were on the lips of that cup. Nine thousand Imperial troops held the depths; soon there were twenty and then thirty thousand Liberals on the heights looking down.

Miguel Miramon looked up from the bottom of the cup and it seemed to him that they were doomed unless by an offensive they managed to force the enemy to consolidate and fight en masse. Perhaps in one battle the Imperials could crush the Liberals. Miramon went to Tomas Mejia and asked him to command reserves which would back the offering of battle to the Liberal hosts. But Mejia, who was terribly ill, could hardly pull himself up from his bed in the Convent of the Cross, the thick-walled sanctuary which served as their headquarters. Miramon went without him, fought a bravely conceived fight, and was knocked back with severe losses.

A final Liberal army under General Vicente Riva Palacio, son of the lawyer Mariano Riva Palacio, had come up from Toluca to take position on the heights overlooking Queretaro. The circle was closed. Forty thousand troops surrounded the city. In Paso del Macho, four hundred miles away, the French Marquis de Galliffet, recovered from his wounds of Puebla, fought a minor skirmish against some bandits, firing in the process the last shots France would discharge upon Mexican soil. Then the final contingent of troops boarded the train for Vera Cruz; and as the engine's whistle faded away, the Juaristas crossed the little river and rode into the town. At Vera Cruz the troops hurried through to avoid *el vomito* and boarded the ships with the marshal of France the very last of all.

By March 11, 1867, the Liberals had smashed the Queretaro aqueduct so that the defenders had no source of water save the city's few wells and the river which ran down from the hills. But the river's flow was made unpotable by the slashed-open bodies of Imperial soldiers which Escobedo's men regularly dumped in the waters. Fished out, the bodies were piled with those men who had fallen to Liberal fire that rained from the heights. Soon the city was rank with their odor. Prince Salm-Salm ordered the bodies burned and a great column of smoke rose into the sky. The Liberal guns fired into the burning mass.

Escobedo's men began thrusting forward. They ranged about the city and attacked through the main cemetery, which lay on Queretaro's southern outskirts. They forced their way in past the gravestones, the entire force of forty thousand concentrating at this one point. It seemed they were about to break through. Standing on the flat roof of a building and looking on with a spyglass, the sick Mejia saw the situation was desperate. He went downstairs, pushed himself onto a horse and galloped to the battle. He grabbed a soldier's lance and charged the enemy. "Boys! This is how a man dies!" The Imperial army fell in behind him and sent the Liberals flying. Then, half-conscious, dehydrated from lack of water and unable to sit the horse, he was taken back to his sickbed.

Escobedo withdrew to the hilltops, deciding not to risk another major frontal attack. Time was on his side. The city was cut off from all supplies. He contented himself with flinging artillery barrages down from the heights.

When it became obvious that there would be a siege, not an all-out set-piece battle, the Emperor had shifted his living quarters from the little Hill of the Bells at the edge of the city and went to live in the Convent of the Cross, which was called La Cruz. His room had a high ceiling, a rough, uncovered floor and simple, hard wooden furniture which would not hold the heat. Outside was a primitive balcony looking down upon the convent courtyard. Sometimes the shells from the hills sprayed adobe-brick dust over the inhabitants of La Cruz, but the Emperor did not wince. Once a shell burst directly over his head as he was lifting a leg over the saddle of his horse Anteburro; his gay smile in response was contagious and his officers found themselves roaring in laughter along with their monarch. Each evening he promenaded in the plaza before La Cruz, always concerning himself with the begging women who came to him. Any officer who accompanied him had to open his pockets. Salm-Salm spent in this manner twenty-five American dollars during one stroll. The Emperor worried constantly about his increasingly ragged soldiers, talking with them in the most informal manner, sympathizing with them at the shortness of their rations and attempting to reassure himself that the slight amount of food was being equitably distributed. Maximilian himself was down to eating oxen and horse meat marinated in vinegar. Its taste was so frightful that he said there was nothing to do but laugh about it.

Often the Emperor left La Cruz at night to join the troops manning the breastworks flung up all around the town. Frequently he slept among them, lying on the rocky cactus-covered ground wrapped up in his plaid blanket. But neither he nor his army could go on in this fashion for very long; sooner or later the siege must be lifted. Leonardo Marquez said he had the solution. Let him sally forth to Mexico City where he would collect money and men. He would return within a couple of weeks. With the reinforcements joined to the besieged troops, they would attack the Liberals and in one great battle break them. Then the Empire would be secure. Maximilian gave Marquez more than one thousand horsemen and the title of Lieutenant General of the Empire. Marquez broke through the lines on March 23 and rode south. His going and the battle deaths and desertions reduced the Imperial army to hardly more than seven thousand men. The soldiers contracted their lines so that the breastworks enclosed a smaller space; but it meant the enemy artillery shells could be concentrated upon a more restricted area.

The defenders' ammunition began to run low, and they stripped the town's buildings of their metal roofs and ornamentations to make bullets for their rifles. Sometimes they thrust out at Escobedo, each man carrying a maximum of three rounds. But to probe the Liberal lines was very dangerous, for prisoners were butchered immediately upon being caught. They could be seen the next day, their throats slit, hanging upside-down on the hills surrounding the town while the Liberals yelled from the heights, "There are your *cabrones!*"

In Queretaro life of a sort went on. Two women fought a bull in the arena near the Alameda and were followed by inept picadors and matadors. Six horses were gored to death. A Spanish comic company performed nightly and coffeehouses sold increasingly inedible delicacies. Ample stores of liquor existed in the city and there were prostitutes also. But always one could see Liberals on the hills and intervening plains. Sometimes they walked around nude, the single white uniform of each man newly washed and lying on the ground, the whole mass looking like a flock of nesting sheep; and then the defenders would know that something was planned, either a military review or a limited attack. The enemy always fought in clean uniform.

Day by day the Imperial army dwindled in number. Studying the enemy, Mejia thought to himself that never had he seen the Liberals in such force or perfection. With the troops at his command the Emperor could not hope to defeat such an army. Their fate hinged on Marquez and the reinforcements. A soldier was asked to slip through the enemy lines, get to Marquez and urge him to come. The man left at night. In the morning the Liberals put his body on a post and raised the post so that defenders could see what was written on the sign hanging around his neck: THE EMPEROR'S MAIL.

The enemy thrusts became bolder. Every outpost was in perpetual danger and the Emperor slept each night on the little Hill of the Bells. When the alarm sounded he seized arms and his spyglass and ran to the scene of the enemy incursion despite the pleas of his aides that he be more cautious. He would not listen, saying his military honor bade him take his chances with the rest. The soldiers of his shabby army came to revere him for his bravery and cheerful smile and kindly way. He could not appear among them without hearing *"Viva el Emperador!"* from hundreds of throats. He lived on the miserly equivalent of fifty American dollars a day which he allowed himself from the Treasury funds and from this paid his doctor, cook and three or four servants. The rest he gave away. His food was the same wretched stuff the others ate save for some bread contributed by the nuns of the Convent of St. Teresita, and his uniform and underclothing grew shabby and worn. Yet he never complained of any inconvenience, including the fits of violent dysentery which tortured him almost constantly. And in fact he seemed in those days to be very happy. It showed in his jaunty walk and the gay nicknames he gave his men—The Young General for Miramon, The Little Black One for Mejia.

In April's latter half the enemy began to attack again in force, coming in behind artillery barrages and establishing lines of sharpshooters to rake the streets with fire from the brand-new American army repeating rifles which General Sheridan had given Juarez in an indirect and unofficial fashion. Miramon threw his men against the enemy placements, which proved unexpectedly strong. His charge halted, then wavered as the Liberal cavalry came sweeping around their own left wing to throw the Imperial cavalry back upon its own infantry. Suddenly the defenders were running for their lives as the Liberal cavalry rode forward, killing every wounded man who lay in their path and leaving more than a twentieth of the Imperial army in the dust. The Emperor stood in the midst of the swirling action with Miramon on his right and Salm on his left. He drew out his sword. Salm grabbed his other arm. "I implore Your Majesty not to expose yourself in such a useless manner." The Emperor kept advancing. "You owe it to your army not to throw away your life!" The Emperor halted, took the reins of his horse and walked it back as his men fled past him.

In the encircled city His Majesty held a review, decorating several men with the bronze medal for valor which showed his head on one side, and on the other a laurel crown. When he finished, Miramon stepped forward. "I take the liberty of bestowing this token of valor and honor on the bravest of all." Miramon put the medal around the Emperor's neck. They embraced. In the evening all the generals came to him and handed him a piece of vellum upon which they had written:

> No monarch has ever descended from the height of his throne under similar circumstances, to endure with his soldiers, as we here see it, the greatest dangers, privations and necessities, which do not find their equal in the world; with soldiers to whom Your Majesty understood how to give such striking examples of self-denying patriotism and endurance in suffering. Both the nation, whom Your Majesty endeavors to save and to enhance, and impartial history will once do justice to the monarch of Mexico—Maximilian the First.

The Liberal commanders had long since expected to take the city. They flogged men who had not done their duty, the miscreants tied down in the center of a hollow square of troops while drums and fifes played to drown their cries. The Emperor would permit no such measures against his own men who did not fight well. Neither would he permit the shooting of those captured Liberals who proved to be Imperial deserters. "I will have no executions," he said. "If things go well here, good; if badly, I shall have nothing on my conscience." But Marquez did not come with the reinforcements. On occasion Maximilian would discuss his vanished Lieutenant General of the Empire and an unspoken thought would come into his mind; but he would check himself and say, "No, no, it is impossible." An Indian woman and an officer volunteered to go to the capital; they left, never to be heard of again.

By the end of April the defenders' food supplies had reached the point where they ate mule; Miramon concocted cat pie. The soldiers were down to retrieving unexploded shells for their artillery, for they had none of their own. Prince Salm-Salm said, "Your Majesty, will you favor me with the permission to speak to you more freely than I would dare under less precarious circumstances?"

"I wish you to speak always openly and freely with me, even under the most prosperous circumstances."

"Well, Your Majesty, then I implore you to leave this city, where you will certainly meet your death." The Emperor must break out and smash through the lines and flee, Salm said. Maximilian replied that he must think of his honor, of how by staying he had proved he was not the tool of any man, least of all the French, of how it would be unthinkable for him to give up a place still defended by thousands of men possessing heavy artillery. "And then, what will become of this unfortunate city, which has been so faithful to us, and of our poor wounded, whom we cannot take with us?"

Meanwhile in Mexico City, Leonardo Marquez was running amok in the Emperor's name, confiscating rents, bursting into gamblinghouses and taking all the money in view, sending his cavalrymen to stop people in the streets at gunpoint with demands for the contents of their purses. At length Marquez ventured forth, taking with him the assembled European troops who had elected to stay in the Emperor's service. But he did not make directly for Queretaro. Rather he went in the direction of the coast. Outside the city he met the forces of Porfirio Diaz coming up to besiege the capital. He pushed Diaz's infantry back, but advancing into a defile he was set upon by the collected Liberal cavalry which had remained in reserve. "My God, they are upon us," Marquez cried out, and put spurs to his horse. Pursued, he ordered his men to split open a wagon filled with gold and toss it in the trail. He made his way back to the capital as the Liberals stopped to pick up the treasure. Once back he lost all previous slight restraint, ordering that anyone who refused to contribute money to him be placed in a spot exposed to Diaz's gunners. He still spoke now and then of going to the relief of the Emperor's army, but made no move in that direction.

In the embattled city of Queretaro cavalry horses turned into bags of bones. Old mattresses were ripped up and the straw contents used for feed. One by one the horses began to die of starvation, their bodies going to nourish the famished men. The troops were still capable of countering Liberal thrusts, but there was never any reserve to exploit a success. They began to suspect the truth about Marquez: he had never had any intention of coming back.

The first of May came. They had been in Queretaro two

and a half months. A lean ox ran into the defenders' lines, sent there by the Liberals. A paper was attached to the animal's horns: it said that here was something for the Imperial army to eat so that they would be captured alive. Bravely the defenders sent back a horse the Liberals might use to chase the Imperials when they broke out of the city.

The Emperor was told ten times a day that he and an armed host must fight their way out to a safe haven. General Ramon Mendez promised that he and Mejia could guarantee a welcome in the Indian lands of the Sierra Gorda, a day's ride away. They could remain there while waiting for a favorable turn of events. All the men around the Emperor spoke in favor of the plan; but Maximilian, fondling his little King Charles spaniel, Baby, said he would rather die than leave his army. By the end of the first week of May there were periods when there was literally nothing for the troops to eat; and the weak patrols sent out for food returned decimated by the fire of the Liberals. The enemy shelling was almost continuous. Maximilian realized, then, that he must go.

Red-eyed and in constant pain, the Emperor visited the wounded in the improvised hospital and, terribly upset, said he would leave Queretaro only on condition that the doctors and nurses of his army stayed behind to do what they could for the men who had bled for him. It was agreed they would cut their way out on the night of the fourteenth. But all of that day Ramon Mendez was ill. "Well," the Emperor said, "one day, more or less, will be no matter." He said they would go on the night of the fifteenth. Miramon said every minute counted. "God help us for these twenty-four hours."

Next to Prince Salm-Salm, the man closest to the Emperor in those last days was the handsome Colonel Miguel Lopez. Maximilian had liked him from the moment he arrived in Mexico. After commanding the Mexican troops escorting Their Majesties from Vera Cruz to the capital, Lopez had served as colonel of the Empress's Regiment and then with the Imperial Guard. Often Lopez was his monarch's only companion as he made his impromptu inspection tours to inquire anxiously after the welfare of the soldiers. In earlier days the Emperor had stood as godfather to one of the colonel's children. An uncle of Marshal Bazaine's wife, Lopez had been one of four Mexican officers awarded the French Legion of Honor.

Some days before May 15, Lopez had secretly gone into the Liberal lines and asked for Escobedo.

Escobedo told him to sit down. Lopez asked if the Emperor's safety could be assured on condition that the Empire was ended. Could Escobedo promise safe passage to the coast, where the Emperor would board a European vessel, sign an abdication and recognize Juarez as ruler of the country?

Escobedo replied that his was strictly a military role. He would send a courier to San Luis Potosi to receive Juarez's decision on the matter.

Some nights later, Lopez came to Escobedo again and asked what the safe-conduct route would be. Silently Escobedo handed him Juarez's answer: there could be no conditions. The Emperor would be tried before a military court once the Liberals took Queretaro.

Lopez read the words and turned pale. He had been a great favorite of the Empress and was fond of the Emperor. He drew himself up and attempted to speak in a firm voice. "But this is death! You don't think so, General? Murder!"

"No!" said Escobedo. "This is justice, Colonel. Go back to the city and tell your chief there is no room for cherishing illusions. If he wants to spare Mexican blood, if he does not wish to increase the number of victims which is already so enormous, he should not delay his surrender."

Lopez left. Escobedo could see how he was trying to control his emotions. Twenty-four hours later, on the night of May 14, Lopez came to Escobedo, saying again that the Emperor would abdicate and publish a statement urging all Mexicans to support Juarez if his life and the lives of his supporters would be spared.

"Why didn't he do this three months ago?" Escobedo asked. "Now it is too late."

They talked. After a while, Lopez went back to La Cruz.

The Emperor did not sleep well that night, tossing in his cot with the frightful pain which accompanies dysentery. At half-past two, in agony, he sent for Dr. Basch, who did what he could for him. The Emperor finally dozed.

Prince Salm-Salm also slept, in a room down the long hall,

fully dressed and prepared for a night attack with a revolver under his pillow and his saber nearby. He had drunk a bottle of champagne to soothe his nerves. Dawn came. At four-thirty Miguel Lopez burst into Salm's room. "Quick!" Lopez shouted. "Save the life of the Emperor! The enemy is in La Cruz." Lopez rushed out. Suddenly La Cruz was alive with men shouting the Liberals were upon them.

Blasio, Maximilian's secretary, rushed into the Emperor's room and awakened him. Maximilian was as pale as death but completely calm. He took his saber in his hand and went into the hall. Salm ran to him. "We are betrayed," the Emperor said. He told Salm to order all available troops to the Hill of the Bells. There they would see how things might be arranged. Salm quickly passed the message to officers who were nearby and then descended a twisting stone stairway which opened upon the plaza facing La Cruz. Not a shot had been fired.

The plaza was entirely empty of Imperial soldiers, but in the dim half-light Salm saw that an artillery piece set in an embrasure had been upset and that through the gap Liberals were pouring in. He turned back to the staircase and saw the Emperor, a greatcoat slung over his shoulders and a revolver in each hand, coming down the steps with four Imperial officers. Salm rushed up the stairs. "Your Majesty, this is the last moment; the enemy is there." He pointed to the growing mass of Liberal soldiers below. The gray uniforms of the Supremos Poderes, the premier Liberal regiment, dominated. But there was nothing for it but to move down the stairs and they cautiously did so. A Liberal lieutenant colonel saw them and stepped forward. He was José Rincon Gallardo.

With Gallardo, at his side, was Miguel Lopez.

Gallardo looked at the Emperor and his little group. "You are civilians, you may pass," he said. They went into the streets of the city, the sound of La Cruz's bells ringing as the Liberals signaled triumph. The Emperor remarked that it was obvious that Gallardo knew who they were, but that he must have let them go because of the friendship of one of his sisters with the Empress. It must have been her kindness to the sister, he explained. "You see, it never does any harm to be good. It is true, you may find amongst twenty people nineteen ungrateful; but still, now and then, one grateful."

They went on. Some officers from La Cruz caught up with them and offered the Emperor a saddled horse. He refused, saying that if his companions walked he would do so too. A moment later Lopez came rushing up. He had left Gallardo behind with the Liberal soldiers. "Sire," Lopez said, "all is lost; the enemy is in La Cruz and very soon will occupy the city. But I have a perfectly safe place to hide Your Majesty."

"Hide myself? Never. Let us continue to the Hill of the Bells and there perhaps we shall find troops."

Lopez vanished, leaving them to continue on to the Hill of the Bells. Behind them they heard the enemy bugles sounding the "Diana"—the sound of victory. All around them their own troops were throwing away their rifles.

They came to the hill, passing an Imperial battalion in formation. It about-faced when its officers saw the Emperor and marched away.

Rifle fire from the Liberals sounded as they went up the hill. Mejia joined them. The three men, Mejia, Salm and the Emperor, stood on the hill together, surrounded by a handful of soldiers. The Emperor asked Mejia if they could break through the Liberal army and escape. It could not be done, Mejia said. The Emperor pressed him for a different answer but Mejia said, "To pass is impossible, but if Your Majesty orders it I am ready to die."

They stood in the clear light and looked down at the masses of Liberals gathered at the foot of the hill. All firing stopped. Before them white flags could be seen rising on the city's buildings. It was the end. "Now for a lucky bullet," Maximilian said. He leaned on his sword, his greatcoat unbuttoned to show his uniform and the medal for valor which Miramon had hung there. He took out some white material and attached it to a stick. The siege had lasted seventy-one days.

With Mejia on his right and Salm on his left the Emperor walked slowly down the hill to where some Liberal officers stood. One officer detached himself from the group and came to meet them. He took off his hat. "Your Majesty is my prisoner." Maximilian nodded.

Escobedo rode up with a large group of officers. They dismounted and Maximilian went to him, unbuckled his sword and handed it over. Escobedo gave it to an aide, Colonel Jesus

F. Garcia. "Take this sword, which belongs to the people," he said. The Empire was over.

He stood before Escobedo in a tent which had been quickly erected on the Hill of the Bells. For a long while he waited for Escobedo to speak, but the Liberal general said nothing. Finally Maximilian, speaking slowly and steadily, said that if there were to be executions in the wake of the victory, only he should be shot. "If more blood must be spilled, take only mine. Let the others go," he said.

Escobedo said his request would be sent to Juarez in San Luis Potosi one hundred and thirty miles away. He then turned Maximilian over to General Vicente Riva Palacio with instructions that he be escorted back to La Cruz. Maximilian was given his horse Anteburro, which had been saddled and brought to him. An unidentified Liberal officer stepped up to Maximilian as he left the tent. "I greet you," he said, "not as Emperor, but as Archduke of Austria, and admire you for your heroic defense." The man opened his arms. Maximilian fell into them.

They went back to La Cruz. As they approached the building the Imperial troops standing unarmed and under guard came to attention and uncovered their heads. Maximilian got off Anteburro, thanked Riva Palacio for his courtesy and gave him the horse.

It was ten in the morning. Under guard, he went back to the room he had left as the Emperor. Dr. Basch was there. He embraced his physician and burst into tears; but after a little while he got control of himself and said that at least there was something to be happy about: the surrender had taken place with virtually no bloodshed. Maximilian had learned by then from the Liberals that it was Lopez who had betrayed him—he had sold them all for money promised by Escobedo. "People like him are made use of, but then kicked," remarked Lieutenant Colonel José Rincon Gallardo, the officer who had permitted Maximilian to leave La Cruz after Lopez let the Liberals in. ("I hope you will recommend me for a good position," the traitor had said to the lieutenant colonel. Gallardo replied, "The only position I would recommend you for would be on a tree with a rope around your neck.")

Gallardo was only one of dozens of Liberal officers who came to see the vanquished enemy chieftain. To all of them Maximilian showed a cheerful appearance and courteous air. He asked them to sit down and chatted with them, showing no concern over his plight. Some of the Liberals were cruel, ordering their men to beat drums in the hall during those hours when Maximilian attempted to sleep, but most came to admire the fallen ruler who never seemed to lose his composure.

A couple of days after the capitulation Ramon Mendez was taken out to be shot. He had been all too anxious to execute the Liberals under the brutal terms of the Black Decree; it was said he shot men with whom he had personal feuds. Mendez claimed he executed men who had killed those near and dear to him. But, after Marquez, he was the most hated of all the Imperial generals. Mendez came swinging past the room where Mejia was being held. He walked quickly as he always did, with a cigar in his mouth. Mendez stopped and embraced Mejia. "I am sure that you will be today before all those people what you have always been," Mejia said. They had soldiered together for years. "Yes, Don Tomas, don't worry," Mendez said. He was taken to the wall of the bullfight arena and forced to kneel with his back to the firing squad, a sign of disgrace. But as the order to shoot was uttered, he twisted around so as to take the bullets with his face to his executioners. The shots knocked him on his back but did not kill him. A Liberal officer came up to give him the coup de grace. Mendez lifted his hand and pointed to a place behind his ear. The shot blew out his brains.

Those around Maximilian tried to keep word of the execution from him, but he learned of it. Perhaps the Liberals thought that the knowledge would impel him to try to escape, for they ordered his place of imprisonment changed. Heavily guarded, he was taken to the San Teresita Convent and was placed in a little room overlooking the yard. The next morning the Princess Salm-Salm was announced. She had spent the days of siege in Mexico City dreaming the same dream over and over: her husband dying in battle as Maximilian stood by imploring him to live. Finally she had suggested to various European officers in the capital that she go to Queretaro and suggest to the Emperor that he surrender and order the surrender of Mexico City on condition that his life and those of his supporters be spared. She went through the encircling lines under a flag of truce and found Porfirio Diaz in a blue cutaway coat with brass buttons, dark-blue trousers and high boots. He shook hands with her. She thought him handsome, with brilliant dark eyes. She explained her plan. He gave her an escort and sent her to Escobedo.

Before sunrise the Princess Salm-Salm rode along the Calle de San Francisco. Outside the capital she saw a Liberal officer hanging from a tree, his head and face covered with a black cap. Blood ran down his body. She looked away and saw another man hanging from another tree. They were rapists, shot at the scene of their crimes and strung up.

The Princess came to Escobedo as the siege went into its last days. He refused to permit entrance into Queretaro, but told her to go to Juarez in San Luis Potosi. For three days she rocked in a swaying diligence going across the desert. She presented a letter from Escobedo at Juarez's headquarters. Her dog Jimmy ran in ahead of her and was already lying on the sofa near the President when she entered the room. Juarez was wearing his usual English collar, black necktie and black broadcloth. The Princess told him she wished to be allowed to visit Maximilian, then under siege. Juarez said he would think it over. He gave her his arm, escorted her to a staircase leading to the street and bowed her out. Nine days later all the bells in San Luis Potosi signaled the fall of Queretaro. She rushed south to the city and to the Convent of San Teresita.

When her husband the Prince came out it seemed to her he was dirty enough to have just emerged from a dustbin. She wavered on her feet and almost fainted in his arms. When the Princess got hold of herself her husband presented her to Maximilian, who lay, sick and pale, on a miserable bed. He rose and kissed her hand. She was indignant at the conditions under which he was existing, and went to Escobedo, who said to her that Maximilian might come to him to discuss the matter. The Princess returned to the convent and reported what the general had said. Maximilian, taking the tack that the general had once called upon him, said he would not feel it wrong to return the call; therefore, with the Prince by his side and the Princess on his arm, he went to visit the Mexican general, who had made his headquarters at the Hacienda Hercules, the residence of a banker. Two bands played in the fine garden and all the Liberal officers bowed when the little party alighted from the carriage which had brought them.

They went down a wide walk past a fountain and sat down with Escobedo and his staff. The conversation was polite and unemotional. Escobedo said the prisoners might move from the convent to whatever place they chose. But General Refugio Gonzales, in charge of the guard detail, objected, telling Escobedo he was treating the prisoner like a reigning Prince and that the place for him was not some randomly selected private residence, but rather the Convent of the Capuchins. Escobedo said that if that was what Gonzales recommended, the convent would do.

Maximilian and those with him went to the Convent of the Capuchins, a rather bleak, austere place. Maximilian was led down to the burial crypts. He halted at the threshold. "Certainly that cannot be my room; why, this is a vault for the dead." A Liberal officer went to ask Gonzales, who had not accompanied them, if this was the place he had chosen for Maximilian. "Yes, that is his room," Gonzales said, "and he must sleep there, at least this night, in order to remind him that his time is at hand." Maximilian slept among the graves. The next day Escobedo intervened and Maximilian was transferred to one of the three rooms on the top story of the building. Miramon, one of the few men wounded when La Cruz was taken—he had been shot in the face—was given the second room, and Mejia the third. The rooms opened upon an interior balcony overlooking the tiny courtyard.

It seemed to the Princess that everyone but Maximilian recognized the danger he was in. Scores of prisoners from the Imperial army were being released every day and sent off, many with small sums of money contributed by Escobedo; but it was openly said that Maximilian must die. Finally it was announced that Maximilian, Miramon and Mejia must immediately stand trial before a military tribunal which would base its case upon the law forbidding aid to the intervention. The law had been promulgated by Juarez in 1862 when the French, English and Spanish first came to Mexico.

The Princess went to Maximilian and said she was going to

Juarez to argue his case and ask at least for a delay so that a defense might be prepared. She went in a mule-drawn carriage with two drivers. Juarez heard her out and said he would delay the trial until the prisoners had time to obtain legal aid. The Princess returned to Queretaro. She was filthy from the dust of the road, her shoes torn from walking in places where riding was dangerous. "Have you had any success? What did Juarez say?" her husband demanded when she came in.

"They have granted the delay," she said. "Oh, Your Majesty, I am so glad."

He kissed her hand. "God bless you, Madame," he finally managed. "You have been too kind to one who is afraid he can never serve you."

"Do not be too sure of that, Your Majesty. I shall have some favor to ask for the Prince here, yet."

"You will never need to ask that, Madame. But you look weary. You are very tired. We can offer you little. Prince, you must care for your . . . I . . ." He turned away to hide his tears.

They sent to the surrendered Mexico City to get lawyers. In the capital Diaz was now master. Marquez had vanished, taking with him a million dollars raised for the defense of Queretaro. It was said he had ordered masons to build a secret tunnel from his headquarters to a street through which he could flee to safety. The task done, he shot the masons and fled to Havana with the money.

In the days that followed, as lawyers were sought, Queretaro gave its heart to Maximilian. Each day ladies sent in bread, meat, cake. Word spread that the deposed Emperor had no linen; soon he was so inundated with it that he said that never in his life had he owned so many sets of underclothing or so many handkerchiefs. He played cards with Salm, listened to his stories of the American Civil War—Maximilian had always been interested in the United States—and read histories, biographies and books on the natural sciences. He seemed to believe that he would meet with Juarez and together they would make everything all right. He often talked of what he would do when Juarez released him. "You shall go with me," he said to Blasio, his secretary. "First to London. We'll stay there a year and have my papers brought from Miramar and write a history of my reign. Then we shall go to Naples and rent a house in one of the beautiful suburbs which surround the city, with a view of the landscape and sea. On my yacht *Ondina*, with Basch, old Bilimek and four servants we'll make little voyages to the Greek archipelago, to Athens, to the coast of Turkey. Later I shall spend the rest of my life in view of the Adriatic on my island Lacroma." He said the same thing to Salm, describing how wonderful a moment it would be when they set foot on his yacht.

"Your Majesty," Salm said, "I request, in advance, your pardon if I should get a little tipsy on that blessed day."

Each day the Princess came to visit the prisoner, her dog Jimmy rushing before her to make Maximilian's face light up. "Our guardian angel is coming." He had Blasio list the Prince as a Grand Officer in the Order of Guadalupe and the Princess as Lady of Honor of the Order of San Carlos. He would have made her a Palast Dame of the Empress, he explained, but it was not possible. Carlota was not there to sign the higher appointment.

Maximilian's position was that he had raised the white flag of surrender and that Juarez would not shoot a prisoner who had surrendered. Everyone around him disagreed. There were Austrian ships in the bay outside of Vera Cruz. He must contrive to get on one. Otherwise he was doomed. Salm talked of nothing but bribing the guards, and went about with a roll of gold which he literally held under the noses of various officers to whom he promised the world if they would let Maximilian escape. But it was going to be difficult, for literally hundreds of Liberal soldiers were in and around the convent. Men with unholstered revolvers stood on the balcony outside the rooms of the prisoners. In addition, Salm's search for soldiers susceptible to a bribe was only reluctantly endorsed by the man he was trying to save. "Do it in an honorable manner," he told Salm. "I would rather die than degrade myself." Anyway, he said, the lawyers would be coming from the capital to discuss the case. What would it look like if he were not there after having invited them to come to him?

Escobedo knew of Salm's attempts, and had Salm and all other prisoners removed from the convent to the city casino.

They were marched there under a burning sun, to find their new lodgings bare of even knives and forks. They ate with their fingers. Maximilian lived more luxuriously. But on his table the jailers placed four silver candlesticks, the traditional lighting for condemned men.

On June 5 three of the foremost lawyers of Mexico arrived in Queretaro. They were led by Mariano Riva Palacio, perhaps the most worthy attorney in the country. The group met, at ten in the morning, with Maximilian in his little cell. The heat was intense and the flies so numerous that it was necessary to cover the glasses containing the sugar-flavored water with cardboard squares. Maximilian seemed, in Riva Palacio's eyes, to be taking a strangely desultory approach to the entire matter. He discussed various people, complimenting the lawyer on his son Vicente, who had escorted him away from the Hill of the Bells, and to whom he had given his horse. He chatted so amiably and in so unconcerned a fashion that the lawyers grew uneasy and finally broke in to talk of the danger he faced.

Juarez's position was that Maximilian was guilty of disturbing the peace of Mexico by even coming to Vera Cruz; the law of 1862 against the intervention covered that. Worse, Maximilian had signed the Black Decree. If Juarez did not execute him for that, Juarez by implication endorsed the deaths of tens of thousands of Mexicans shot by the French and the Imperial army. There were other unstated reasons for the Liberals to wish him dead. Fifty years of battle had not crushed Conservatism in Mexico, and if Maximilian were allowed to live he would remain a Conservative symbol and rallying point for the rest of his life. The Emperor Iturbide had sworn he would never come back after being deposed, but he had returned. Would this ex-Emperor do the same? As for Mejia and Miramon, the first was the Empire's best soldier and the second had been a Conservative President and unreserved enemy of Liberalism. Allowed to go free, would they ever be reconciled with Juarez's leadership of their country?

From the very first the lawyers realized they were beaten on a legal basis. Maximilian himself studied the charges and said he had to hide his mouth with his hand, for they were so ridiculous they made him laugh. He refused to go before the tribunal, which held its proceedings in the town's fine pink sandstone theater five minutes' walk from the Convent of the Capuchins. He based his refusal upon his poor health, saying to the people around him that he would not have it reported that he looked weak as he sat, an Archduke of Austria and a former Emperor, in the prisoner's dock. Miramon and Mejia went, Miramon to say that indeed it was true that he had expected to succeed Maximilian as the country's ruler, Mejia to sit in silence. The tribunal, composed of young and half-literate Liberal officers, many in their early twenties, sentenced the three defendants to death by the firing squad. There had never been the slightest doubt they would do so.

An officer came to Maximilian's cell and read him the verdict. The officer then went next door and read it to Miramon. Mejia was next. His wife, in the last stages of pregnancy, was visiting with him. When the officer began to read the verdict to Mejia he was interrupted by Maximilian, who had burst in after him. "General," he cried, "with your permission may I take your wife outside?"

"Go on, girl," Mejia said. She began to cry out that she would not go, and Maximilian, desperate to spare her the sight and sound of the officer droning out the news that her husband was doomed, practically carried her to his room. She was weeping there as he tried to comfort her when, a few minutes later, Mejia came and put out his hand. "Thank you, Señor," he said.

The sentence did not take Princess Salm-Salm unawares. A few days earlier, in the evening, she had had a long conversation with Maximilian. He talked of his mother, saying he wished the Princess to go to her if he were shot. She kept at him about the possibility of escape through bribery and, almost reluctantly, he gave her his signet ring and two signed bills, each for one hundred thousand U. S. dollars' worth of gold drawn on the Imperial family of Austria. The Princess would offer one of the bills to the officer in direct charge of the guards, Colonel Miguel Palacio. If he accepted the money, she would give him the ring also; seeing him wearing the ring, Maximilian would know the way to freedom was open.

At eight that evening, when they had finished their talk, she left Maximilian and asked Palacio to see her to the home where she had rented rooms. Maximilian had nicknamed

Colonel Palacio The Hyena but the word was not entirely descriptive of him; he was just a simple, hardly literate soldier. His young wife had just given him his first child and his life revolved about the infant. The Princess drew him out, asking his opinion of Maximilian. He said that all through the years of the Empire he had been a great enemy of the Emperor but, seeing him now, "how good and nobly he behaved in his misfortune," having "looked into his true, melancholy blue eyes," he felt "the greatest sympathy, if not love and admiration for him."

They talked for about twenty minutes, alone in the parlor of the home where she was staying. Finally she said she had something to say of the greatest importance but that before telling Palacio she must have his word of honor as an officer and gentleman, that he must swear by the head of his wife and child never to reveal what she was about to divulge. He did so and, trembling, she took out one of the signed bills. He need only turn his back and close his eyes for ten minutes and it was his. Bluntly she said she knew he was a poor man. What she offered him, one hundred thousand dollars' worth of gold, would mean luxury for his wife and child for all their lives. And it need not offend his honor to accept, for in doing so he would really be serving Mexico. What good would it do, after all, to kill Maximilian?

Palacio put his hand over his heart and said that he really did think it would be best for Mexico if Maximilian escaped, but that he could not make up his mind so quickly. In any case, he said, he would not take money. It came into her mind that he was after all the son of a nation where paper money was suspect, where only metal coinage was trusted. A bag of gold would have been better, she thought to herself. She gave him the signet ring and urged him to wear it as a sign to Maximilian that there would be an escape. Palacio fingered the piece of paper, put the ring on, took it off and handed it back. "Isn't the sum enough?" she cried. She began to unbutton her blouse. "Well, Colonel, here am I!" He jumped up and said that now his honor was even more in question and that if she undressed he would leap from the window into the street. She calmed him and he said he would think of the matter. He left her. And went to Escobedo and told him everything.

In the morning the Princess was put under arrest and taken to the general. Escobedo ordered her out of the city. She went again to San Luis Potosi to see the President. Word of the death sentence had reached Europe, where Benito Juarez was looked upon as a bloodthirsty Indian akin to those who were occasionally exhibited in loincloths at expositions and fairs. A flood of interoceanic cables had gone out, from Victor Hugo, Garibaldi, from government officials. All asked that Mexico spare the brother of the Emperor of Austria, the brother-in-law of the King of the Belgians, the relative through marriage of Queen Victoria. The Princess Salm-Salm found Juarez pale and suffering at the thought of the sentence. He told her that her husband would be freed but that Maximilian must die.

The execution was set for June 16, at three in the afternoon. At noon the prisoners were told. Maximilian took out his watch and looked at it. He told Dr. Basch, who was taking some dictation from him, that there would be time to finish their work. "I can assure you that dying is a much easier thing than I imagined," he added. "I am quite prepared."

Three o'clock came. They waited. Nothing happened. Juarez, learning the lawyers were coming to appeal to him for mercy, had ordered a postponement. The wives of Mejia and Miramon were also en route to San Luis Potosi. Neither of their husbands had the slightest hope that Juarez would change his mind, but Miramon, thinking it would be better for his wife to be active, had told her she might go. The idea of asking mercy would never have occurred to Mejia, but his wife also wanted to make an appeal and he did not forbid her.

In San Luis Potosi the lawyers met with Juarez. He was as formal and unmovable in victory as in the days of defeat. The execution would be carried out in three days, he told the lawyers. "At this moment," he said, "you cannot comprehend the necessity for it, nor the justice by which it is supported. That appreciation is reserved for Time. The law and the sentence are at this minute inexorable, because the welfare of the nation exacts it. That may further counsel the economy of blood, which will be the greatest pleasure of my life."

"Señor President," cried the lawyer Martinez de la Torre, "no more blood!"

But Juarez's mind was made up.

Half-demented by fear, Miramon's wife met the lawyers after their appeal to Juarez. "Is there any hope for the life of Miguel?" she asked. They told her there was not. Mejia's wife went from one member of Juarez's staff to another. Her husband had during the endless Conservative-Liberal wars spared the lives of several of them. They tried to comfort her and offered money, but said nothing could be done. The time for her confinement was almost upon her, but she left San Luis Potosi, frantically saying she would appeal to Escobedo by reminding him that Mejia had let him live when Marquez would have shot him. Distracted, she rushed south toward Queretaro. She traveled all night and through the next day. At midnight her labor pains began. She stopped at a hacienda and at one in the morning gave birth to Mejia's son. At dawn she was again on the road for Queretaro.

She did not know it then but Escobedo had already gone to Mejia and said he would permit him to escape. Mejia asked if Maximilian would also be allowed to go free. Escobedo told him it was impossible. Mejia said, "I am obligated to the Emperor, and I will follow the same destiny as he." Escobedo went away. When Juarez learned, later, he said: "He was Indian and he was loyal."

From his cell Maximilian sent a last appeal to San Luis Potosi: "Citizen Juarez, I should desire that the lives of Don Miguel Miramon and Don Tomas Mejia, who the day before yesterday suffered all the tortures and bitterness of death, be conserved; and that, as I intimated upon being made prisoner, I may be the only victim." There was no answer to the telegram.

With Blasio, Salm and Basch acting as secretaries, he dictated a will which called upon his brother to aid the widows Mejia and Miramon would leave behind. He did not mention his own wife, for he believed she was dead. That was the news which had reached Queretaro. It was Mejia who told him Carlota was gone. "One string less that binds me to life," he said. Then word came that she lived. No one knew which story was true.

Maximilian wrote to Francis Joseph, his first letter in years, to beg his brother's pardon for any hurt he had caused him. He wrote Riva Palacio and the other attorneys thanking them for all they had done; he wrote to say farewell to a dozen people in Europe and Mexico, the Pope, the King of the Belgians, his former cabinet Ministers, his younger brothers, Gutierrez de Estrada. There were no recriminations, only words of thanks and Godspeed.

Thinking that it was at least a possibility that his wife still lived, he wrote to her also:

"My beloved Charlotte! If God grant that you recover your health and are able to read these lines, you will understand the cruelty of the fate which has been dealing me its blows without respite since your departure for Europe. So many events, alas, so many sudden blows, have broken the whole of my hopes! Death is to me a happy release. I shall fall proudly as a soldier, like a king defeated but not dishonored. If your sufferings are too severe, and God calls you to come and join me soon, I shall bless the hand of God which has been heavy upon us. Adieu, Charlotte! Adieu. Your poor Maximilian."

The Ministers of the European nations, and others, came to say farewell. Baron Karl von Gagern, who had long ago at Miramar told him not to go, went to see him and thought he looked more the part of an apostle than of a hero. Friendliness shone from his eyes and he said, "Baron Gagern, you have been a good prophet."

In San Luis Potosi on the evening of the eighteenth, the night before the scheduled date of the execution, the Princess Salm-Salm made a last attempt to change Juarez's mind. He said he could not prolong the agony, could not order another delay. Maximilian must die. She fell before him and gripped his knees. He tried to raise her. The Princess remained kneeling before him, and Juarez said in a low, sad voice, "I am grieved, Madame, to see you thus on your knees before me; but if all the kings and queens of Europe were in your place I could not spare that life. It is not I who take it, it is the people and the law, and if I should not do its will the people would take it and mine also."

Princess Salm-Salm arose and went out into the anteroom where waited Miramon's wife, her two children and more than two hundred ladies of San Luis Potosi. They had come to ask for mercy. Juarez tried to speak with Señora Miramon but she fainted when his first words indicated he could not spare her husband's life. The President left and locked himself in his room, refusing to see anybody. A telegram was handed in.

"Señor Benito Juarez, On the point of being executed, as the consequence of having been desirous to prove if new political institutions would have the effect of terminating the sanguinary civil war which has devastated this unfortunate country for many years past, I shall deliver up my life with pleasure if its sacrifice can contribute to the peace and prosperity of my adopted country. Fully persuaded that nothing solid can be founded in a territory drenched with blood and agitated by violent commotions, I conjure you, in the most solemn manner and with the sincerity becoming these moments, that my blood may be the last that is shed, and that the same perseverance (which it has been my pleasure to acknowledge and respect in the midst of prosperity) with which you have defended the cause that has just triumphed may be consecrated to the most noble task of reconciling minds, and establishing in a stable and durable manner the peace and tranquility of this unfortunate country! Maximilian."

They rose at dawn of the next day, June 19, 1867, awakened by the "Diana" sounding on the trumpets as the troops assembled in the street. Maximilian, thirty-four years old, was dressed in black and wore a white felt sombrero. He had tucked a half-dozen handkerchiefs into his shirt to stop the blood from pouring out. He came onto the balcony and stood with Miramon as they waited for Mejia. In his room Mejia washed, and then dried himself with the sheet from his bed. He had not been given a towel and had not asked for one. He made the sign of the Cross all over his body and then draped under his coat the blue band of a divisional commander. Together, they ate breakfast, chicken, bread, wine, coffee.

Outside, four thousand men stood in the street surrounding three simple fiacres. A priest, Father Soria, held Mass in Maximilian's room. When he was finished, they went to the head of the stairs leading down to the courtyard. The Emperor's valet Antonio Grill and his cook Josef Tudos stood with Dr. Basch. Salm was not present by Maximilian's order. He said he was afraid the Prince would do something violent which might cost him his life. Grill and Tudos were in tears. "Be calm," Maximilian told them. "You see I am so. It is the will of God that I should die, and we cannot do anything about that. Are you ready, gentlemen? I am."

The three men went down the stairs, and Dr. Basch made as if to fall into line behind him. But as the doctor started down the steps he hesitated, then halted. He found it impossible to go on and stayed there as the three men went into the street. The sun blazed down on the waiting troops of the Supremos Poderes, Cazadores de Galena and the Nuevo Leon Battalion. Maximilian turned his head right and left, breathed deeply, looked up at the magnificent, cloudless Mexican sky. "What a glorious day! I have always wanted to die on just such a day."

Each of them, accompanied by a priest, took a separate carriage. As Mejia mounted the steps of his carriage, carrying a crucifix in his hands, a disheveled woman whom the onlookers took for a maniac came rushing up through the ranks of the soldiers. She was screaming. In her arms she carried a one-day-old baby boy. The carriages began to move. Augustina Mejia shifted the baby to one arm and grabbed at the back wheel of her husband's carriage. Inside, he stared straight ahead. The turning wheel carried her forward a step or two and then flung her down into the street, her face striking a rock in the gutter. She lay there, blood flowing, holding her baby, and the rear guard troops marched past her.

The streets of Queretaro that day were silent. The window shutters were drawn closed, a sign of mourning within. No one turned out to watch the procession. A military band began to play the Dead March.

They went across the city. Rushing after them came a dark figure. It was Tudos. "Good God!" he cried in Magyar. "I didn't believe it could come to this! I didn't believe—"

They came to the Hill of the Bells and wound their way up its slight rise. Just short of the summit a crude adobe wall had been erected. The carriages stopped. Maximilian tried to open the door on his side. It was jammed. He took off his sombrero and lifted himself through the window and down to the rocky ground. "Here is where I wanted to plant the standard of victory, and it is here where I am going to die," Maximilian said. "Life is only a comedy."

Father Soria came out of the other door of the carriage, looked around him, staggered. He seemed about to faint. Maximilian reached into his pocket, found smelling salts and held them under the priest's nose until he signaled he was more in control of himself. The group of men moved up to the wall. Mejia suddenly became weak and was helped by two soldiers. A file of peons put down three simple pine coffins, bought at a price of one peso fifty centavos each.

An officer turned to the assembled troops and onlookers. He read out an order of the day: if anyone attempted to interfere with the proceedings about to take place, that person would join the three condemned men in sharing their fate.

Maximilian took out his watch and pressed the spring which opened it. Looking out at him were the hands which indicated it was just seven o'clock; and a tiny photograph of Carlota. He raised her face to his lips and kissed it. He gave the watch to the priest and asked that if she lived he arrange for it to be given to her. "Should she ever be able to understand, tell her that my eyes were closed with her likeness, which I will bear with me to heaven."

Father Soria said, "Sire, in my person bestow upon Mexico the kiss of reconciliation. Let Your Majesty forgive all in this supreme moment." Maximilian leaned down. They kissed. A very great silence hung over the Hill of the Bells. Tudos arrived, sobbing. Maximilian gave him his sombrero and a handkerchief. "You will give these to my mother." The cook fell on his knees and bent to kiss Maximilian's feet. He gently raised him up and moved toward the firing party. Maximilian went down the line of seven men, handing to each a gold piece of the Empire with his profile on it. Pointing to his heart as he walked, he said, "Boys, aim well, aim right here."

The officer commanding the firing squad, Captain Gonzales, came up behind Maximilian and said to the men that General Escobedo, in accordance with the wish of the condemned man, had ordered that no bullets must strike his face. Should a bullet hit Maximilian in the face, the officer said, it would be impossible to know which of the men of the squad had disobeyed orders; therefore all of them would be executed.

Maximilian turned to Mejia and Miramon. "General," he said to Miramon, "a brave man must be honored even in the face of death. Allow me to give you the place of honor." Miramon moved to take the center position in front of the wall. Maximilian turned to Mejia. "General, what is not rewarded on earth will surely be in heaven." He motioned Mejia to stand on Miramon's right. He knew Mejia would not want to be on the other end of the little line; for that was where the unrepentant thief had been when Jesus Christ was crucified.

He himself took up the position on Miramon's left. He looked at Captain Gonzales. "At your disposition, Señor." The officer saluted with his sword and began to stammer out that he regretted the duty he was about to perform. He had not desired this, he said. He asked forgiveness. "Young man," Maximilian said, "I appreciate your compassion, but the duty of a soldier is to obey. No forgiveness is necessary. Carry out the order which has been given you." Gonzales stepped back and stood by the squad.

Some people who had been standing about began to draw back. The firing squad, twenty-one men in all, seven for each of the three figures in front of the wall, lifted their rifles and cocked them. The people ran, leaving the three prisoners by themselves. None wore coverings over their eyes.

Maximilian folded his hands over his heart and in a clear voice cried out, "I forgive everybody, I pray that everyone may also forgive me, and I wish that my blood, which is now to be shed, may be for the good of the country. Long live Mexico, long live independence!"

Miramon cried, "Long live the Emperor!"

Mejia repeated the words, then dropped the crucifix in front of him, saying, "Holy Virgin."

An absolute silence fell upon the assembled people. The official physician, Dr. Manuel Calvillo, looked at the three men before turning his head away, and it seemed to him that standing there by their wall they looked like silhouettes.

The captain commanding the firing squad raised his sword in the air.

"Listos!

"Apunten!

"Fuego!"

Afterword

THE NEWS OF THE EXECUTIONS on the Hill of the Bells reached Paris ten days after the event. It came to the Emperor and Empress of the French as they prepared to go to distribute the prizes for the Great Exhibition of 1867, in the area where the Eiffel Tower stands today. The Great Exhibition was a world's fair to rival London's famed Crystal Palace event of 1851. Twelve Emperors and Kings came to Paris, six reigning Princes, a Viceroy and nine Heirs Apparent.

Eugenie and Napoleon did not accept as true the early rumors of the execution. But as they were about to leave the Tuileries for the fair grounds a servant announced an unscheduled visit by the Count and Countess of Flanders. Eugenie came out and saw the Belgians were in black. "You are in mourning," she gasped. "Not me. No, it is not possible. I do not wish to believe in such a misfortune!"

She ran to her husband. Perhaps it was true after all. In two priceless stagecoaches from the Trianon Museum, each of crystal and gold and drawn by eight horses, the Emperor and Empress and Prince Imperial rode through great crowds to the exhibition grounds. The Prince of Wales and the Sultan of Turkey were there. As the Emperor and Empress arrived a gigantic orchestra of twelve hundred musicians began to play. Wondering if the report was correct, the monarchs handed out prizes to the winners of the fair's various competitions. During the procedure a messenger came to the Ambassador and Ambassadress of Austria, the Prince and Princess Richard Metternich. They immediately rose and left. A telegram was handed to Napoleon. It was confirmation. They continued to award prizes, smiling as the enormous orchestra played. When it was over they drove back to the Tuileries. Eugenie came out of the carriage smiling, made her way to her private apartments, and, fainting, was carried to bed.

Three years later Juan Prim, who once had gone to Mexico to participate in an intervention there, sought and found a candidate for King of Spain. Queen Isabella had been deposed. Prim, at the head of the government, offered the throne to Prince Leopold of Hohenzollern. His acceptance would mean that Prussia had outflanked France to the south. The French Ambassador to Prussia was ordered to protest. He obtained from King William a statement that the Prince would withdraw himself as a candidate. Fatally demanding too much, the ambassador then asked King William for a guarantee that the Prince would never again consider an offer. King William indicated he had finished speaking. The news was telegraphed to Bismarck in Berlin. Bismarck rewrote the telegram to make it appear that the King had insulted France's ambassador, and released the text to the newspapers.

The next day the streets of Paris were filled with people crying, "To Berlin!" The armies mobilized. Utterly weary and terribly ill with a frightful gallstone, the Emperor of the French went to the wars with the fourteen-year-old Prince Imperial. "Louis, do your duty," Eugenie said, tracing a cross on her son's forehead. They stood in the Imperial train and Napoleon said to a courtier, "Dumanoir, I forgot to say goodbye to you." Dumanoir bowed. Those were the last words Paris heard Napoleon utter, for he was never to return to the capital. A pale baggage, he trailed after armies completely outgeneraled by the Prussians. Defeat followed defeat. He sought death in the lines, ordering his suite to safety while he waited for a shell. It did not come. He called upon a marshal of France who had commanded in Mexico. "To your charge I commit the last army of France," he said to Bazaine. "Think of the Prince Imperial." The Prussians bore down. Bazaine surrendered.

In Paris, Eugenie said, "The dynasty is finished. We must think only of France." Outside the Tuileries, draped and closed for the summer, she heard the mob screaming, "Death to the Spanish woman!" Once they had screamed death for an Austrian woman—Marie Antoinette. Admiral Jean Pierre Edmond Jurien de la Gravière, who once had taken twenty-five hundred French troops to the port of Vera Cruz, was with her as they listened to the sound of the gates of the palace being smashed down and the windows caving in. She forbade him to go with her—the mob would kill any Frenchman in her company—and fled with Prince Metternich of Austria and the Italian ambassador. They ran through half a mile of the Tuileries and Louvre, past statues of Egyptian pharaohs and Louis XIV paintings. Breathless, Eugenie arrived in the Place de St. Germain l'Auxerrois, where she leaned against the railing of the church from which was given the signal for the massacre of St. Bartholomew's Night. She looked back at her Palace of the Tuileries. "A dream! A dream!" she gasped. She took a horsecab, as King Louis Philippe had done, and went to safety and exile in England. Her husband and son joined her there.

Three years later Napoleon III was dead, his last glazed-eyed words to his doctor remindful of the battle which ended his reign: "Ah, Conneau . . . Were you at Sedan?" Six years passed and the Prince Imperial, twenty-three, went in a British uniform to Zululand. He found his death there at the hands of hostile natives who surprised the patrol he was accompanying. He took seventeen assegai slashes, all in front. Eugenie buried him by his father. After that she often went back to Paris to wander the Tuileries gardens, all that was left of the palace the mob had burned. Once an old gardener ordered her not to pick a flower from the beds. She told her friends she liked being there despite the memories. "The Empress died in 1870," she said. The flesh lived fifty years more.

If she died in spirit in the year of 1870, Prim perished in actuality. "Prepare to die!" a voice cried out of the night as his carriage passed through Madrid; and a pistol shot took him. No one ever knew who fired it, or why. Thirty-four years later a street in Mexico City was named for him: Calle de General Prim.

That year, 1870, destroyed Marshal Bazaine. He was the scapegoat of France's disasters. He was sent to prison. With the aid of former Señorita Peña he escaped, to die in exile in

Madrid. She went back to Mexico, to die lonely and forgotten there in a mental institution.

Prince Felix zu Salm-Salm died in 1870, taking precisely the kind of death wound he would have desired: a French bullet in the body as he struggled up a hill with his sword in his left hand, his right having been disabled as his horse was shot from under him. His wife's last memento of him was a note scribbled an hour before his death. It ended with mention of their dog, who had been fondled by the condemned prisoner Maximilian and who had sat by Benito Juarez as Princess Salm-Salm begged Juarez to spare Maximilian's life: *"Kiss little Jimmy."*

The dashing Marquis de Galliffet was the only French hero of that war. He had led a last gallant cavalry charge at Gravelotte and had wrenched from the watching enemy chieftain, King William of Prussia, a gasped-out, "Oh! The brave men!"

It was Jules Favre who on September 4, 1870, had the great pleasure to announce to the Legislative Body that the Empire was finished. It was the happiest moment of his life. It was succeeded by wretchedness. "I believe," he said, "that the strongest nation is the nation that comes closest to total disarmament." Thinking so and also that with the Bonapartes gone Prussia would have no argument with France, he went to Bismarck. So inept a negotiator was Favre, Bismarck said later, that he had been tempted to take him in hand and show him how the world worked. Instead he took from France Alsace and part of Lorraine and an unheard-of indemnity. In the Palace of Versailles, Bismarck proclaimed Prussia and its satellites a German Empire. It was said of Napoleon's surrender in that war that when he handed his sword to King William it was only a fragment that he offered. For it had been broken in Mexico, the Moscow of the Second Empire.

The news of the execution reached Francis Joseph as he prepared to go for his annual summer shooting holiday at Ischl. He did not postpone the trip by one hour. He was a creature of habit.

A very great proportion of those who had been at the party the Archduchess Sophia gave in the Christmas of 1866—the one at which tears came into her eyes as the bells in Max's clock chimed—found tragic fates. The Archduke Rudolph, who pulled the children along in a sleigh, shot himself twenty-two years later at Mayerling, leaving behind several Last Wills, one of which spoke of his Adriatic island of Lacroma and asked that the Imperial family always keep it as a remembrance of "poor Uncle." On the day Rudolph died, his father attended to all the business his staff brought before him. He grieved, but he was still Francis Joseph the Emperor. The Empress Elizabeth found her death ten years after Rudolph found his—at the end of an anarchist's stiletto. She must have welcomed it as a release from a life that had been intolerable for half a century.

The Archduke Karl Ludwig's son Otto, whom Francis Joseph had rocked in the sleigh on the day of the Christmas party, died of venereal disease after a wild and scandalous life. His older brother, the Archduke Francis Ferdinand, who had climbed up to sit by Sisi on the sofa, had become Heir Apparent on Rudolph's death. In the summer of 1914 Francis Ferdinand entertained the Emperor of Germany, William II, at the castle of Miramar. From Miramar Francis Ferdinand went to Vienna. From Vienna he went to Sarajevo. When he died of the bullets which set off the First World War, the dead Otto's son Charles became Heir Apparent. Two years later Francis Joseph died, murmuring that he must get up, for there was so much to be done. In somber wartime Vienna, Charles was crowned Emperor. His reign lasted two years; and the Empire crashed to earth.

The Archduchess Sophia was long dead by then, of course, dying in 1872. She never recovered from the horror of the news from Queretaro. "My good son Max, shot like a criminal," she screamed, her voice chilling those who heard her. It was said of her that she never raised her head again after the death of her favorite child. When on the night of January 17, 1868, she saw his body in his coffin, she sank sobbing upon it and stayed with it until dawn.

Maximilian had come home on the *Novara*, crossing the ocean in a salon draped in black and with candles burning. A hearse in black crepe waited at Trieste, and when the coffin touched Austrian soil his brothers Karl Ludwig and Ludwig Viktor were there to receive it. The funeral party traveled north in a special train through snow-covered mountains and came to Vienna, where a detachment of Hussars waited with torches to escort the coffin to the Hofburg. On January 20 in the Capuchin Crypt of the Augustiner Church of Vienna the body was committed to a marble sepulcher locked with a golden key. Next to it rested the coffin which held the remains of the Duke of Reichstadt. They lay side by side for seventy-two years. In 1940, as a gift to France, Adolf Hitler ordered the body of the Great Emperor's son taken to lie by his father.

Benito Juarez went from San Luis Potosi to Queretaro and then to Mexico City, where Porfirio Diaz reigned. There was no flag of the Republic over the National Palace. Once Diaz had promised that Juarez would raise that flag there again, and he had allowed no one else to do so until the President arrived.

Juarez lived five more years. A heart attack struck him as he pulled an orphan up from where the child had fallen on his knees, his arms clasping Juarez's legs.

"Doctor, is my disease mortal?" Juarez asked, and took the affirmative answer with not the slightest sign of emotion, almost as if, the doctor thought, it were the body of another person being discussed.

Soon after Juarez's death, Diaz became President and with hardly any interruption reigned until 1910. The heroes of the war against the French and Maximilian were the Mexican Government for all that long era. As the decades passed they grew old and corrupt. Perhaps Diaz forgot those things the young Diaz had said he fought for. As President he maintained a murderous dictatorship.

It can be said of Diaz that he held no grudges. Archbishop Labastida stayed at the head of the Church, and in time ingratiated himself with the increasingly Conservative government. And when Leonardo Marquez came back from Havana to live in Mexico City, Diaz did nothing about it.

Because Diaz for the first time since the end of Spanish rule had given Mexico stability, he became a greatly respected world figure. The first departure of an American President from United States soil while in office occurred when President Taft had lunch with Diaz in Ciudad Juarez, formerly

Paso del Norte. They ate off the plates which Maximilian of Hapsburg had brought from Miramar.

In 1910, to celebrate the cry of Father Hidalgo for freedom, Diaz held a world exposition. As with the Great Exhibition in Paris, this one was soon followed by the spectacle of an apparently secure ruler fleeing his people. Old, heavy, braided and bemedaled, Diaz fled the Villas and Zapatas on a German steamer out of Vera Cruz. He died in exile in Paris in 1915.

From the anarchy and horror which followed the Mexican Revolution arose the Mexico of today. It was a difficult birth. For years the chaos of the wars between the Liberals and Conservatives was duplicated by the grandsons of the men who fought those wars. Not a few people in those years wondered if it would not have been better had an Emperor reigned in Mexico.

But it was out of the question. There was no foreign intervention. The Mexicans were left to battle it out by themselves. And while they did, their country slowly degenerated. But among the places which did not were Chapultepec Castle and the little shrine which stands over the exact places where Maximilian, Miramon and Mejia died on the morning of June 19, 1867. The castle was Diaz's summer abode. The shrine was put up by the Austrian Government in 1901. Francis Joseph sent a cross made of timbers from the *Novara*, and a picture of Jesus and Mary which the Archduchess Sophia had commissioned for her rooms when she heard of Maximilian's death. An enormous statue of Juarez towers over it. Today Chapultepec reminds one of Maximilian and Carlota: here are their balconies, paintings, state carriage, furniture and, below the heights of the building, their Emperor's Road, now the Paeso de la Reforma, the principal street of the capital.

In Miramar Castle there is a constant flow of tourists coming to the only attraction of a city whose importance faded away with the end of the Austro-Hungarian Empire. It looks very much as it did when last the Emperor of Mexico saw it. At Vienna the Votiv-Kirche Maximilian built in thanks to God for sparing Francis Joseph after an assassination attempt still stands. So do Schoenbrunn and the Hofburg, the latter strangely haunted by Sisi. It is her pictures which draw the most attention, and her rooms which make visitors linger. In the intervening years since Austria's disasters of the First World War, Francis Joseph's harshness has been glossed over and today in Vienna he is remembered as The Old Gentleman. It is hard to think of him as he was when he was young, when Maximilian knew him.

Their story—dreams, madness, death—held a certain place in the mind of the later nineteenth century. It was peculiarly of its time. Surely the 1860's were almost the final moment when it was possible to conceive of an Austrian Archduke going to rule a primitive country five thousand miles away. For that reason and also because there was gallantry and knight-errantry in him, and a classical fate for her, their tragedy seemed to have a lesson. A sad lesson. Perhaps that was a part of its attraction for the peoples of Middle Europe, among whom the Mexican monarchs remained great subjects of interest for a long time. But the years passed. Wars, the uprootings of old loyalties, the almost complete end of the monarchial system, have made Maximilian and Carlota distant figures of history. Mexico remembers her as having introduced a certain elegance which lingers on. They tend to call her The Frenchwoman and think of her as a refining influence upon a raw country. "La Paloma" is instantly definable as her song.

Maximilian is thought of in Mexico as having something of the nobility of Hidalgo, Morelos, the Boy Cadets. He died very well. "I can repeat the words of one of your kings," Maximilian said to a Frenchman in his cell at Queretaro. " 'All has been lost, save honor.' Remember? I hope that they say this of me after my death."

For a long time they did not dare to tell Carlota what had happened. The summer of 1867 passed. When the new year arrived Queen Henriette, whom Carlota had once thought so insipid, came to Miramar to take her home to Brussels. The servants had removed their mourning attire, and so she did not know.

Carlota rode with the Queen in a pony cart, walked with her in the park by the palace and, as winter came on, went with her in a sled along the canal, watching the skaters. It was quite astonishing to all who saw her that she should be more beautiful, at twenty-seven, than ever before. It was not possible for them to be uniformly mistaken. She was mad, she was in the eyes of those who saw her a poor ghost beaten into the ground, fearful of everything—but her appearance was radiant.

There were lucid moments. Carlota spoke of her childhood, of how she now slept in the room that had been the bedroom of Leopold and Philippe, her brothers. Their billiard table had rested where her bed was now. Most of the time she was calm and able to read or play games and speak in a rational fashion. But the sure mind and precise intelligence were gone. There was a look in her eyes—they were larger, José Blasio thought, than he had remembered—and the look seemed to question her fate. What did she see? No one ever knew. She did not speak of her husband, never of Mexico.

In the winter of 1868 the Queen of the Belgians gave an audience to the former Minister to Mexico, Frederic Hooricks. Then, in preparation for what she was about to have him do, she made a novena. The day it was finished she brought him to Carlota. He began to speak. He talked of the departure from Mexico City, the march to Queretaro, of how well the men had fought, of how they would have done better if Lopez had not betrayed them.

"And then?" she whispered.

"The Emperor is dead with the courage of a man and the dignity of a Prince," he said. Carlota got up and ran. The Queen chased after her and caught her. For a long time they wept in one another's arms.

For a brief time the shock appeared to steady her. Carlota said that if men had killed the son of God, then why not the son of Kings? She seemed more tender and loving to those around her. They hoped for a short moment that there would be a cure. The hope died. For although usually there was a look of gentle melancholy upon her features, it could be replaced by one of rage and violence. She would go berserk, smash and rip and break everything about her. All glass mirrors were removed from her rooms and bars were installed on the windows.

They moved her from the palace of Laeken to the chateau of Tervuren. She lived in rooms upon whose walls hung pictures from her childhood nursery, and on the tables were her

children's books, which she often read. Mixed with them were
mementos of Max. She had a life-sized doll with long whiskers
such as he had; she draped her doll in Imperial robes and
spent long hours whispering to it. In her terrible mad rages
she never touched it or any of the pictures of him on the walls.

In 1879 the chateau burst into flames. The Queen drove her
away in a pony cart, and behind them the fire fighters heard
Carlota scream that the flames were wonderful, wonderful. The
chateau burned to the ground. They rescued her pictures and
her doll.

Carlota was approaching forty by then. They took her back
to Laeken, to the King, Philippe, their children. She went
out into the park every day, and practiced the harp and took
up the piano again, and took her meals with people for the
first time in ten years. Queen Henriette asked those who had
known Carlota to write her. It would be no great pleasure for
them, the Queen explained, but Carlota was sensitive about
being entirely forgotten.

But the periods of rationality grew fewer. They took her to
the Castle of Bouchout, a twelfth-century building half an
hour's drive from Laeken. The park around it was magnificent,
with sweeping lawns and a lake and ancient trees. There she
stayed. Once, and only once, she left it. It happened one day
that she approached a guard on duty and asked him if she
were not a free person. Entirely, he replied. She ordered him
to open the gate. He did so and she stepped into the road. She
stood there for perhaps five minutes and then went back.

Sometimes she played duets or cards with the ladies of her
suite, and she read or was read to. She dressed very carefully,
in soft morning dresses which were changed to more formal
ones in the afternoon. She wore bonnets with ribbons matching the color of her dress, and shoes with matching ribbons
also. She was sensitive to compliments people paid her.

Carlota had no grasp of the passing of the years and the
decades, but kept track of various dates—her name day, holi-
days, the first of every month. Sometimes she appeared to show
understanding of her situation: "Don't pay attention, Monsieur,
if one is irrational. . . . Yes, Monsieur, one is old, one is stupid,
one is crazy. . . . The crazy one is still alive. . . . Monsieur,

you are at the home of a madwoman. . . ." But generally she spoke in meaningless phrases, entirely incoherent bits and pieces in French, English, German, Italian and Spanish.

Almost never did Carlota speak of her husband; but once she burst out, "Monsieur, one tells you that one had a husband, a husband, Monsieur, Emperor or King! . . . A great marriage, Monsieur, and then madness! . . . The madness is made from events! . . . Monsieur, you are the cause of the assassination!"

Then there was a pause as her lost mind groped, and then, "Maximilian, Archduke, House of Hapsburg!"

She grew enormously wealthy as her brother Leopold made the Belgian Congo the private property of his family. Yet she could not abide the sight of him, and when once or twice he came to her castle she flew into one of her terrible rages. In the end she became one of the richest women in the world. The Prince de Ligne, who took care of her finances, discussed them with her every few months. He was always received in a room filled with twenty or more chairs carefully lined up. Carlota would come into the room and greet each chair. Then she would discuss business matters with him. She understood everything he said.

She maintained a Court and was addressed by the style of Imperial Majesty. She had a doctor who when her worst frenzies seized her often effected a calm by saying, "Madame, of all the Empresses I know, you are the only one who does this!"

Decades went by. Her brother Leopold died and Albert, son of the Count of Flanders, became King of the Belgians. But often Carlota forgot and, when he came to visit her, she addressed him as Prince. It was only upon occasion that she had lucid moments and cried to her attendants, the majordomo and ladies-in-waiting, "Imagine, one has a nephew—a King!" She did not mention her late brother. She had long forgotten that when as children they had danced together the courtiers spoke of how much more graceful she was.

Leopold's passing was not the only death which went unmentioned in her presence. Du Barail, risen to high rank, died, and so did Loizillon, Blanchot, all the dashing French officers, and the Austrian Malortie, and the Prussian von Gagern. At Cuernavaca the Borda gardens fell into dreaming ruins, the heavy fountains toppling and the long terraces, deserted, turning silent and sad as the years passed. Nearby, a dozen and a half Austrian Hussars lay in a common grave with Colonel Paulino Lamadrid; and an outdoor dance pavilion where they had danced during off-duty hours dwindled away into a pile of forgotten stones. The Countess de Castiglione ended as a ghost of herself, forbidding in her home any mirrors which would reflect the loss of her magnificent beauty, and ordering that she be buried in the gray cambric gown she had worn on the night in 1857 when she first seduced the Emperor of the French.

The twentieth century arrived. Carlota lived on.

In 1914 the Great War swept by Carlota's castle as the German troops took Brussels. By order of the German Emperor William II she was not disturbed. For she was the sister-in-law of William's ally, the Emperor Francis Joseph. So she was never told of the war. Yet she seemed to sense it. "One sees red," she said in her wandering, mad way. "One supposes there is something going on because one is not gay. . . . The frontier is black, very black."

General Mariano Escobedo died, Riva Palacio the father and Riva Palacio the son, Pepe Hidalgo, going in his last months to cafés on cold days because he could not afford to heat his room. José Blasio, Marquez, who turned deeply religious in his old age . . . even the sons of men who had been the old woman's subjects were dead: Pancho Villa, Emiliano Zapata, Madero, Carranza. She would not have known their names.

Eugenie died. She had lived on in a museumlike atmosphere at her homes in England and on the Riviera—she had finally lost her fear that one day France would do to her what it had done to Marie Antoinette—and even on her yacht the salon had Winterhalter portraits of the ladies of her Court, pictures of the Tuileries and busts of her husband's marshals. She had lived to see the German lines crack in 1918, forty-eight years after the great defeat of 1870, and had walked to Napoleon's grave in the chapel by her English house and there read aloud the terms of the Armistice, sadly saying that it would have made the Prince Imperial so proud and happy.

The wife of the gardener at Cuernavaca was dead, and her son—Maximilian's son—also. He had lived an unsavory conniver's life in Europe, dying before a firing squad. French rifles killed him in 1917. He had been a German spy.

And still she lived on although she had long outlived her world. Sometimes she talked of the death that awaited her, and of the crypt of the Church of Our Lady in Laeken, in Brussels, where her father Leopold and her mother Louise Marie were. "One goes up and up and up and then finally disappears behind the towers," Carlota said. She wished to go there, to Laeken, in the end.

Finally, at long last, still hopelessly insane, the old woman died. The weather was very like that of the day of her husband's funeral, cold and snowing.

Troops lined the road to Laeken. Her nephew Albert, King of the Belgians, led the procession. By her casket marched a little group of elderly men—the last members of the Belgian Legion which had once gone out to Mexico to help their Princess. Upon the coffin, next to the flag of Belgium, rode the colors of Imperial Mexico. It was early winter of 1927. She had turned eighty-seven.

Sixty years had passed since the day when a banner was lowered from the flagstaff on top of La Cruz in Queretaro.

"I was to blame, my beloved darling, for everything," she had once written from her mindless wilderness to her husband lying in his copper-lined casket five hundred miles away. Lord of the World, she had called him, Sovereign of the Universe. "But now I am happy. You have triumphed! You are part of God's victory over Evil. . . . Your eyes look down at me from every place and I hear your voice everywhere."

Bibliography

ACOSTA, ROBERTO SALGUEIRO. *La Intervencion Francesa Armada y Maximiliano en Veracruz*. Mexico City, Universidad Nacional Autónoma de México, 1969.

ALGARA, IGNACIO. *La Corte de Maximiliano*. Mexico City, Editorial Polis, 1938.

ALVENSLEBEN, MAX VON. *With Maximilian in Mexico*. London, Longmans, Green and Company, 1867.

ANONYMOUS (Margaret Cunliffe Owen). *The Martyrdom of an Empress*. New York and London, J. B. Lippincott Company, 1899.

ARONSON, THEO. *Golden Bees: The Story of the Bonapartes*. Greenwich, Conn., New York Graphic Society, 1964.

AUBRY, OCTAVE. *The King of Rome*. Philadelphia and London, J. B. Lippincott and Company, 1932.

———. *The Second Empire*. Philadelphia and New York, J. B. Lippincott and Company, 1940.

BAKER, NINA BROWN. *Juarez, Hero of Mexico*. New York, The Vanguard Press, 1942.

BANCROFT, FREDERIC. *The Life of William H. Seward*. New York, Harper & Brothers, 1900.

BARAIL, FRANCOIS DU. *Mes Souvenirs*. Paris, Librairie Plon, 1898.

BASCH, SAMUEL *Maximilien au Mexique*. Paris, A. Savine, 1889.

BAUER, LUDWIG. *Leopold the Unloved*. Boston, Little, Brown and Company, 1935.

BEALS, CARLETON. *Porfirio Diaz*. Philadelphia and London, J. B. Lippincott and Company, 1932.

BICKNELL, ANNA L. *Life in the Tuileries under the Second Empire*. New York, The Century Company, 1895.

BISHOP, WILLIAM HENRY. *Old Mexico and Her Lost Provinces*. New York, Harper & Brothers, 1887.

BLANCHOT, CHARLES. *Memoires sur l'Intervention Française au Mexique*. Paris, E. Nourry, 1911.

BLASIO, JOSÉ LUIS. *Maximilian, Emperor of Mexico. Memoirs of his Private Secretary.* New Haven, Yale University Press, 1934.

BOCK, CARL H. *Prelude to Tragedy.* Philadelphia, University of Pennsylvania Press, 1966.

BUSSIN, CARON CAMILLE. *La Tragédie Mexicaine.* Brussels, A. de Wit, 1925.

CALDERÓN DE LA BARCA, FANNY. *Life in Mexico.* Garden City, N.Y., Doubleday and Company, 1966.

CALLCOTT, WILFRID HARDY. *Liberalism in Mexico.* Hamden, Conn., Archon Books, 1965.

CARETTE, A. *Recollections of the Court of the Tuileries.* New York, D. Appleton and Company, 1889.

CASTELOT, ANDRÉ. *King of Rome.* New York, Harper and Brothers, 1960.

CHAPMAN, MARISTAN. *Imperial Brother: The Life of the Duc de Morny.* New York, The Viking Press, 1931.

CORLEY, T. A. B. *Democratic Despot: A Life of Napoleon III.* London, Barrie and Rockliff, 1961.

CORTI, COUNT EGON CAESAR. *Maximilian and Charlotte of Mexico.* New York, Alfred A. Knopf, 1928.

———. *Elizabeth, Empress of Austria.* London, T. Butterworth, 1936.

CRAIG, GORDON A. *The Battle of Könniggrätz.* Philadelphia and New York, J. B. Lippincott Company, 1964.

CREELMAN, JAMES. *Diaz, Master of Mexico.* New York and London, D. Appleton and Company, 1911.

DABBS, JACK AUTREY. *The French Army in Mexico, 1861–1867.* The Hague, Mouton & Co., 1963.

DAHLBERG-ACTON, JOHN, first Baron Acton. *Historical Essays and Studies.* Freeport, N.Y., Books for Libraries Press, Inc., 1967.

DESTERNES, SUZANNE, and CHANDER, HENRIETTE. *Maximilien et Charlotte.* Paris, Librairie Academique Perrin, 1964.

DIAZ, FERNANDO. *La Vida Heroica del General Tómas Mejía.* Mexico City, Editorial Jus., 1970.

ELTON, JAMES FREDERICK. *With the French in Mexico.* London, Chapman and Hall, 1967.

ERNST, OTTO. *Franz Josef I in seinen Briefen.* Vienna, Rikola Verlag, 1924.

FLANDRAU, CHARLES MACOMB. *Viva Mexico!* Urbana, Ill., University of Illinois Press, 1964.

FLEURY, COMTE. *Memoirs of the Empress Eugenie.* New York and London, D. Appleton and Company, 1920.

FLINT, HENRY M. *Mexico Under Maximilian*. Philadelphia, National Publishing Company, 1867.

GAGERN, CARLOS VON. *Todte und Lebende*. Berlin, Abenheimsche Verlagsbuchhandlung, 1884.

GOSTOWSKI, GUSTAV. *Los Ultimos Dias y los Ultimos Momentos de la Vida de Maximiliano*. San Luis Potosi, Universidad Autónoma de San Luis Potosi, 1966.

GUEDALLA, PHILIP. *The Second Empire*. New York and London, G. P. Putnam's Sons, 1922.

———. *The Two Marshals*. London, Hodder and Stoughton, Ltd., 1943.

GUÉRARD, ALBERT. *Napoleon III: A Great Life in Brief*. New York, Alfred A. Knopf, 1966.

HALL, W. H. BULLOCK. *Across Mexico in 1864–65*. London and Cambridge, Macmillan and Company, 1866.

HANS, ALBERTO. *La Guerra de México Según los Mexicanos*. Paris, Berger-Levrault & Cie., 1899.

HESSE WARTEGG, ERNEST DE. *Quinz Ans Après la Catastrophe de Querétaro*. Brussels, Revue Générale, 1882.

HYDE, HARFORD (*sic*) MONTGOMERY. *Mexican Empire*. London, Macmillan and Company, 1946.

KENDALL, JOHN JENNINGS. *Mexico Under Maximilian*. London, T. Cautley Newby, 1871.

KOLLONITZ, COUNTESS PAULA. *The Court of Mexico*. London, Saunders, Otley and Company, 1867.

KURTZ, HAROLD. *The Empress Eugenie*. Boston, Houghton Mifflin Company, 1964.

LALLY, FRANK EDWARD. *French Opposition to the Mexican Policy of the Second Empire*. Baltimore, The Johns Hopkins Press, 1931.

LAURENT, PAUL. *La Guerre du Mexique*. Paris, Amyot, 1867.

LEGGE, EDWARD. *The Comedy and Tragedy of the Second Empire*. New York, Charles Scribner's Sons, 1911.

LEMPRIÈRE, CHARLES. *Notes in Mexico in 1861 and 1862*. London, Longman, Roberts and Green, 1862.

LICHTERVELDE, COMTE LOUIS DE. *Leopold the First: The Founder of Modern Belgium*. New York and London, The Century Company, 1930.

LOISEAU, MODESTE. *Notes Prises au Mexique par un Officer de la Légion Belge*. Brussels, E. Guyot, 1867.

LOIZILLON, HENRY. *Lettres sur l'Expédition de Mexique, 1862–67*. Paris, Ernest Flammarion, 1898.

LOLIÉE, FRÉDÉRIC. *Women of the Second Empire*. London, John Lane the Bodley Head, 1897.

LONGFORD, ELIZABETH. *Queen Victoria*. New York, Harper & Row, 1965.

LYNCH, SISTER M. CLAIRE. *The Diplomatic Mission of John Lothrop Motley to Austria 1861–67*. Washington, The Catholic University of America Press, 1944.

MARES, JOSÉ FUENTES. *Juarez y el Imperio*. Mexico City, Editorial Jus., 1963.

MARIA Y CAMPOS, ARMANDO DE. *El Emperador y al Poeta*. Mexico City, Coleccio Temas Teatrales, 1956.

MARSHALL, WILLIAM. *An American in Maximilian's Mexico*. San Marino, Calif., The Huntington Library, 1959.

MARTIN, PERCY F. *Maximilian in Mexico*. New York, Charles Scribner's Sons, 1914.

MARTINEZ, VIDAL COVIAN. *Efemerides del Sitio de Queretaro*. Ciudad Victoria, Tampico, Ediciones Siglo XX, 1967.

MARX, ADRIEN. *Révélations sur la Vie Intime de Maximilien*. Paris, Librairie du Petit Journal, n.d.

MASSERAI, E. *Un Essai d'Empire aux Mexique*. Paris, G. Charpentier, 1879.

MAXIMILIAN, EMPEROR OF MEXICO. *Recollections of My Life*. London, n.p., 1868.

MERCER, CHARLES. *The Foreign Legion*. London, Arthur Barker Ltd., 1964.

METTERNICH, PRINCESS PAULINE VON. *My Years in Paris*. London, Everleigh Nash and Grayson, 1922.

MISMER, CHARLES. *Souvenirs*. Paris, Librairie Hachette et Cie., 1890.

MURAT, PRINCESS CAROLINE. *My Memoirs*. New York, G. P. Putnam's Sons, 1910.

NUÑEZ MATA, ELFREN. *El General Don Juan Prim*. Mexico City, Ediciones Botas, 1962.

PALÉOLOGUE, MAURICE. *The Tragic Empress*. New York and London, Harper and Brothers, 1928.

PAZ, OCTAVIO. *The Labyrinth of Silence: Life and Thought in Mexico*. New York, Grove Press, 1961.

QUIRARTE, MARTÍN. *Historiografía Sobre el Imperio de Maximiliano*. Mexico City, Universidad Nacional Autónoma de México, 1970.

RADZIWILL, PRINCESS CATHERINE. *The Austrian Court from Within*. New York, Frederick A. Stokes Company, 1916.

REDLICH, JOSEPH. *Francis Joseph of Austria*. New York, Macmillan of Canada–Viking Compass Books, 1929.

REINACH FOUSSEMAGNE, COMTESSE H. DE. *Charlotte de Belgique Impératrice du Mexique*. Paris, Plon-Nourrit et Cie., 1925.

ROEDER, RALPH. *Juarez and His Mexico*. New York, The Viking Press, 1947.

ROLLE, ANDREW F. *The Lost Cause: The Confederate Exodus to Mexico*. Norman, Okla., University of Oklahoma Press, 1965.

RUMBOLD, SIR HORACE. *Francis Joseph and His Times*. New York, D. Appleton and Company, 1909.

SALM-SALM, AGNES PRINCESS ZU. *Ten Years of My Life*. New York, R. Worthington, 1877.

SALM-SALM, PRINCE FELIX ZU. *My Diary in Mexico in 1868 Including the Last Days of the Emperor Maximilian*. London, Richard Bentley, 1868.

SCHNÜRER, FRANZ. *Briefe Kaiser Franz Josephs an seine Mutter*. Munich, Jos. Koesel and F. Pustet, 1930.

SCHOLES, WALTER B. *Mexican Politics During the Juarez Regime*. Columbia, Mo., The University of Missouri Studies, 1957.

SCHROEDER, SEATON. *The Fall of Maximilian's Empire*. New York and London, G. P. Putnam's Sons, 1887.

SENCOURT, ROBERT. *The Life of the Empress Eugenie*. New York, Charles Scribner's Sons, 1931.

SMART, CHARLES ALLEN. *Viva Juarez!* Philadelphia and New York, J. B. Lippincott Company, 1963.

STACTON, DAVID. *The Bonapartes*. New York, Simon and Schuster, 1966.

STEPHANIE, PRINCESS OF BELGIUM. *I Was to Be Empress*. London, Ivor Nicholson and Watson Ltd., 1937.

STEVENSON, SARA YORKE. *Maximilian in Mexico: A Woman's Reminiscences of the French Intervention*. New York, The Century Company, 1899.

STURMFEDER, BARONIN LOUISE VON. *Die Keindheit Unseres Kaisers*. Vienna, Gerlach und Wiedling, 1910.

THAYER, WILLIAM ROSCOE. *The Life and Times of Cavour*. Boston and New York, Houghton Mifflin Company, 1914.

THOMAS, LOUIS. *Le Général de Galliffet*. Paris, Dorbon-Aîné, 1909 (?).

TERREROS, DON MANUEL ROMERO DE. *Maximiliano y el Imperio*. Mexico City, Editorial Cultura, 1926.

TRENS, MANUEL B. *Historia de Veracruz*. Mexico City, Enríquez, 1950.

TYRNER-TYRNAUER, A. R. *Lincoln and the Emperors*. New York, Harcourt, Brace & World, 1962.

VERISSIMO, ERICO. *Mexico*. New York, The Orion Press, 1957.

VIEL CASTEL, COUNT HORACE DE. *Memoirs*. London, Remington and Company, 1888.

VICTORIA, QUEEN. *Letters.* New York, John Murray, 1926.

WILLIAMS, FRANCES LEIGH. *Matthew Fontaine Maury.* New Brunswick, N.J.: Rutgers University Press, 1963.

WRIGHT, MARIE ROBINSON. *Picturesque Mexico.* Philadelphia, George Barrie & Sons, 1911.

NEWSPAPERS

Periódico Oficial del Imperio Mexicano
El Diario del Imperio
Reglamento para el Servicio y Ceremonial de la Corte

Acknowledgments

THE MOMENT WHEN THE IDEA for this book first came into my mind can be traced to a day in late winter or early spring of 1957. I was living at that time in New York City, and one day I found myself in a bookstore, since vanished, where I purchased a secondhand copy of Philip Guedalla's *The Two Marshals*. Printed on the cheap paper and enclosed in the thin covers which showed it to be a book published in an England at war, it attracted my interest because of its concern with Marshal Pétain, an individual then and now of great fascination to me.

However, the book was only partially concerned with Pétain. The other marshal was Bazaine. I confess I had only the haziest idea of whom he might be. I knew of him only in connection with the Franco-Prussian War. I read the book and for the first time learned in detail the story of the Mexican Empire. Not long thereafter, perhaps a year or so, I went to see Al Jolson in *The Jazz Singer*—filmdom's first talkie. There was a second feature: *Juarez,* with Paul Muni, Bette Davis, John Garfield and Brian Donlevy. I do not think that I realized the interesting coincidence that the character played by Bette Davis died the year *The Jazz Singer* was made, but I liked the movie very much. (Seen more recently on television, it stands up as a quite accurate portrayal of the events covered in this book.)

In any event, I began thinking about a book on Maximilian and Carlota of Mexico. Many years, other books, intervened. One day in 1965 I mentioned the project to my publishers, William Morrow & Company of New York. Both the president of the publishing house, Lawrence Hughes, and my editor,

Hillel Black, encouraged me to do a biography of the two monarchs. For some months I looked into the matter. In the end I decided the language problem was too great to overcome, for to do the book would require research into French, Spanish and German tomes. I dropped the project in favor of other matters.

About a year later I met the lady who was to become my wife, the then Miss Jayne Barry. Having spent much of her life abroad, she was fluent in several languages. She said she would be my translator. I demurred, remarking that I had once discussed the project with the late historian Allan Nevins and that he, although pointing out that Prescott had done his great work on the Conquest of Mexico without knowing a word of Spanish, had said that working through a translator was a most difficult matter.

At the 1967 reception following my marriage to Miss Barry, Hillel Black was a guest. The next day, in Paris for our honeymoon, my wife remarked that she had chatted with Mr. Black. "I told him you would do Maximilian and Carlota," she said.

So I did.

Primarily, then, my thanks for assistance in completing this book are due my translator-collaborator, not only for the long hours spent in translating, but also for the psychological insights offered as together we attempted to look into the minds of our two protagonists, the Emperor and Empress. During the months we spent in Mexico, we were greatly aided by the officials of the Biblioteca National, who allowed us special typewriter privileges, and by the director of the library of El Colegio de Mexico, Lic. Ario Garza Mercado, who permitted us to take books from his stacks to our apartment for more comfortable perusing. We were fortunate in being permitted a special tour of Chapultepec Castle, through areas closed to the public, this through the courtesy of understanding Mexican officials. The librarians of the Benjamin Franklin Library in Mexico City also extended kind assistance. And I am indebted for the many services rendered in Mexico City by Arthur Rosenberg.

We took away many speculations as to what an Archduke of Austria and a Princess of Belgium must have thought of some of the things which, unchanged after a hundred years, came under our eyes. One memory particularly lives in my thoughts. We had gone westward out of Vera Cruz to trace the Imperial journey inland over the original road. (The present super-highway deviates somewhat.) We covered about fifteen miles on an increasingly primitive track and ended rocking along at a speed of perhaps seven or eight miles an hour. To go faster would certainly have endangered the springs of our car. According to the map, we appeared to be nearing the town of Camerone, which in France is famous as the site of a deathless battle fought by the Foreign Legion. (In fact, the Feast of Camerone is the annual celebration day of the Legion, and has been for a century.) But the road was truly incredible. We came to La Soledad, where the French and Mexicans negotiated before the French inaugurated hostilities in 1862, and found it to be utterly untouched by modernity. The children were naked; there were open gutter drains, no paving, grass shacks.

Surely, we said to each other, the internationally celebrated Camerone will be different. But the road degenerated even further, if possible. This, then, was what Maximilian and Carlota saw, we reflected. The thought gave us pause. Finally, after an hour of seeing not a soul, our car filled with dust and laden with the corpses of countless insects, we saw a peon in front of a shack. A few chickens scratched in the dust; a burro wandered in the yard. I told my wife to ask him how long it would take to get to Camerone.

"He says," she said, "by horse, three hours."

"And by car?"

She spoke to him. He answered.

"Impossible."

I thought of that moment some months later, standing in the magnificent Castle Square at Miramar near Trieste, and I thought of it again at the palace of Laeken in Belgium. Even to us, with years of study behind us, with countless picture books, Mexico came as a shock. What must it have been to them, who had lived their lives in castles and palaces?

In Mexico City, with its pollution and cars, one loses sight of the two young monarchs. They return, however, in the country-side, on the desert of the great plateau, in the little one-street towns. One feels kin to them in those places which are as strange and alien to us of the 1970s as they were to them of the 1860s. In imagination one finds them also in the great chambers of their Europe, Schoenbrunn, Versailles. Such places can never be built again, of course, and so they are timeless—and timeless also are those who tenanted them: Max, Carlota, Napoleon, Eugenie, Sophia, the Duke of Reichstadt, Francis Joseph, Sisi.

I have tried to bring these people to life in this book. Necessarily I have failed. No one can truly bring back those days that are no more. Sometimes after these years of living with them they seem like dream-figures to me. I suppose they will be likewise to my readers. In any event, any errors in this manuscript are my responsibility, but I repeat my indebtedness to my wife, and add my thanks for assistance rendered in Belgium to Mme. Christiane Vanoye and in Vienna to Herr Karl-Ludwig Schibel of Frankfurt University.

Lastly, I owe many thanks to all the officials of the Mid-Hudson Library System, particularly its representative in my hometown, Mrs. Mary Lou Alm.

Index

Acton, Lord, 250–251
Acts of Adhesion, 142–145
Albert (Prince Consort of England), 47, 56, 161, 236
Algara, Ignacio, 174
Almonte, 123, 126, 137, 138, 158, 241
Alvarez, Juan, 104, 107–108
Antonelli, Giacomo, 232, 234
Assembly of Notables, 138, 141
Augustin. *See* Iturbide, Augustin
Austria: and Crimean War, 51–52; after death of Francis, 24–25; under Francis Joseph, 43; and Italy, 67–68, 72–74; and Revolution of 1848, 24–29; and War with Prussia, 215–218; and French withdrawal from Mexico, 210, 211
Aztecs, conquest of, 93–96

Basch, Dr. Samuel, 238, 249, 261, 264, 269, 274, 276, 277
Bazaine, François Achille, 132, 144–145, 158, 167, 177, 178–179, 191–192, 196, 199, 222, 224, 240, 281; death of, 282–283; leaves Mexico, 246, 247; and Maximilian's abdication decision, 243–245
Bazaine, Pepita Peña (Mrs. François), 191, 192, 219, 261, 282–283
Beauharnais, Alexandre de, 3

Beauharnais, Eugène de, 3
Beauharnais, Hortense de, 3, 4, 6, 8, 18, 20, 38, 48, 115, 154
Beauharnais, Josephine de. *See* Josephine
Belgium: under Leopold I, 54, 60; and Revolution of 1848, 55–56; royal family of, 53–61
Benedek, Ludwig August von, 215
Bilimek, Dr., 241–242, 269
Billault, Auguste, 131
Bismarck, 218, 223, 228, 283
Black Decree, 204–205, 240, 265
Blanchot, Charles, 136, 176, 213, 245, 291
Blasio, José Luis, 179, 193, 262, 269, 274, 288, 291
Bombelles, Count Karl, 151, 194–195, 206, 240–241
Bonaparte, Jerome, 18, 36, 48, 52
Bonaparte, Joseph, 20, 86, 98
Bonaparte, Louis, 3, 4, 22
Bonaparte, Louis Napoleon, 4, 8; becomes Emperor of France, 34, 35; and death of Reichstadt, 17–18; and death of his mother, 20; description of, 18; elected to French Chamber of Deputies, 35; elected President of France, 36–37; escapes from prison, 22; imprisonment of, 21–22; in London, 20; and Mathilde, 18; in New York, 19–20; plots against

Fischer, Augustin, 240–241, 244, 245
Forey, Elie, 131–132, 135, 137–138, 144
Fould, Achille, 225, 226
France: cancels Treaty of La Soledad, 125–126; and Cochin China, 133n; and Convention of London, 114–118; and coup of 1851, 37; and end of Napoleonic dynasty, 283; after fall of Napoleon I, 8; invades Mexico, 130–138; Maximilian's opinion of, 53; and Maximilian's policies in Mexico, 174–175, 185–186, 187–188; and Mexico, 88–89, 113, 120, 122–129, 130–131, 136–138, 177–178, 192–193; under Napoleon III, 37, 47–48; offers throne to Maximilian, 139–140, 146; and Pastry War, 101; and Prussia, 216–217, 223, 281; and Revolution of 1848, 22–23; and troop withdrawals from Mexico, 167, 209–211, 224, 245–246; and United States' attitude toward Maximilian's regime, 198–199; after Waterloo, 18–19
Francis (Emperor of Austria), 4–5, 9, 10, 13, 24, 29, 46
Francis Charles (Archduke of Austria), 10, 11, 12, 24, 26, 27–28
Francis Ferdinand (Archduke of Austria), 238, 284
Francis Joseph (Emperor of Austria), 13–14, 15, 27, 35, 37, 154, 230, 238, 286, 287, 291; attempted assassination of, 147–148; becomes emperor, 28–29; birth of, 12; childhood of, 29–31; and death of Rudolph, 284; education of, 31; in 1866, 237; Italian policies of, 26, 71–74, 75–76; life style of, 83; marries Elizabeth, 41–42; Maximilian's letters to, 51–53, 60, 62, 63, 274; and Napoleon III, 37–38, 50, 79–80; personality of, 31–32, 33, 34;

and Prussian-Austrian war, 215; relationship with Elizabeth, 42, 194; relationship with Maximilian, 30–31, 33, 45, 81, 83–84, 119, 147–151, 244; romances of, 40–41; and Sardinian-French alliance, 77–78; tours Italy, 73; at war with France, 77–78

Gagern, Baron Karl von, 275, 291
Gallardo, José Rincon, 262, 263, 264–265
Galliffet, Alexandre Gaston de, 133, 134, 254, 283
Garcia, Jesus F., 263–264
Genlis, Waubert de, 222
Gonzales, Refugio, 267, 278, 279
Grant, Ulysses S., 102, 199
Great Britain, and Convention of London, 113, 114, 118, 119–120, 122, 125, 131
Grill, Antonio, 194, 249, 276–277
Gutierrez de Estrada, José Maria, 86, 107, 115, 118, 119, 120, 123, 141, 151, 152, 154, 170, 175
Gyulai, Count, 76, 77

Helena of Bavaria, 40–41
Henriette (Queen of the Belgians), 59, 287, 288, 289
Herzfeld, Stephen, 242
Hidalgo, José ("Pepe"), 85, 111, 113, 118, 123, 151; death of, 291; and dispute between Francis Joseph and Maximilian, 149; and Eugenie, 86–87, 88; and fall of Puebla, 130, 135; as Minister to France, 175; and Napoleon III, 88–89
Hidalgo, Miguel, 98–99, 176, 231, 286
Hooricks, Frederic, 288
Howard, Miss, 20, 22, 35, 36, 37
Hübner, Count, 50

Imperial Mexican army, 247–250, 252–263

Indians of Mexico, 203; and Catholic Church, 104–105; and Maximilian, 161–162, 163, 176, 184

Isabella (Queen of Spain), 281

Italy: under Austrian control, 67–68, 72–76, 172; and Revolution of 1848, 26, 36; and Villafranca settlement, 79–80. *See also* United Italy

Iturbide, Augustin de (Emperor of Mexico), 99, 100, 123, 202, 270

Jackson, Stonewall, 202

Jecker, Jean Baptiste, 115–116, 123, 198

Jilek, Dr., 152

Johnson, Andrew, 198

Josephine (Empress of France), 3, 4, 14, 39, 314

Juarez, Benito Pablo, 106–108, 110, 112, 121, 124, 128, 160, 174, 244, 245, 257, 261, 283; and aid from United States, 199; and Catholic Church, 110–111, 169; death of, 285; and death of his son, 208; evacuates Mexico City, 136; and fall of Puebla, 135; and French invasion of Mexico, 122–123, 126, 136, 143, 144; after French withdrawal, 212; letter to Maximilian, 167–168; and London Convention, 121; during Maximilian and Carlota's reign, 178, 182–184; and Maximilian's death sentence, 267, 269, 273, 274, 275–276; and Maximilian's surrender, 261, 264; and Maximilian's trial, 270–271; meets with Princess Salm-Salm, 266, 268, 273, 275; and Mejia, 166; as President of Mexico, 112–113; rumors of flight from Mexico, 204–205; sends family to U.S., 182

Juarez, Señora, 198

Juaristas: and French withdrawal from Mexico, 211, 243. *See also* Juarez, Benito Pablo; Liberals

Jurien de la Gravière, Jean Pierre Edmond, 120, 124, 125, 145, 282

Karl Ludwig (Archduke of Austria), 28, 30, 31, 44, 45, 151, 207, 238, 284

Karl Salvator (Archduke of Austria), 151

Kirby-Smith, Edmund, 200–201

Kollonitz, Countess Paula, 153, 156, 158

Labastida, Antonio Pelagio, 169, 170, 171, 179, 181, 285

Lamadrid, Paulino, 239, 291

Latrille, Ferdinand (Count of Lorencez), 125, 126, 127, 128–129, 130, 131–132

Lee, Robert E., 102, 121

Leopold I (King of the Belgians), 53–54, 292; and Charlotte, 55, 72; and Charlotte's dowry, 62–63; death of, 206, 213; and death of Louise Marie, 57; and education of his children, 58; and Francis Joseph's demand for Maximilian's renunciation, 150; marries Louise Marie, 54–55; and Maximilian, 60, 61, 71, 83; and Maximilian's decision on offer of Mexican crown, 119–120, 140, 146; and Revolution of 1848, 56

Leopold II (King of the Belgians), 54, 57, 59–60, 62, 63, 82, 139, 206, 288, 290

Liberals, 158; attitude toward Maximilian, 172–173, 175; and Black Decree, 204–205; and Carlota Colony, 202; French assault against, 177; after Maximilian's departure from Mexico City,